Business and Politics

Also by Graham K. Wilson

Interest Groups in the United States
Special Interests and Policymaking
The Politics of Safety and Health
Unions in American National Politics

For Gina and Adam

Business and Politics

A comparative introduction

SECOND EDITION

Graham K. Wilson

MACMILLAN

First published 1985 by
THE MACMILLAN PRESS LTD
Houndmills, Basingstoke, Hampshire RG21 2XS
and London
Companies and representatives
throughout the world

ISBN 0-333-53581-2 hardcover
ISBN 0-333-53582-0 paperback

A catalogue record for this book is available
from the British Library.

Printed in the United States

First edition reprinted 1987
Second edition 1990
Reprinted 1992, 1994

Contents

Preface to the First Edition

One of the few useful by-products of the economic difficulties which have afflicted the world in the 1970s and 1980s is a revival of interest in political economy. The central place of discussion of the performance of economies in political debate has encouraged many to ask again some of the basic questions about the relationship between government and the economy. Does government dominate business, or does business dominate government? Is the relationship between business and government effectively structured so that such widely shared goals as economic growth and full employment are likely to be attained, or not? How do business and government interact?

Although the relationship between business and government now forms part of almost all university courses on individual political systems, the topic is rarely studied *comparatively*. Courses on the comparative study of legislatures, executives and political parties are far more common than courses which compare the relationship between government and business, in spite of the importance and popularity of the topic. It is my belief, which I hope the following book will substantiate, that there is at least as much variation in the business–government relationship as there is in the character of political parties. Failure to appreciate the variation in this relationship from country to country may result in practical disadvantages for those who wish to make their careers in business; it also enfeebles debate within individual countries about the nature of their own political economy. Failure to appreciate the unique aspects of one's own system leads in political economy

– as in the study of political institutions and practices – to an unnecessarily shallow understanding of it; a comparative approach is the only remedy.

Any attempt to cover as broad a range of countries as concisely as I have attempted in this book is to run a high risk of writing a book which the experts on individual countries will find in their own area to be shallow and incomplete. I hope that they will accept my apologies for trespassing outside my own usual specialisms. I have taught courses on business and politics for several years now in both Britain and the USA, and have been aware of the lack of a short book which would provide students with some picture of the range of relationships between business and government found in the capitalist, industrialised democracies. I have attempted to fill that gap with this book, and hope that the range of countries covered will compensate for my failure to provide more extensive detail on each. As those used to planning long car journeys will know, there are advantages to both detailed and more comprehensive maps. I hope the Bibliography of this book will provide some assistance to students who wish to obtain more detailed 'maps' of the topics covered in outline here.

Inevitably, portions of such a general work as this rest on my reading of secondary sources. I am deeply indebted to the Nuffield Foundation, however, for their generous support in conducting research on aspects of the relationship between business and government which has informed many sections of this book. I am also profoundly grateful for the intellectual companionship of Virginia Sapiro during the writing of this book.

GRAHAM K. WILSON

Preface to the Second Edition

The 1980s proved to be a fascinating decade for students of business and politics. The importance of the topic was illustrated by the prominence of economic issues in election campaigns and by the growing visibility of political activity by corporations through techniques such as political action committees in the United States. The quantity and quality of writing on relations between business and government continued to grow dramatically; those who tried to 'bring the state back in' made particularly important contributions. The trends towards neocorporatism and other forms of more organised capitalism had seemed clear in the 1970s; the more neocorporatist or state led economies seemed to perform better on a variety of dimensions. In the 1980s, however, neoconservative politicans such as President Reagan and Mrs Thatcher achieved a degree of political and economic success that dismayed and surprised most social scientists. The resurgence of faith in market mechanisms and enthusiasm for 'shrinking the state' has been the most striking feature of economic policy thinking in the 1980s, not only sweeping the USA and Britain but influencing countries such as France with apparently very different traditions.

I hope I have learned much since the first edition of this book appeared. I have certainly enjoyed much of the literature on business government relations that has appeared in the 1980s. I have also benefited from discussions with colleagues here at Wisconsin, including several graduate students who

have widened my intellectual horizons. I am more grateful
than ever to Virginia Sapiro for love, support and my son,
Adam. This edition is dedicated to both of them.

GRAHAM K. WILSON

1

Introduction

The Business–Government Relationship

The relationship between business and government has emerged as one of the central issues of contemporary politics. The questions raised by political scientists, commentators and citizens about this relationship vary considerably, however.

For some people the question is whether the relationship between business and government is such that basic economic objectives are likely to be achieved. This raises at its simplest questions about the government's record. Is unemployment higher or lower than when the government came to power? Are real incomes increasing or falling? Are prices steady or increasing?

More reflective commentators have asked whether the structure of the relationship between business and government – as opposed to day-to-day events – serves in the long term to promote or to hinder the attainment of shared economic objectives. This raises questions such as whether the relationship between business and government is structured in such a way as to minimise the risk that government will adopt policies which will inadvertently hurt business activity – for example, increasing costs or decreasing competitiveness when policy alternatives without these disadvantages were available and acceptable. Is government kept aware of the needs of industry and commerce in the making of policy in matters as important to them as transport, education, and the promotion of science and technology? Is, in short, business sufficiently effective in expressing its concerns to government to warn government when its essential purposes may be endangered? We may summarise these concerns by asking whether or not the relationship between government and business is efficient in promoting the achievement of objectives (such as higher employment and increased living standards) which need not divide business and government.

The agreement which exists in most quarters on the desirability of economic growth does not mean that there is anything approaching general agreement on the means of obtaining that growth, or on the relationship between business and government which will best promote it. From the mid 1970s onwards, there was a significant increase in the influence of those who believed that the most efficient role for the state was to leave economic decisions to market forces. Governments should concentrate on helping market forces allocate economic resources rather than displacing market forces as allocators of resources. In some countries such as the United States, the restoration of the influence of market forces might be accomplished simply by having the government do less, for example by regulating the mergers of corporations less closely. In other countries such as Britain, the state would have to clear the ground so that market forces could operate by more forceful actions such as privatising industries, government-owned housing and weakening the power of unions to impede industrial change. The best industrial policy for government, declared the Thatcher Government in its White Paper, *DTI The Department for Enterprise*[1] was to create the conditions for successful entrepreneurship.

The belief in the adequacy of market forces for the promotion of economic growth was expressed vigorously by politicians such as Mrs Thatcher and President Reagan who told Americans early in his Administration that 'Government isn't the answer, it's the problem'. But this belief was anathema to many academic commentators who argued that the most successful economies of the period since the Second World War have been characterized by more vigorous government involvement. Such involvement might involve acting as a mediator between powerful interests such as business and labour in order to promote consensus on the measures needed to achieve growth. Governments could also play a leadership role, identifying markets and products which are likely to grow in the future. Government might then use its leverage over corporations, for example intervening through the financial sector to make finance cheaper and more readily available for corporations which comply with the government's wishes, to bring about investment in industries in which government believed the growth prospects were best.[2] It has been argued that this approach has characterised Japan[3] and, to a somewhat lesser extent, France, since the Second World War. Advocates of such a major, direct role for government in making investment decisions argue that government is capable of taking a longer term, more informed, view of the prospects for growth and investment than is the individual corporation. Left to themselves, corporate managers will be too pressured by the need to provide high dividends for stock holders today in order to avoid hostile take-over bids to plan investments which will bear fruit in the more distant future.[4] Thus a profound difference emerges between those who believe government promotes more, and those who believe it promotes less economic success.

In contrast to these questions of efficiency are the questions of *distribution* raised by political scientists and commentators. A wide variety of books have been written arguing that business has extensive and, by implication, excessive power. Some of these arguments are based on the analyses of particular policies or the links between politicians and business executives. Defence contractors in the USA,[5] major oil companies in a variety of countries,[6] car manufacturers in Britain and the USA, shipyards, steel mills and aircraft manufacturers more or less round the world have all been accused of 'feeding at the public trough', extorting unfair assistance from government. Others have argued that employment, tax, consumer and environmental laws reflect the power of business. A wide variety of mechanisms has been adduced to explain this alleged dominance of government by business. The shared background of business executives and top officials in government,[7] the contributions which business executives or their companies make to the electoral campaigns of politicians,[8] the number and skill of lobbyists employed by business concerns to put across their case, and the sensitivity of politicians to the votes of those employed in the relevant concerns are all advanced in both political science and popular debate as reasons for the power of business in democratic political systems. The question of whether there is a power élite which links (presumably to the disadvantage of the public) top government officials and business executives has been much discussed in relation to both Britain and the USA.[9]

In some theoretical traditions, the apparently important activities of business interest groups are seen as in fact possessing limited significance. The state itself fulfils important functions without which capitalism could not survive. Rather than thinking of business exerting 'pressure' which results in marginal advantages for it in public policy, we should rather conceptualise the entire state – bureaucracy, courts, executive and legislature – as fulfilling certain functions without which capitalism could not exist. It is the state which by laws establishes 'the market' whose existence is sometimes treated as though it is an act of nature. Markets require a vast institutional underpinning. Without courts to interpret and enforce agreements, for example, commercial life would be chaotic. Without law to define, and police to enforce them property rights would be non-existent. The modern corporation itself – the limited liability joint stock corporations – is, in historical terms, a comparatively modern creation of the state. In the Marxist tradition,[10] the state also serves to *legitimise* what to Marxists is the inherently unfair capitalist system. Welfare systems alleviate the worst poverty among the disadvantaged; elections foster the belief that citizens control their own destinies by choosing their governments freely, even if for many Marxists, those governments have limited capacity to act. The state also services the need of capitalists – some would say *increasingly* services the needs of capitalists[11] by providing services or subsidies. Modern industries need better trained or educated workers; the state provides them by improving education and training. Modern industry is dependent on science and technology; the state expands its expenditures on research. Industry has insufficient funds for investment; advocates of industrial policy suggest that the state should make good the deficiency. When labour markets have been tight in countries with strong unions, the state has been asked to operate incomes policies, sometimes backed by legal sanctions, to limit the rise in wages or has acted to reduce the legal immunities or rights of unions. Clearly, there is plausibility in the view based in the Marxist tradition that the modern state exists to maintain capitalism.

For many others, however, the view that the modern state exists to service capitalism is simplistic. The state can be seen as a forum within which competing or conflicting social forces contend as well as an institution with the powers to compel obedience. Environmentalists, farmers, workers and many other groups contend with business for control of the state so that they can use its powers for their own purposes. Yet other writers believe that all these views underestimate the degree to which the state is an independent actor, that is, enjoys autonomy.[12] The state has its own values, objectives and interests that cannot be reduced to those of any interest group, even one as important as business. Those political scientists – be they pluralist or Marxist – who try to reduce the state to being merely the operating arm of any interest group are in error. States often act without regard for the wishes or interests of groups, even when the decision has the most profound consequences for society; for example, no one suspects that any interest group played a significant role in prompting Britain to declare war on Germany in 1939. Yet the effect of war on British society was enormous. Sometimes, as we shall see, the state selects a sympathetic interest group to work with in furthering its own objectives, or, if none is to hand, sets out to create one. Of course the intellectual movement to 'bring the state back in' by emphasising its importance and autonomy is not without its own problems. What the state is, what its interests are and the degree to which the state has autonomy are fundamental but unresolved questions. Nor is it clear that all states have the same characteristics at all times and in all places. States change over time, and vary from one nation or society to another. In short, the recent theoretical emphasis on the state adds interesting but difficult questions to those we have already encountered.

Ideally, the political scientist would cast a dispassionate light on these questions. Unfortunately, there are a variety of reasons why it is particularly difficult to gather evidence or assemble arguments on these issues. Take, for example, the questions of *efficiency* which we have already examined. It is reasonably easy to compile satisfactory statistics which should show levels of economic growth, employment, and changes in real income or prices in different countries as, for example, in Tables 1–5. There is also increasing knowledge of the patterns of relationships which prevail between business and government in different countries. Attempts to link economic performance in a particular country to the nature of the business–government relationship will however, encounter, objections that the real explanation for a country's economic success or failure is to be found in other factors such as the culture of the country, its unions, the quality of its management, etc. It may even be argued plausibly that emulating the business–government relationship in a different country without adopting its culture and society will make matters worse. It might be that attempts by Britain or the USA to emulate the Japanese pattern of government–industry relations would thus only exacerbate their economic problems, in spite of the apparent success of that relationship in Japan.

Even more severe problems await those who try to assess the political power of business through studying systematically the *distributive* questions. At the heart of these disputes is the lack of consensus in political science about the meaning of 'power' – and particularly about the importance of its more directly observable aspects compared with other less visible dimensions.

The most widely accepted form of power is the form emphasised by pluralist political scientists. A has power over B to the extent that B behaves in a manner which B would not have done without A's intervention. In principle, though there could be major practical difficulties in securing access to the relevant information, the exercise and the extent of power can be observed. The original intentions of A and B can be ascertained, as well as the nature of their dealings. The extent of A's 'victory' can be ascertained and – if the dealings are continuous – the frequency of A's victory can be assessed.[13]

Table 1 *Union density[a] rates*

	Austria	Denmark	France	W. Germany	Italy	Netherlands	Norway	Sweden	UK	Japan	USA
1970	63.6	65.3	22.0	33.0	34.0	37.0	63.5	67.6	50.0	35.4	28.9
1980	59.6	86.9	18.7	37.4	48.6	33.0	64.0	80.8	56.4	30.8	23.2
1985	60.6	92.9[b]	16.5	38.0	41.4	27.5	64.9	82.8	52.4	28.9	21.9[c]

[a] Percentage of *employed* workforce paying union dues. Groups such as farmers are excluded.

[b] 1984

[c] 1982

Source: J Visser (1988) 'Trade Unionism in Western Europe: Present Situation and Prospects', *Labour and Society*, 13 (April) 2, pp. 125–82; Hovo Shinada (1988) 'Japanese Trade Unionism: Postwar Evolution and Future Prospects', *Labour and Society* 13 (April) 2, pp. 202–3; *Statistical Abstract of the United States*, US Department of Commerce, Bureau of the Census, Washington DC (1989) Table 683.

Table 2   *Real average annual growth rates, GDP and (GDP per capita)*

	1950–60		1960–65		1965–70		1970–81	
Austria	6.0	(5.8)	4.3	(3.7)	5.1	(4.6)	3.5	(3.3)
Denmark*	3.2	(2.4)	5.1	(4.3)	4.0	(3.2)	2.1	(1.8)
France	4.5	(3.5)	5.9	(4.4)	5.3	(4.5)	3.3	(2.8)
W. Germany	8.7	(7.6)	4.8	(3.5)	4.5	(3.9)	2.6	(2.6)
Italy	5.7	(5.0)	5.1	(4.4)	6.3	(4.4)	2.9	(2.5)
Japan**	6.4	(5.0)	10.1	(9.0)	11.5	(10.3)	4.5	(3.4)
Netherlands	4.6	(3.3)	4.9	(3.3)	5.7	(4.6)	2.7	(1.9)
Norway	3.5	(2.6)	4.4	(3.6)	3.9	(3.0)	4.5	(4.0)
Sweden	3.4	(2.8)	5.2	(4.5)	4.1	(3.3)	1.8	(1.5)
UK	2.4	(2.0)	3.2	(2.4)	2.6	(2.2)	1.7	(1.6)
USA	3.2	(1.5)	4.7	(3.2)	3.1	(2.0)	2.9	(1.9)

* 1953–60: ** 1952-60 and does not include Ryuku Islands.

Source: World Bank, *World Tables*, VI 'Economic Data', 3rd Edition, Washington, DC (1983) pp. 480–1.

Table 3   *GNP per capita, US$*

	1966	1970	1975	1980	1986
Austria	1400	1460	4760	9980	10000
France	2210	3000	6040	11860	10710
W. Germany	2060	2550	5720	11560	12090
Italy	1510	1980	3560	6090	8550
Netherlands	1710	2330	5080	10430	10030
Norway	1990	2530	5290	10990	15420
Sweden	2960	3810	6930	12530	13170
USA	3930	4790	6900	11150	17500
UK	1940	2210	3920	7900	8920

Source: World Bank, *World Tables*, 4th edition, Washington DC (1987).

Table 4 *Balance of payments (millions US$), trade balance*

	1972	1977	1982	1987
USA	-6420	-31100	-36420	-160280
Japan	8936	17160	18080	96390
Austria	112	-3826	-3450	-4471
Denmark	-430	2715	-794	12
France	1037	-3289	-15785	-2354
W. Germany	8397	19449	24716	70157
Italy	54	-131	-8911	95
Netherlands	438	-243	4663	5237
Norway	-1015	-4053	2386	-869
Sweden	1218	275	-220	4466
UK	-1859	-3937	3895	-15800

Source: International Monetary Fund, *International Financial Statistics* (1988) pp. 140.

Table 5 *Consumer prices (% change over previous year)*

	1970	1975	1980	1985	1987
USA	5.4	9.1	13.5	3.6	3.7
Japan	3.9	11.8	7.7	2.0	0.6*
Austria	4.4	8.4	6.4	3.2	1.4
Denmark	6.5	9.6	12.3	4.7	4.0
France	5.9	11.8	13.3	5.8	3.3
W. Germany	3.4	5.9	5.4	2.2	0.3
Italy	5.0	17.1	21.3	9.3	4.7
Netherlands	3.8	10.5	6.5	2.2	-0.5
Norway	10.5	11.6	10.8	5.7	8.7
Sweden	5.7	9.8	13.7	7.4	4.2
UK	6.4	24.3	18.0	6.1	4.2

* 1986
Source: International Monetary Fund, *International Financial Statistics* (1988) p. 117.

The pluralist concept of power has been subject to sustained criticism now for over twenty years. Many of these criticisms are particularly relevant to the study of business and politics. The first criticism made was that the pluralist measure of power is of value only when there is an observable clash of interests or opinions. In some situations, one interest may be so powerful that issues are not expressed in the political system.[14] Crenson has argued that the power of US Steel in Gary, Indiana was so extensive that the issue of controlling the pollution from its furnaces was not raised.[15] Crenson argues that the people of Gary probably wanted clean air, but did not dare raise the issue because US Steel had such a dominance of the town that to do so would have been futile or costly. Similarly, it is beyond doubt that business is well aware of the importance of public opinion. Television viewers in Britain and the USA are treated to commercials showing heroic oil company workers struggling with the freezing temperatures of Alaska or the waves of the North Sea to bring the public its petrol or heating oil. Other commercials show the care taken by the oil companies to protect the environment. To the extent that public opinion is willing (or is persuaded) to take a favourable view of business, business has acquired a valuable political resource. It was probably the case that many Americans in the 1950 would have shared the view attributed to a member of President Eisenhower's Cabinet, Secretary of Defence Charles Wilson, that 'what is good for General Motors is good for the United States'. Public trust in the integrity of business executives, and belief that business executives tried to strike a fair balance between the public interest and profit, were high. It was unlikely, therefore, that there would be determined efforts to impose on business policies unwelcome to it, for such policies would have little popularity. A major observable clash of interests between business and government or business and other interest groups would be unlikely to occur because the climate of opinion was so favourable to business.

The critics of pluralism have proposed other measures of power to take account of the problems they have raised. Crenson borrowed the concept of 'non-decision' or a 'second face of power' from its originators, Bachrach and Baratz. The second face of power was the power to protect one's interests through the exclusion from political discussion or the policy agenda proposals which could be damaging to them. In Gary, proposals to require US Steel to spend large sums on preventing pollution was thus excluded from the political agenda and were not even seriously discussed.

Steven Lukes[16] argued that to take account of the climate of opinion – or what in Marxist terms might be called the 'dominant ideology' – it was necessarily to acknowledge a third face of power: the power to shape opinion in such a way that people with conflicting interests were unable to formulate a challenge to the dominant interest. Those believing that what was good for General Motors was always good for them would not even be able fully to imagine, let alone support, policies unwelcome to General Motors.

Other writers have stressed the importance of *structural* aspects of the power of business. Business leaders, writers such as Lindblom[17] have stressed, are not just another interest group analogous to the League Against Cruel Sports or an anti-abortion movement. On the contrary, business leaders in market societies dispose of real power because they have been entrusted with the power to decide whether (and where) to invest in the new processes which are vital to the future prosperity of the whole community. If business leaders feel that the conditions are not right for investment, if business confidence is lacking, then that investment will not be made – or, more probably, will be made elsewhere. In Europe governments thus compete for the international car companies such as Ford to build new plants in their country and not in a rival one; in the USA the states compete with each other to attract industry by having the lowest corporation taxes and in other ways creating a 'favourable business environment'. Business executives can consult league tables which rank each US state in terms of its 'business climate'.

Most of these theories have an obvious value and plausibility in supplementing the pluralist analysis of the power of business. They are also, however, subject to serious criticisms. Both the second and third faces of power theories are open to the objection that the observer using them is imposing his or her own values on the people in the situation being studied. To say (following Bachrach and Baratz) that a particular proposal should have been discussed – and the fact that it was not indicates the power of those whose interest would have been hurt by the proposal – seems to involve making a judgement that the proposal was of such obvious value and importance that its neglect needs explanation; it is always possible that those involved in the situation might not agree. Luke's third face of power theory similarly involves asserting that people who have absorbed a pro-business ideology have a form of 'false consciousness' which blinds them to their true interests. Only those confronted with particularly bizarre ideologies (such as an argument from a poor white in the old deep South of the USA that he had common interests with plantation owners) or those such as Marxists who ascribe to an over-arching theory of society and human nature will be happy making such assertions. Most social scientists would be wary of imposing readily their own values on the subjects of their study.

Crenson's attempt to avoid this problem illustrates how severe the problem is. Crenson argued that we could assume that the desire to avoid pollution – which is damaging to the health – is so universal that failure to propose pollution controls could be sign only of domination by a hostile interest. Further reflection indicates that this is not necessarily so. People living in Gary – particularly if they were working for US Steel – might believe that if the company was not bothered with pollution controls and their expense, it could pay higher wages, invest more and create new jobs, and at least would refrain from locating elsewhere. This would be true particularly if – and there seems to have been some evidence that this was the case – the population of Gary consisted of people attracted by hopes of high wages, who perhaps planned to stay in the town for only a limited time. Such considerations could rationally lead them not to favour pollution control laws.

Lindblom's argument that business has structural power can be similarly criticised, in spite of its plausibility. If business executives decide not to carry out an investment because the political climate is not right, they pay a price;

potential profits are foregone. Even decisions about where to locate a factory or other plant cannot be made in response simply to the political climate in the planned location. A copper company may be forced to open a copper mine in Chile even if it fears expropriation by a left-wing government, because there is no other source of copper so readily available from a mining point of view. Closing a factory and transferring its production to a new plant in a low-wage, low-cost environment may be very costly in the short term, and such things as markets or the supply of raw material may also exert a more powerful effect on location than differences in government policy. Moreover, the needs of business in relation to government are neither as homogeneous nor as simple as we have so far supposed. Some businesses, such as textiles, need a comparatively unskilled, low-wage workforce and as few government regulations and as low taxes as possible. The computer industry has very different needs. A skilled, highly-educated workforce is sufficiently important that it is better to locate in a country or state with a good educational system than one with low taxes and a poor educational system. (The American microchip industry is a case in point, locating in California and Massachusetts, not the South.) High government spending and taxation may provide businesses with benefits as diverse as lively cultural centres (of value in attracting top executives and their families to the area), or a good road system. Politicians are likely to be given a surprisingly wide-ranging 'shopping list' by companies whom they solicit, and such apparently obvious demands as low taxation may not, in fact, figure very prominently. A survey of business executives in the USA in 1983 suggested that low company taxation was listed as only the thirteenth most important factor in deciding where to locate a new plant.

In spite of the difficulties which each of these theories creates, few would deny that each contributes to a fuller understanding of the power of business. It is also obviously the case that the importance of these factors will vary considerably from country to country. It might be plausible to argue that a dominant, pro-business ideology dominates thinking in the USA inhibiting fundamental challenges to capitalism; the question 'Why is there no socialism in the

United States?' has been debated at least since Sombart wrote the classic book of that name.[18] It is surely less plausible to argue that a dominant ideology precludes challenges to business in countries such as Italy or France where Communist and Socialist parties have received a major proportion of the votes cast in elections. Less obviously, it is almost certainly the case that attitudes to business fluctuate *within* each country over time. In the USA, for example, the high levels of trust in business executives common in the 1950s gave way by the 1970s to high levels of distrust and scepticism, recovering somewhat in the 1980s.[19] Similarly (as we shall see) the degree to which business is organised to take part in politics in pluralist fashion through lobbying, campaign contributions, etc. varies very significantly over time. It is probably wise, therefore, to think of the different theories of the power of business not as permanently mutually exclusive theories, but as descriptions of factors which may vary in importance from country to country, and from period to period within the same country, in determining the power of business.

Types of Policy and Organisation of Business

Bauer, Pool and Dexter published in 1963 a study of American business and public policy which was one of the most carefully researched books on any aspect of American politics till then published.[20] We shall have cause to refer to this book in detail later; it also prompted one of the most influential book reviews in political science. The reviewer, Theodore Lowi, took Bauer, Pool and Dexter to task for basing a book on American business and public policy on a single topic: tariff policy. Lowi argued that policies shape the pattern of politics associated with them. In particular, there were three major types of policy which shaped the pattern of politics.[21] These were *distributive* policies (such as tariffs, government contracts, etc., *redistributive* policies (such as progressive taxation and welfare policies), and *regulatory* policies (such as the imposition of rules concerning pollution by government on industry). In each of these types of policy, Lowi contended that the same interest (such as business) would find itself in a different web of political relationships and dealings.

The adequacy of Lowi's typology and the question of how to define the types of policy in practice need not detain us here. We should note, however, that Lowi is undoubtedly correct in his claim that different policy areas will involve business in different types of politics. There will obviously be a difference between the politics of issues which divide industry and the politics of issues which unite it. When it comes to exerting political pressure to win a defence contract, the situation is obviously one in which it is every firm for itself. In the USA, for example, such aircraft builders as Lockheed and Boeing have waged mighty battles, involving newspaper campaigns and the Representatives and Senators from areas where the firms' factories are located, in the quest for military contracts. There are, however, issues which unite business. Issues such as the level of corporation tax affect all companies. Regulations to limit the exposure of workers to noise considered by the Health and Safety Commission in Britain, would affect so many firms (and practically all engaged in manufacturing) that again there can be a common front on the issue. Some issues (such as the level of rates) are a matter of concern to both very large and very small businesses, whereas other issues (such as exchange rate policy) affect primarily only medium-sized and large concerns.

The frequency with which issues which unite rather than divide business arise varies from country to country. In general we should expect that this in turn will affect the character of business organisations. Where issues affecting all businesses are raised frequently, business may be expected to create more impressive organisations to raise common interests than in countries where such issues are rare. A strong socialist or union movement would therefore be likely to be accompanied by a strong employers' organisation. Countries in which socialism (or a similar general challenge to business interests) and unions were both weak would be unlikely to have a strong central employers' organisation. As we shall see, there is considerable evidence to support these propositions. The central employers' organisations of Britain,

Germany and Sweden are much more impressive organisations than the employers' organisations of the USA, where both unions and radical challenges to capitalism have been comparatively weak. The degree to which the small business owner is willing to throw in his or her lot with the multinational enterprise in paying membership dues to an organisation purporting to represent both depends to a major degree on the extent to which both feel that they have important (but threatened) common interests.

Many other factors help shape the character of business organisation. The political cultures of Western democracies differ considerably in the degree to which they bestow legitimacy on the representation of views and interests through interest-group activity as opposed to through political parties, legislators and other elected politicians. In some countries close, confidential discussions between interest group officials and government officials are regarded as part of everyday life; in other countries such gatherings are regarded as potential conspiracies, so that a public record of such meetings and their purpose is required.

One of the most important influences on the character of business interest groups is the character of the state in which they are embedded. Most social scientists follow Weber and define the state as the institution which has the monopoly on the legitimate use of force within a geographically defined area. The state has several characteristics, however. First, state agencies can be *actors* which implement policies such as waging war or levying taxes. Second, the state is an institutional *arena* within which different interests or parties compete for power. Third, the state is a *structuring agent* which defines the forms of other actors in society by its procedures and laws. All of these characteristics of the state can be important in shaping the form of business interest groups.

Considerable variation exists in the ways in which different states *act* towards business with, in consequence, considerable variation in how these actions influence the organisation of business. Dyson has emphasised the importance of what he terms *industrial culture* in shaping expectations about how states should act towards business.[22] In some countries, such as the United States, the assumption will be that state agencies should keep themselves distant from the activities of corporations. The role of the state is to maintain conditions conducive to business's success by maintaining the institutional infrastructure needed for commercial activity (such as a system of law) and by steering the economy at the *macro* level in order to avoid recessions or inflation. Decisions about the allocation of investment and the co-ordination of different factors of production are left to market forces. In contract, in France and Japan the assumption will be that, in addition to fulfilling tasks expected of the state in the USA, state agencies will take a close interest in the plans and activities of industries and corporations. In brief, state agencies are expected to be involved at the *micro* as well as the macro level.

States which practice interventionist micro as well as macro economic policies will have or acquire a greater capacity for influencing industry than states which do not. This capacity will consist of agencies such as the Japanese Ministry of International Trade and Industry (MITI) or the French Commissariat du Plan staffed by officials who have considerable detailed knowledge about individual firms and industries. Generally, however, more interventionist states seek partners by promoting the growth of interest groups which, while enjoying a virtual monopoly on representing the sector of the economy for which they claim to speak, are in agreement with the basic thrust of government policy. Monopolistic rather than competitive groups suit the needs of interventionist states because they not only speak more authoritatively but are less likely to be constrained by divisions of opinion among their members. If there is only one interest group which can plausibly represent a corporation, corporations are less likely to resign if they disagree with a particular policy of the interest group. Monopolies can give interest group leaders the freedom from the control of their members they need to form alliances with the state. For such interest groups not only provide interventionist states with greater knowledge, but also assist government by promoting and helping to implement government policies among their members.

Interventionist states promote interest groups in a variety of sectors; in France the farmers' organisation, FNSEA, is a good example of a sponsored group.[23] But the most important examples of interest groups promoted by states in order to facilitate their plans for economic growth are business organisations such as the Keidanren in Japan. We may expect, therefore, that the greater the wish of the state to engage in interventionist micro-economic policies, the greater the likelihood that we will find strong, monopolistic employers' organisations which have been fostered by the state. It is not a coincidence that the creation of the Confederation of British Industry (CBI), which was supposed to speak authoritatively for all British industries, occurred at the instigation of government during one of the high points of belief in detailed government involvement in industry.[24]

As noted earlier, the state is also an arena in which different interests compete for power. The type of arena provided by each state also influences the nature of the business organisations which emerge. In general, the more fragmented the arena in which interest groups and parties compete for power, the more fragmented are interests – including business groups. If the political arena – as in Britain – seems capable of producing decisive, even dramatic, changes in policy, then interest groups, including business, will feel an imperative to units. In states with fragmented policymaking structures, such as the United States, where dramatic change is in consequence unlikely, the imperative to unite is less keenly felt. Indeed, individual corporations or industries may believe that they can protect their important interests individually, perhaps by dominating a particular agency or Congressional committee in which they have unusual influence.

Bureaucrats and politicians find many advantages in monopolistic interest groups. Monopolistic groups can aggregate demands on government which, were they to be expressed by competing groups, would force bureaucrats or politicians to choose between them. The leaders of monopolistic groups, freed from the pressures of competing for members, can take a more moderate or 'statesman like' stance in their dealings with government than can the leaders of competing groups. As Mancur Olson has argued, the larger the sector of society for which an interest group speaks, the more likely it is to think of the long-term impact of its requests.[25] Thus British unions have been less likely to play a constructive role than Swedish unions partly because there are so many more of them. No union sacrificing a short term gain today can be sure other unions will match its restraint; the monopolistic Swedish LO knows that if it makes a commitment, the matter is settled. Finally, it is much easier to turn policy implementation over to a monopolistic interest group than to competing groups.

When the state itself provides a relatively simple, united structure within which competition for power takes place (as in Britain), the state can pressure interests such as business into forming monopolistic, cohesive organisations. Would-be competitors to the dominant interest group are either not consulted at all, or are consulted so late in the policy-making process that their opinions have little impact. In states with more fragmented institutions, it is much harder to exclude an interest group from the policy-making process. If American bureaucrats had attempted to build up systematically the Business Roundtable at the expense of the Chamber of Commerce or the National Association of Manufacturers (NAM) by consulting only the Business Roundtable, the neglected interest groups would still have found a hearing in Congress.[26] A fragmented state cannot bring about cohesive business organisations, for it cannot control access to policy making in the same way that a less fragmented state can.

Finally, the state structures the character of business organisations by a wide variety of laws and regulations. In the United States, for example, where most people do not think of the state structuring interest groups, a large number of laws in fact shape the interest group system. Anti-trust legislation has inhibited powerfully the growth of trade associations. Campaign finance laws, by limiting to $5000 the maximum an interest group can contribute to a political campaign, encourage the formation of numerous interest groups rather than a single large group. Parts of the tax code – particularly Section 501 c (i–v) – encourage certain types – and discourage others – of interest group activity. The fact that the expenses of lobbying in Washington can be set against corporate tax liabilities can be viewed as a subsidy for corporate political activity. The doctrine that corporations are persons and can therefore seek protection in the courts for many of the rights guaranteed citizens under the Constitution has provided business with many legal weapons to fight policies it dislikes.

In brief, the state as agent, arena for conflict and structuring agent exerts a powerful influence on the character of business groups. We should not suppose, however, that is the only influence.

Two further factors which merit attention are the industrial relations systems and industrial structures which prevail in different countries. The strength of employers' organisations representing specific industries (trade associations) has been fostered by the existence of powerful trade unions seeking industry-wide collective bargaining agreements. Employers have been forced to unite to counteract the power of unions. The impact of industrial structure is less simple. In principle we might suppose that industrial concentration so that very few corporations dominate an industry will promote the formation of business organisations; the few will always have less trouble coalescing than the many. However, if corporations are large enough, they will also feel more confident about establishing direct relations with government and will be able to afford to open their own offices in Washington or London. It is impossible to determine in the abstract which of these tendencies will dominate, partly because the receptiveness of government to contacts from individual corporations will have a vital impact. There are strong indications that in both the United States and Britain, individual corporations came to play a larger role in interest group politics during the 1980s. Business organisations faded in importance somewhat because of the increased importance of individual corporations. Whether this shift represents a structural change in business representation or merely the temporary dominance of issues such as taxation or trade which divide rather than unite business is an issue which we shall explore in subsequent chapters.

Considerable efforts have been made by political scientists to describe and explain differences in government – business relations in western democracies. A number of different themes have been used to categorise these differences. One approach would be to focus on the extent of the activities of government. As we have noted already, some governments avoid extensive involvement in the detailed planning of investment or production. Other governments work in partnership with corporations and other economic interests to identify the most promising prospects for future economic growth and to steer resources to those sectors. We might focus therefore on how far governments 'intervene' in industry or limit themselves to macroeconomic policies intended to promote economic growth.

Fruitful as such an approach can be, this book focuses instead on another difference characterising the business–government relationship. That difference is how far the relationship between business and government is structured or *institutionalised*. The more institutionalised the business–government relationship the more it is conducted between organisations which enjoy generally-acknowledged status as representatives of business and government. In countries with less institutionalised business–government relationships, dealings between government and business are conducted by government either with numerous competing business organisations of uncertain status or directly with individual corporations. Institutionalisation in this context often implies the existence of somewhat formalised channels of communication; councils, commissions or planning procedures are established as forums for concerting business and government plans. However, as in all institutions, much consultation and co-ordination occurs outside formal procedures. Institutionalisation at its highest involves close informal relations between business representatives and government officials with consultations occurring as readily in a Prime Minister's country retreat or on a park bench as in a committee room.

My focus on institutionalisation obviously has much in common with political scientists who have employed the concept of *neocorporatism*. Schmitter defined neocorporatism as a system of interest intermediation in which interests were linked to government through groups that enjoyed a monopoly of representation of the sector of society for which they speak and that were licensed or encouraged by the state.[27] Although Schmitter originally argued that neocorporatist systems could involve linking a wide variety of interests to government, in practice neocorporatism is used to characterise the concertation of government, employers and unions, with some other sectors such as agriculture being involved less frequently and centrally.

The concept of neocorporatism has provided one of the most important focuses of debate for students of comparative politics in recent decades. Unfortunately, the debate has seemed to raise more questions than it answers. Neocorporatism was used originally to characterise linkages between government and umbrella organisations representing the collective interests of employers and unions. Perhaps because of difficulties in establishing empirically the importance of such linkages in more than a handful of countries, political scientists using the concept of neocorporatism shifted their focus, looking for neocorporatism at the *meso* level linking government and trade associations representing individual industries. One writer has even argued that neocorporatism can be used to characterise the relationship between governments and individual corporations.[28]

A further problem concerns the status of neocorporatist relationships. The claim that political systems are neocorporatist seems to involve more than a description of their interest group systems. It also seems to involve a claim that the interest group relationship is of dominating significance. More – or more important – decisions are made by government in consultation with interest groups than in other parts of the political system such as the legislature, the electoral system or political parties. Yet such claims are rarely substantiated by writers using the neocorporatist concept. Clearly important decisions are made through neocorporatist channels in countries such as Norway or Austria. But whether most, or the most important decisions are made this way remains in question.

Further questions have been raised about the inevitability or stability of neocorporatism. Some political scientists writing on neocorporatism seemed to adopt a developmental perspective, suggesting that mature industrialised democracies would tend to become more neocorporatist. As we shall see, this prospect seemed less likely in the late 1980s than the prospect that neocorporatism would break down even in countries which had seemed its exemplary. Even at the height of its academic popularity, neocorporatism had been seen by some as an inherently unstable alliance between the state, employers and labour which could not long persist.[29]

Whole books can be, and have been, written on neocorporatism. It would be hazardous in this book to embrace the concept of neocorporatism wholeheartedly. For to do so would be to take sides in complex theoretical disputes without the opportunity to resolve them. Moreover, neocorporatism, in practice generally understood to be a form of concertation between government, business and labour in practice fits badly two countries with interesting, highly institutionalised links between business and government. Those countries are France and Japan. In both countries, as we shall see, close consultation occurs between business and government which is generally routed through highly developed business organisations. However, in neither country have unions played a major role in economic policy-making. Although it is possible to deal with this problem by terming those countries corporatist without labour it can equally well be argued that neocorporatism exists only when there is a triangular relationship between business, labour and government. It might be less controversial to say that in those two countries the business–government relationship is highly institutionalised than to say it is neocorporatist without labour.

This book is organised, therefore, along a continuum of how institutionalised is the business–government relationship. The countries covered are the United States, Britain, West Germany, Italy, Sweden and Austria, France and Japan. The range, as we shall see, is from the loosely-structured competitive system of the United States to the highly-structured government–business partnership in Japan. It is not accidental that this continuum coincides with a continuum of countries ranked in terms of how deeply interventionist on micro-economic issues governments have been. However, the focus here will be more on the characteristics of the business–government relationship than on the economic policies of governments. The two are indeed related, but not identical.

The Political Context

The recent prominence of the debate over neocorporatism has led to an understandable, even desirable, focus on the relationship between government and business interest groups. Sometimes, however, such a concentration results in the neglect of the political context in which business interest group activity is embedded. That political context is shaped partly by the success of political allies of business, whom business often tries to help through tactics such as campaign contributions, and partly through the strength of interests or viewpoints inimical to business interests.

In most if not all of the democratic nations, one political party is more closely associated with business than are the others. That party receives a disproportionate share of the votes of managers and stockholders, and generally receives substantial financial support from business interests. The Republican Party in the United States, the Liberal Democratic Party in Japan and the Conservative Party in Britain are all examples of political parties closely associated with business. It might well be argued that the strength of pro-business political parties in western democracies has been more beneficial to business interests than the activities of business interest groups.

The norms and rules governing the relationship between business and the pro-business party differ, however. In the United States, for example, it is illegal for companies to make political contributions out of their general funds. The situation which has existed legally since 1926, though enforced effectively only since 1972, contrasts with the situation in Britain where companies have openly and legally supplied the Conservative Party with a large proportion (until recently a majority) of its funds from their general accounts. The contribution of Japanese corporations to the different factions within the Liberal Democratic Party are extensive. Indeed, Japanese politicians raise a far larger amount of money per voter than do their American counterparts, and most of the money comes from business. The financial ties between LDP politicians and business became notorious in the late 1980s because of a financial scandal known as the Recruit affair. Few expected the scandal to reduce significantly the dependence of LDP politicians on cash from business.[30]

What proportion of the electorate are natural allies of business? Even in the United States, home of popular capitalism, only a minority of the population are stockholders. The proportion in Britain is even lower, though the Thatcher government succeeded in significantly raising the proportion of the population owning stock. The top managerial class which can be expected to identify its interests automatically with those of stockholders is also a minority of the population. Of course it can be argued that a large proportion of the population has an *indirect* interest in the performance of corporations through insurance policies, retirement plans and other forms of indirect investment. *Institutional* investors representing millions of retirees such as the British Rail Pension Plan or the managers of retirement funds for states such as New York or Wisconsin are more important today than individual investors. However, indirect investments have a lesspowerful impact on political consciousness than being a top manager or a wealthy individual investor. Political parties supported by business have therefore needed to broaden their appeal by identifying with broader ideals or sentiments and by forging alliances with other interests, such as farmers. The British Conservative Party and the Republican Party in the USA have often suggested that they are the more patriotic party; the LDP has protected the interests of Japanese farmers even at the cost of embarrassment in international trade talks. Even pro-business parties therefore have to put some distance between themselves and business interests in order to secure electoral success.

As we have noted above, business is not a homogeneous unit. At least three differences in types of business are likely to have political relevance. These are differences between financial institutions (such as banks, insurance companies and other investing institutions), manufacturing and mining firms, and small businesses (ranging from restaurants to garages). In Britain, obvious differences have arisen between financial institutions and manufacturing firms. High interest rates and a high value for sterling have worked to the advantage of financial institutions, labelled 'The City'. High interest rates have brought high incomes for the City institutions, and the high value of sterling prevailing in the early 1980s made investment overseas, a long-standing strategy of the City, an easier option than would otherwise have been the case. In the USA, differences between very large institutions (both financial and manufacturing) on the one hand, and small-scale business ('Main Street') have long been noted in the degree to which unions and social expenditure on welfare, food stamps and health care have been tolerated. Though the entire business community in America opposed such policies at their inception, most big business – referred to sometimes as Wall Street and sometimes as the East Coast Establishment – has been more willing to tolerate their continuance than has 'Main Street'.

The divisions between 'Main Street' and Wall Street parallel those between Wall Street and the 'sun belt' enterprises of the South and South-west which again are more hostile to federal government programmes than Wall Street has been – unless, of course, a federal government programme such as the space or defence programmes benefits their corporation.[31] How intense these divisions are depends on prevailing circumstances. In the mid-1960s, when American economic leadership was still unchallenged, the well established 'Wall Street' firms were dismayed by the Republican Party's flirtation with the far-right-wing candidacy of Senator Barry Goldwater. In 1980, as the same long-established corporations felt severe competition from foreign competitors and struggled to reduce their costs, Ronald Reagan was able to evoke a much warmer response among 'Wall Street' business types than had Senator Goldwater while reiterating Goldwater's attacks on unions or government assistance for poorer Americans. Similarly, the rise of Thatcherism within the Conservative Party has been associated with the decline of the landowning interest and the rise of those representing finance or service industries such as advertising. Moreover, different types of business interest may have influence in different political institutions. The United States Congress, composed of individual political entrepreneurs who must build their own local coalitions of support, has been more responsive to local business élites than other parts of the political system.

In contrast to both Britain and Japan, conservative politics in France, Germany and the USA also has a religious dimension with which economic interests of business must be accommodated. This is perhaps most obvious in the USA where the moral concerns of the 'Moral Majority' coexisted with most business concerns without trouble. Banning abortion or 'dirty' books does not cause serious problems for Exxon, while the 'Moral Majority' causes may lure some votes away from liberal Democrats likely to be perceived by business executives as their political enemies. In Christian Democratic parties in Europe, in contrast, business has to compete for influence with socially-reforming Christian politicians and the Christian trade unions. While it is thus possible to say quite accurately that there is always one party particularly associated with business in contemporary democracies, the extent of business influence within that party, and the type of business which has influence within that party, may vary significantly.

Purpose of Business–Government Relations

It is very easy to assume the universality of what is in fact a particularly Anglo-American perspective on business–government relations. That is to assume that government and business are involved in a necessarily *adversarial* relationship.

The major political task for business is to limit government policies such as company taxation or regulations which cost business money. In fact, as we have seen even in Britain and the USA, the business–government relationship is more complex. Business wants things from government – such as research funds, commercial representation overseas, and protection from unfair foreign competition. Outside the

USA and Britain, the tradition of regarding business and government as necessarily locked in conflict is unfamiliar. In both Germany and Japan industrial development was fostered by government; from the earliest days, the relationship between the two was seen as mutually beneficial. In France, too, there has been a tradition stretching back to Colbert of the duty of government to promote industries. Since the Second World War, business has joined with government (and, to a lesser extent, unions) in the formulation of a Five-year Economic Plan. Similarly, the Japanese Ministry of International Trade and Industry (MITI) has developed, and to some degree fostered, a particular view of how Japanese industry should develop, encouraging growth in areas such as computers where the prospects seem bright, and encouraging movement out of industries with limited potential such as textiles, an inherently low-wage industry MITI believed to be fundamentally unsuited to the contemporary Japanese economy.[32]

Such collaborative links between government and industry have been called 'industrial policy' in Britain and the USA. There is widespread agreement that the USA and Britain are much less likely to have coherent industrial policies than Japan and France. This is partly a matter of ideology. Business executives, politicians (except on the left of the Labour and Democratic Parties) and civil servants are likely to oppose detailed government involvement in industry. Broad-scale management of the economy has long been accepted in Britain; government policies concerned with the encouragement or discouragement of specific industries have been much less accepted than in France or Japan. Political structures are also relevant here. In both Britain and the USA the political system is very responsive, particularly to geographically-concentrated interests (because in two-party systems a small, strategically placed minority may determine the outcome of a parliamentary or presidential election). In both Japan and France, the power within government of the bureaucracy, the dominance of a single party of Japan, and the weakness of politicians in the French Fourth Republic (followed by the insulation from electoral pressures of the president in the Fifth Republic) have made it easier to make politically unpopular but economically wise decisions.

We can ask, therefore, not only how the character of the business–government relationship varies, but also how its *purposes* vary. Just as countries can be contrasted in terms of the degree to which business–government relations can be described as corporatist, so can countries be contrasted in terms of the degree to which their governments follow a purposeful industrial policy, promoting long-term industrial growth.

Enemies of Business

A full consideration of the role of any interest in society should consider not only the characteristics of that interest, but also the attitudes and strength of its potential enemies. As we have stressed above, the character of business organisations can be profoundly affected by the degree to which business executives perceive that common interests of the business community are threatened. However, the success of such organisations in defending business interests will be affected in turn by the organisation, support and resources of any interests with which conflict might develop.

Traditionally, the business community has felt that its common interests are most likely to be threatened by trade unions and socialist movements. There are well-known variations in the degree to which unions constitute a political threat to business. A large section of the American union movement was influenced by a 'business union' conception of their role, represented by the founder of the American Federation of Labor (AFL), Samuel Gompers.

Gomper's belief in pure and simple unionism led him to oppose any broad role for unions in politics, and to argue that union members had an interest in the profitability of their companies; profitable companies could afford larger wage increases than unprofitable companies. Gompers, moreover, believed in the provision of unemployment and sickness insurance through the unions rather than through government. In short, his type of unionism posed few problems for the collective interests of business. In contrast, the industrial unions in the USA, and most European trade unions, have played a much more active political role, typically pressing for welfare state measures unwelcome to business. The variation in the character of the unions, both between countries and within the same country over time, means that unions have posed a problem of varying complexity politically for business executives. Moreover, unions obviously differ in strength. Unions have succeeded in recruiting a proportion of the workforce which varies from 17 per cent in the USA and just under 46 per cent in Britain to over 75 per cent in Austria and the Scandinavian countries. Although the percentage of the workforce unionised is not a precise measure of the political power of unions, it is obviously an important influence.

One might argue, however, that in most countries there has been something of an 'historic compromise' between organised labour and organised business. That is in a sense what corporatism is all about. Certainly in Germany there are few contentious issues between the employers' organisation and unions; the Swedish employers' organisation and the union federation (LO) similarly enjoyed smooth relations from the 1930s to the 1980s. Even in Britain, it is probably the case that the Trades Union Congress (TUC) and the CBI agree as much as they disagree, and certainly are on better terms with each other than their American counterparts. Most social democratic parties have similarly made their peace with business in the context of a mixed economy in which there are both publicly- and privately-owned enterprises supporting a welfare state. Only in Britain does the question of the extent of public ownership still seem to arouse the passions. Indeed, it has often seemed that social democratic parties – perhaps because of a belief in planning rather than free markets – have been particularly conspicuous in the creation of highly-institutionalised, corporatist links between business organisations, unions and government. In Britain, the Labour Governments of 1964–70 and 1974–9 were more favourably disposed to close links between government and the CBI than the Conservative Governments which succeeded them. Similarly in the USA, faltering steps towards corporatism under Democratic President Carter (involving exploring the idea of a business, union and government forum) were halted by the election of the vehemently free market Reagan Administration.

The Green Challenge

One of the most important challenges facing business in many western democracies in the late 1980s came from environmentalists. As well as functioning as interest groups, environmentalists had formed their own political movement, the Greens, in many European countries. The Green parties enjoyed surprising success for what had seemed in the late 1970s to be a social movement with limited popular support. In the European elections of 1989 the Greens captured 15 per cent of the vote in Britain, and were denied representation in the European Parliament only by the fact that the British electoral system, uniquely in the European Community, has no element of proportionality in it. The Greens have long been established in the West German Parliament and have been part of governing coalitions at the state and local level.

Environmental concerns come in many forms. At their most radical, environmentalists call for a fundamental change in society so that pollution can be reduced. Such changes might include a reduction in the population and in consumption of goods – including cars – whose production or use leads to pollution. Farmers would abandon such techniques of intensive production as the use of chemical fertilisers in favour of more natural techniques. Less-radical environmentalists have more moderate concerns such as eliminating the use of lead in motor fuels, reducing the use of non-biodegradable plastics and halting the destruction of the countryside through urban sprawl.

In some form or other, environmental concerns have been with us for some time. The Council for the Preservation of Rural England has been campaigning against urban sprawl since the ribbon development of the 1930s made the danger of unregulated development clear. In the United States conservationists (who are not always the same as environmentalists) have been arguing for the preservation of natural resources for future use since the turn of the century. Indeed, the movement to preserve natural resources in the United States may well be linked to the realisation in the late nineteenth century that the frontier was closed, that the USA like other countries was now a nation with geographical boundaries.

In more recent times, environmentalism has had two major periods of strength. The first was in the late 1960s and early 1970s when a massive wave of environmentalist legislation was adopted in the United States (such as the Clean Air Act and the Clean Water Act) and the Environmental Protection Agency was created, somewhat implausibly, by President Nixon. The second period of environmental strength was from the mid-1980s onwards when, as we have noted, Green parties flourished in Europe and to their astonishment, US President Bush and the British Prime Minister, Mrs Thatcher, declared that they were environmentalists too.

Why are people environmentalists? The answer might seem obvious. Our capacity to destroy the planet has never been greater, not only through military means (the hydrogen bomb) but through civilian (as the nuclear accident at Chernobyl in the USSR made clear). By the late 1980s, the general public had become aware of a strong possibility that quite mundane activities (such as the use of deodorant aerosols) contributed by releasing chlorofluorocarbons into the atmosphere to a 'greenhouse effect' which, through raising the average temperatures around the world, could have quite catastrophic results. Humanity must control itself, or destroy itself.

Unfortunately for social science, the link between environmental awareness and risk is not simple. By many measures such as life expectancy, people are living longer and better than ever before. There was a more urgent need to tackle air pollution in nineteenth century British cities than there is today. Perhaps environmentalism is to some degree a luxury product, one 'consumed' most avidly in countries such as West Germany and the United States with the highest standards of living. Even in the United States, the environmental movement's political strength evaporated in the 1970s when acute concern developed about the American economy. Only after the recovery of the American economy in the mid-1980s did environmentalism re-emerge as an important political issue.

Yet if environmentalism is a product of affluence, it is reasonable to assume that its strength will increase. No doubt there will be recessions again – as in the late 1970s–and early 1980s. In the long term, most economies will continue to grow, and with the growth will come more support for environmentalism. How will this affect business?

The most radical forms of environmentalism clearly call for drastic changes that are incompatible with current society. Large-scale reductions in the size of the population and mass consumption would raise profound problems for business. At the other end of the spectrum a shift to slightly more expensive forms of packaging using biodegradable materials would cause large corporations few problems. If all car manufacturers are required to fit equally expensive catalytic burners to the exhaust systems of cars in Europe (as has long been standard practice in the USA), then though the total demand for cars might fall slightly, no manufacturer would be placed at a significant disadvantage and the industry as a whole could live with the problem. On the other hand, if the costs of conversion fall particularly heavily on one manufacturer (perhaps because it produces fewer units over which to spread the costs of conversion) that producer is likely to object energetically, and if the industry as a whole feels threatened, as the American textile industry felt threatened by health regulations in the mid-1970s, the objections will be vociferous. In short, there are some environmental regulations that industry will feel it can live with, and others that it will feel it cannot.

What are the effects of environmentalism on the political activities of business? Most obviously, the more business is confronted with a challenge from environmentalism, the more politically active it is likely to be. As we shall see, challenges to business by groups such as environmentalists in the USA in the late 1960s and early 1970s contributed to a massive expansion of business's own political activities. The potential impact of environmental regulations on investment patterns and profitability is too great to ignore. But what form will business's response to this challenge take? One possibility is that business will tend to unite, strengthening trade associations to protect particular industries and general employers' associations to protect the common interests of all industries. Individual companies will be reluctant to tarnish their own images by defending what might be described in the media as unsafe or environmentally damaging practices. In consequence, firms will prefer to act politically through business associations rather than individually. In the United States in the early 1970s firms were further attracted to collaborative political activity by a feeling that the activities of agencies such as the Environmental Protection Agency (EPA) and Occupational Safety and Health Administration (OSHA) constituted such a broad challenge to so many industries that the general interests of all employers were threatened. Whether this feeling reflected a reaction purely to the breadth of the agencies' concerns or to the somewhat aggressive style of regulation those agencies adopted can be debated.

It is possible that in future the political response of business to environmentalism will be less cohesive than in the past. Many corporations are aware that they themselves are relatively 'clean' and have nothing to gain from standing shoulder to shoulder with 'dirty' polluters. Even within a single industry such as petrochemicals, there is widespread agreement that there are certain 'cowboy' companies that by taking chances with the environment or health or safety both endanger the community and undercut their more responsible rivals. There are even companies that, because they manufacture equipment to promote health and safety or protect the environment, have a vested interest in increased regulation. It may well be that in the future, therefore, environmentalism will encourage cohesive action by employers only if the environmental movement or regulatory agencies make major political errors. Certainly in the USA in the early 1970s, environmentalists and similar movements aroused such irritation in the business community that some of its allies argued that it would be better to have a socialist movement to deal with![33]

The Special Challenge of 1992

The plans for the creation of a truly common market within the European Community in 1992 have posed a special challenge to European business and businesses elsewhere which wish to operate in the giant European market.

Some of these challenges are commercial. As the advocates of a truly common market after 1992 intended, the abolition of remaining trade barriers within the Community will increase competitive pressures. The cheaper, more efficient and lower-cost producers will in theory be able to compete for business on the home ground of rival businesses without government interference.

Yet 1992 has other implications for business. Corporations manufacturing outside Europe but trading with it are anxious to avoid free trade within Europe being accompanied by greater restraints on imports from outside Europe, a 'fortress Europe' as its critics call it. Firms within Europe will be reminded by 1992 of a development that precedes it, the increase in the importance of the European Community as a governing institution. Firms will find increasingly that, like the British water industry, important decisions are being made in Brussels, not London. The prospects for a privatised water industry in Britain were affected significantly by the enforcement by the Commission of *European* rules on water safety.

The growing significance of the European Community as a decision-making institution raises crucial questions for business about its political tactics. In the first place, business needs to build up a set of interest groups in Brussels as strong as any found in individual European capitals. This process has of course begun. Employers' associations exist in Brussels to defend the interests not only of employers in general but of individual industries. However, these organisations are not yet fully authoritative, perhaps because employers, like other interest groups, are often attracted to lobbying their national minsters on how to vote in the Council of Ministers where the final decisions are made. But as political scientists are fond of saying, setting the agenda is an important power, and the agenda in Brussels is set primarily by the Commission's staff, not by the individual national ministers.

A further challenge from the growth in the importance of the Community as a policy-making institution reflects the fact that styles of policy making and implementation in Brussels will often differ from the national tradition with which a business is familiar. British business, for example, will find itself faced with important differences in policy formulation and implementation between the Community and London. Whereas British business executives turn increasingly to political activity at the company level, many Community administrators from continental European nations will expect to deal with trade associations or general employers' organisations. Employers' associations at the Community level will be far more important than in Thatcher's Britain, even if Community officials also maintain some direct links with corporations. A second difference will be in the style of regulation. Community regulation will be enforced in what British businesses will find an adversarial or legalistic style compared with the collaborative and informal style that has characterised regulation in Britain until the 1990s.

The overall success of 1992, or even the degree to which a truly common market has been created, cannot be assessed until the late 1990s. At present there is much speculation but little hard evidence about the degree to which the growth of Community power will reduce the power of business to assert its 'privileged position' by moving to nations that treat it best compared with the degree to which a truly common market will increase the ability of businesses to more to nations with 'the best business climate'. Only time will tell. It is beyond doubt, however, that before the moves towards '1992' but even more because of them, the European Community had emerged as a major locus of decision making on policies affecting business. By the late 1990s it will be necessary for books on business and politics to pay as much attention to Brussels as to decision making in national capitals.

We may therefore conclude by saying that business executives in different countries and at different times face challenges from different sources. A full treatment of the role of business in any particular country requires consideration of these challenges.

Summary

At one time it might have seemed acceptable to theorise about the relationship between government and business in capitalist societies, as though such relationships were relatively constant. This chapter has stressed the numerous ways in which relations between government, business and politics can vary both within the same country over time, and between different capitalist countries at the same time. The degree to which business is organised politically; the attitudes of the public to business; links between different interests and political parties; the degree to which there are institutionalised ties between business and government; and the degree to which business faces the hostility of organised interests against it all vary from place to place and from time to time. Whereas some theorists (both Marxists and non-Marxists) may have thus wished to emphasise the similarities in the business–government relationship in all capitalist societies, the book which follows is based on the assumption – acceptable to both Marxist and non-Marxist theorists – that the differences in business–government relations are worth exploring.

The countries chosen for examination in the chapters which follow have been selected precisely to illustrate the variations in business–government relations which exist. We shall examine the countries usually cited as the classic examples of corporatism: Austria and Sweden. Japan, apart from being the world's second largest economy, has been selected because, as is well known, it is the country in which the business community and government have been involved in a particularly close relationship – so close that the label 'Japan Inc.' has been attached to the country. We shall see whether this jibe is justified. France, too, has been celebrated as a country which has successfully blended business and government, not only because the government owns a large number of industries but because the series of Plans drawn up after extensive consultation were seen as underlying the tremendous economic success of France in post-war decades. Great Britain is of equally obvious general interest, though sadly as an example of economic failure rather than success. Until the 1980s, Britain has alternated between 'corporatist' periods in which government and industry and government and unions have been very closely linked institutionally, and periods when such relations have been deliberately loosened by government. West Germany commands attention as a successful 'social market economy' in which historic tendencies towards corporatism contend with more free market ideas. Italy, one of the most dynamic of European countries, provides a particularly interesting blend of corporatist and political influences. Finally, the USA commands attention not only as the world's largest economy but as the country in which capitalism is most politically secure, yet business is the worst organised as a pressure group to protect its collective interests. We shall start with this paradoxical country.

2

Business and Politics in the USA

Support for a Capitalist Market System

Whenever trouble threatens the world, the American dollar strengthens against other currencies. The strength of the dollar reflects the belief amongst investors that the USA is the country in which capitalism is safest. Such interpretations of the strength of business in the USA are common. The comment attributed to Eisenhower's Secretary of Defence that 'what is good for General Motors is good for the United States' may have been a slight misrepresentation of his remarks. The remark was, however, picked up by many as symptomatic of the degree to which capitalism in the USA is unchallenged.

It is indeed the case that most Americans explicitly support a capitalist market system. Opinion polls show that most Americans (69 per cent) are prepared to make sacrifices to defend the free-enterprise system, regard economic freedoms as essential for freedom in general, and are mainly opposed, (74 per cent) to any large-scale government ownership of industry.[1] As Shonfield notes,[2] the USA is one of the few countries in which the word 'capitalism' has no opprobrious connotations. In most Western countries – and many Eastern European ones – the practical necessity of using market incentives is widely accepted. In the USA, however, market mechanisms have a degree of moral legitimacy as determinants of the allocation of incomes, resources and investment not commonly found elsewhere. King has argued that government spending in the USA is unusually small by the

39

standards of industrial democracies; government spends a lower proportion of gross national product (GNP) than in any industrial democracy other than Japan. Nationalised industries are almost unknown; government services such as a national health service or insurance have not been implemented in the USA;[3] and the tendency under President Reagan was for government to reduce further its commitment to ameliorate poverty. The free-enterprise system is thus unusually free of government 'interference'.

The reasons for the strength of support for capitalism and hostility to extensive powers for government in the USA have been much discussed. Probably the most popular explanations are rooted in an emphasis on the distinctive history of the USA. Louis Hartz,[4] for example, argues that its unique history has caused the USA to remain anchored to the nineteenth-century *liberal traditions* of support for democracy, civil liberties and a market economic system in which government plays a limited role. Having no aristocracy, the USA could not support the paternalistic conservatism of such nineteenth-century Europeans as Shaftesbury, Disraeli or Bismarck. As political rights, including the vote, were extended very speedily to nearly all white men in the USA by 1830 the combination which in Hartz's view was crucial for the development of socialism, a simultaneous quest for economic rights and full citizenship (for example, the right to vote) did not affect the USA. Other writers have stressed different factors in the history of the USA tending in the same direction. American wages have been comparatively high, and the working class has been fragmented by ethnic, racial and regional divisions. The opportunities, real or alleged, for individual advancement through geographic social mobility in addition all protected the legitimacy of capitalism by inhibiting challenges to it.[5] European visitors to the USA in the nineteenth century such as Dickens, de Tocqueville and Sombart noted, too, that the American working class was never as distinct from the middle class in terms of culture, dress or consumption patterns as in Europe. Class consciousness, predictably, was therefore lower. Finally, both the Republican and Democratic Parties established links with the working class at an early stage through the urban machine to a degree untrue of, say, the Liberals in Britain. As in Britain, the electoral system discourages third parties.

Not surprisingly, in view of such factors, the USA is distinctive amongst industrial democracies in that no socialist party has received major support (in 1912, Eugene Debbs received about 7 per cent of the votes cast, or almost one million, which was by far the socialists' best showing in a presidential election). Those identified as socialist or communist have received little support and have suffered persecution in periods, such as the years following the Bolshevik *coup* in Russia in 1917, and during the first decade of the Cold War from 1945 to 1955 (an episode somewhat misleadingly named after Senator Joe McCarthy who was by no means the only 'Red baiter'). Of course, such repression, painful as it was, scarcely matched repression in countries such as Russia in which communism triumphed. Unions have also been influenced by such factors. The oldest unions in the USA are by and large craft unions[6] which struggled to find respectability by confining themselves to a narrow, instrumentalist approach to politics. These craft unions formed the American Federation of Labor (AFL). Union involvement in politics was confined to issues affecting their rights, or which strengthened their bargaining position, such as the exclusion of Chinese labourers.

A very different type of union gained ground in the 1930s, typically industry-wide, based on mass production or heavy industries such as steel or cars. These unions, which formed the Congress of Industrial Organizations (CIO), shared a generally social democratic approach to politics, the most famous exemplar being Walter Reuther of the United Auto Workers who became President of the CIO. But though the AFL's differences with the CIO became sufficiently less intense for the organisations to merge in 1955, the 'business union' approach which the craft unions had embodied remained important both within the AFL–CIO and within certain unions expelled from it, notably the Teamsters. Union membership in the USA has moreover lagged below the levels common in northern Europe. Union membership in the USA peaked at 35 per cent shortly after the Second World War, and has since fallen to around 17 per cent of the workforce. There are large parts of the USA (such as the South and South-West), in which the unions are conspicuously weak. As these areas (and industries nation-wide in which unions are traditionally weak, such as services) are the fastest-growing in the USA, the unions look certain to continue to decline.

A Bed of Roses for Business?

It may seem, on the basis of the facts we have covered so far, that the American business executive has no political problems. Such, in reality, would not be the case. Although the basic features of capitalism are not contested in the USA, there has been at least as much (and possibly more) criticism of the day-to-day conduct of corporations in the USA than in any other industrial democracy. Opinion polls show, for example, that most Americans are in favour of strict regulation of such undesirable by-products of industry as pollution, workplace accidents or occupationally caused illness and unsafe consumer goods.[7]

In the late 1960s and early 1970s, such sentiments found expression in newly-created or rejuvenated public-interest groups. Capitalising on the growth in a middle-class propensity to participate in politics, increased cynicism amongst Americans over business, government and other major institutions, organisations such as Friends of the Earth, the Sierra Club and Common Cause succeeded in imposing constraints on corporations in such diverse aspects of their activities as discharges into rivers or lakes and discharges of funds to politicians as bribes or campaign contributions. Though the influence of public-interest groups declined in the late 1970s for a variety of reasons (including increased fears of inflation and the uncompetitiveness of American industry with consequent loss of jobs) the public-interest groups had secured the adoption of important laws constraining many aspects of business behaviour.

Such a 'surge and decline' in criticism of business producing some permanent results is by no means an unusual phenomenon in the USA. The 'revolt' of poor farmers demanding government controls over banks and railroads contributed to the adoption of legislation affecting those industries, even though within twenty years the Populist movement was dead. The Progressives, a loose alliance of reforming intellectuals, writers and journalists, were equally ephemeral but contributed to an even greater amount of reforming legislation on monopoly, clean food and drugs, and other constraints on business abuses. Franklin Roosevelt's New Deal alliance of the South, farmers, unions, ethnic groups, northern cities and intellectuals lasted in its full glory for only eight years, yet changed fundamentally (and permanently) the balance between business and government power in the USA. Such challenges to business may be temporary, but are nonetheless important in their consequences.

Neither is it the case that government officials in the USA are necessarily sympathetic or close to business. Although it is true that there have been periods in which officials of agencies such as the Interstate Commerce Commission (ICC) were seen as being too favourably disposed to the industry which they supposedly regulated in the interests of the public, there have been other periods (such as the 1970s) when officials of agencies such as the Federal Trade Commission (FTC), the Environmental Protection Agency (EPA) and Occupational Safety and Health Administration (OSHA) were bitterly attacked by businessmen as being either uncomprehending of their problems, or even actively hostile to business. Some academic writers concluded that American government was actually more stringent in its regulation of business than the governments of supposedly more left-wing countries.[8] Moreover, the strength of the *laissez-faire* tradition in the USA denied government an active role in partnership with industry in an 'industrial policy', as developed in France and Japan (except when, as in the case of defence industries, a special factor such as national security legitimated government intervention).

It is also misleading to think of the USA as a country in which government exists on a nineteenth-century scale. The growth in government in the USA may have been slower than elsewhere, but the share of GNP spent by governments (federal, state and local) is now one-third. Government, in short, is a major potential customer, and one whose purchases are often affected by political pressures. Moreover, as Shonfield noted, although there are practically no nationalised industries in the USA, regulation has generally been more extensive and stringent than in other countries. Antimonopoly legislation was tougher than in Britain, water polluters prosecuted more vigorously than in Britain, and health and safety at work legislation imposed more toughly than in much more socialist Sweden. The importance of government as a customer and the problems which could arise with potential regulators meant that there were plenty of political issues for business to worry about. The celebrated popularity of capitalism as an abstract doctrine has not produced a problem-free life for capitalists.

Defending Business Interests: A Multi-Pronged Approach

The modern American corporation is likely to follow a variety of approaches in defending its interests. The approach used will depend partly on the nature of the issue, but will also often involve several complementary strategies which can be used simultaneously.

The wise corporation will try to create a favourable *attitude* and willingness to listen amongst decision-makers before a problem arises. The most obvious way to do this is through campaign contributions. Prior to 1972 it was common for corporations to make campaign contributions from their general funds. This practice was illegal, and so such contributions were often routed through overseas subsidiaries or individual donations by corporate executives in order to disguise their origin. After the Watergate affair led to the discovery of such illegal campaign contributions, corporations were limited to contributing amounts of no more than $5000 per candidate per election, the money to be raised by political action committees (PACs). Though PACs can have their operating expenses paid by the corporation, their funds must be 'voluntary' contributions from executives or stockholders. A corporation's PAC may also ask its workers to contribute on two occasions a year – a rarely-used procedure.

Company PACs generally concentrate their giving on those best placed to help the company. Corporations thus usually give most of their money to incumbents (politicians already in Congress) rather than to their challengers.[9] Such beneficiaries will usually be on the Congressional committees that most affect the corporation. Corporations' PACs have proved willing to contribute to Democrats, even liberal Democrats, who are in the powerful positions and are almost certain to be re-elected, because the object is to buy access to the legislator and, if possible, goodwill. Only in 1978 and 1980, when the political tide was running against the Democrats did corporation PACs follow their hearts and tilt heavily towards supporting Republicans. In 1982 the balance shifted to the Democrats and remained there.

The corporation would also expect support from *Representatives* and *Senators* from areas where its factories are located. Such assistance might be of particular importance when there is competition between corporations for a government contract, for example to build a new transport plane for the Air Force. The top executives of the company can attempt to build ties to the legislators by making individual contributions to their campaign funds, though since 1974 such contributions have been limited by law to $1000 per election. The executives may also participate directly in the campaign, though this is unlikely. In spite of being urged frequently to become more involved politically, company executives have usually been too busy to do so. Social contacts and links with other élites (through working for the local symphony orchestra, for example) may however provide an opportunity for influencing the local climate of opinion and so, indirectly, the legislator. Above all, however, the legislator is likely to feel an identity of interest with local companies. Local companies, after all, determine the income and employment prospects of the legislator's voters. The American system provides numerous opportunities for the legislator to claim the credit for good news for local companies: defence contracts, for example, will generally be announced through the local legislator's office.

A third line of attack which the corporation might use would be to exploit links with the *Executive branch*. These

links will take a variety of forms. The most obvious links are
personal. Both Democratic and Republican Administrations
recruit heavily from the ranks of business executives to fill the
thousands of political appointments made by the president.
Key figures of the Reagan Administration (1981–89), such as
George Schultz, the Secretary of State, came to Washington
from the boardrooms of major corporations (in Schultz's case,
the Bechtel Corporation). These personal links can be used if
the corporation has a problem which needs government action
or assistance. The awareness of the value that personal
connections can provide in American corporations is
demonstrated by the lucrative careers that former Executive
branch officials can have as company lobbyists; a similarly
lucrative career also awaits defeated legislators, whose
Congressional contacts are greatly prized.

Apart from such personal ties, corporations may have
almost institutionalised ties to particular government *agencies*.
The agencies are subjected to constant argument and pleading
from companies whose business is affected by their work.
Corporations can moreover make life unpleasant for agencies
that cross them through their Congressional allies. Congressional committee assignments are typically given to legislators
with a constituency interest in the committee's work. The
committees that supply agencies with operating funds or that
oversee their work are thus typically filled with legislators
representing the people (including corporations, their
executives and workers) with which agencies have to deal.
The agency which offends interests it supposedly controls risks
having its budget savaged and its executives humiliated by
representatives of those interests in Congress.

Such considerations have led many observers to argue that
American government agencies are unusually susceptible to
'capture' by the interest with which they deal. Agencies can be
coerced as well as persuaded to fall in with their 'clients" view
of good public policy. Yet such arguments can be taken too
far by neglecting the importance of party politics. Democratic
Administrations have been quite likely to appoint people more
sympathetic to environmental protection or labour unions to
key positions, while the Republicans have appointed quite
consistently officials sympathetic to business. In spite of

predictions of capture by business, Democratic appointees to agencies such as the National Labor Relations Board (NLRB), the EPA, the OSHA and the FTC have caused apoplexy in the boardrooms of corporate America. Individual companies are usually represented in Washington by law firms. These are not law firms which specialise in court appearances, indeed, many of the law firms' senior partners have not set foot in a court for decades. 'Lawyers' such as the one-time Truman presidential aide Clark Clifford, sell not their legal expertise but their connections built up over the years with a wide variety of influential people in Congress and the Executive branch. Access to such power figures might not secure a favourable decision for the company, but it will at least secure a serious hearing for the company's arguments.

Individual companies in the USA thus have numerous opportunities to influence decisions before they need the assistance of a trade association or an 'umbrella organisation' for employers. Somewhat surprisingly, American trade associations and employers' organisations have not enjoyed a consistently high reputation in recent decades.

Modes of Political Participation

Writers in the late 1950s and early 1960s were struck by the limited development of business organisations in the USA. The groups claiming to speak for the general interests of business were notoriously weak. Both the Chamber of Commerce and the National Association of Manufacturers (NAM) were regarded as highly ideological associations with little to contribute to the discussion of complex policy issues. One authority found substance in the rumour that the NAM was the 'kiss of death' for a cause which it supported.[10] Neither did trade associations seem stronger. In their magisterial study of the impact of business on American trade policy, Bauer, Pool and Dexter[11] found that trade associations were accorded little prestige. Business executives regarded the staff of the associations as people incapable of 'making it' in business, while the lobbyists of trade associations were by and large dependent on the goodwill of politicians already disposed to support them. Politicians were more likely to complain about the paucity of information provided by both trade associations, or about the failure of trade associations even to contact undecided Representatives and Senators than to complain about pressure from them. The picture of trade associations painted by Bauer, Pool and Dexter is more of organisations anxiously trying to maintain membership than of organisations exerting pressure successfully on politicians.

The weakness of trade associations and 'umbrella groups' representing the general interest of business contrasted with the growth of such organisations in Europe and Japan. The USA lacked interest-group representatives who were recognised by the government, Congress, the media and the public as the authoritative voice of business. Instead, the business organisations of the USA seemed weak, ideological and bitterly divided.

This organisational weakness represented, ironically, political strength.[12] Business organised little to protect its collective interests in the USA in the 1950s because its collective interests were little challenged. A variety of factors contributed to the political strength of business. Opinion polls showed a high degree of public confidence in business executives and major companies. The Eisenhower Administration not only pursued pro-business policies, but at the highest levels was overwhelmingly recruited from the ranks of business executives. In Congress, a pro-business conservative coalition of Republicans and southern Democrats controlled the agenda, and its southern Democrat members benefited from the workings of the 'seniority system' under which the most senior members of the majority parties received the tremendously powerful chairmanships of Congressional committees. Moreover, though their legality was sometimes questionable, contributions to the campaigns of both Republicans and Democrats of business executives or stockholders were the most important source of election campaign funds for both parties. A general assault on business was not, therefore, to be feared.

A number of factors in the late 1960s and 1970s convinced American business executives that more vigorous action was needed to protect their collective interests. There was a very sharp decline in confidence in business and business executives amongst the public, exceeding the rate of decline of trust in other American institutions. The balance of power in Congress changed in a way which favoured conservatives less and liberals more, while public-interest groups seeking legislation protecting the environment and public from harmful side-effects of business activity scored notable triumphs, reflecting a considerable upsurge in their membership, funding and prestige. The Watergate affair brought disgrace to not only President Nixon but also to those business executives who had made illegal contributions to his election campaign, generally under pressure from the Administration and fearful of government harassment if they did not comply. New campaign finance laws both reduced the possibilities for illegal campaign contributions by business executives and created new opportunities for pressure groups to raise funds for election campaigns through the PACs.

The factor which above all else caused alarm in business circles was the increased impact of government regulation. One of the largest-ever increases in government regulation occurred between 1967 and 1976. This entailed not only a five-fold increase in the number of staff employed in the regulatory agencies and a similar increase in their budgets, but also a dramatic increase in the impact of regulation on business. Regulatory agencies had been a feature of American government since the late nineteenth century. Most of the older regulatory agencies had been concerned with the prices and conditions of service of a single industry. The regulatory agencies created in the 1960s and 1970s were generally concerned with the regulation of factors such as pollution and safety which cut across industries, and were often referred to as the social regulatory agencies.

The social regulatory agencies such as the OSHA or the EPA brought the power of federal government to bear on the day-to-day operations of businesses for the first time. Until their creation inspectors encountered by business executives had, by and large, been officials of state governments. The officials of the federal social regulatory agencies were made of sterner stuff than most state officials. The new social regulatory agencies gained a reputation for toughness and even for adopting an adversarial approach to business. Moreover, the regulations evolved by the social regulatory agencies to protect the environment were extremely costly to business, forcing executives to divert a substantial proportion of investment funds to meeting their requirements.

In brief, the growth of regulation in the 1960s and 1970s seemed to business executives to constitute a dramatic and threatening extension of the power of government. Both the cost and extent of regulation seemed likely to increase, moreover, as time passed. New regulatory agencies, and new regulations from them, seemed all too likely to be created because the liberal Democratic triumphs in the elections following the downfall of President Nixon seemed to suggest the future dominance of politicians critical of business. American business executives, for the first time since the New Deal, feared that government posed a threat to interests shared by a wide variety of business, or what might be termed business's common interests.

The political challenges and setbacks of the 1970s coincided with increased commercial challenges to American business. The dominance of American manufacturing, so complete in the immediate aftermath of the Second World War, was eroded by the increasing success of competitors from Europe, Japan, and the successful industrialising countries such as the Four Tigers (Hong Kong, South Korea, Taiwan and Singapore). By the late 1980s, the comparative economic decline of the United States was much discussed by Americans.[13]

The increased competitive challenge to American corporations encouraged their political activism in two respects. First, a large number of industries sought *protection* from foreign competitors. The American textile industry had long been given extensive, though generally unsuccessful, protection from foreign competitors. All Administrations, Republican and Democratic, had accepted the political need to make concessions to the textile industry in order to prevent it from becoming the core of a coalition which might endanger the United States's general commitment to free trade. In the 1980s industries as varied as steel and semiconductors also received protection. Naturally, the pursuit of protection required extensive political activity to mobilise support in Congress and to persuade executive branch agencies such as the International Trade Commission, the Commerce Department and the Special Trade Representative to accept the need to help the afflicted industry.[14]

Increased competitive pressures also increased the attractiveness of types of business from which in practice foreign competitors are in practice excluded, such as government contracts. It is often remarked that government is the largest single customer for business. As keeping or winning ordinary customers became more difficult for American corporations, they devoted increased resources to winning government contracts. Obtaining government contracts in the United States is a highly political process in which mobilising the support of powerful political allies is essential.

Business responded to a variety of challenges by becoming more active politically. This increased activity took a variety of forms. First, *individual corporations* increased their political activism. The best known sign of this increased activism is the growth in the number and importance of business political action committees (PACs). When election law changed in the early 1970s to allow the formation of PACs few expected that business would use the new law much. However, corporate PACs grew much more rapidly than any other category. Business overtook unions as the largest source of legal campaign contributions to such a degree that business contributed twice as much to campaigns in the 1980s as did labour. Individual corporations also opened Washington lobbying offices in larger numbers; the number of corporations with their own representation more than doubled between the early 1970s and the early 1980s so that nearly 600 corporations had permanent embassies in the capital. Other corporations used either Washington lawyers or the new profession of contract lobbyists to represent them. The Washington bar expanded considerably in the 1970s to meet demand for lobbying. The 1980s saw the growth of firms of contract lobbyists that represented wealthy clients (usually corporations) who needed to persuade government officials or Congress to help them.[15]

A second development was that *individual industries* that faced particularly severe challenges to their collective interests improved the quality of their trade associations significantly. The oil industry, one of the main targets of critics of business in the 1970s and considerably regulated by government in that period, increased its spending on its trade association, the American Petroleum Institute, considerably. The chemical industry, again a frequent target for regulators in the 1970s, similarly boosted spending on its trade associations. Schlozman and Tierney[16] found in the survey of interest groups in Washington in the 1980s that there had been considerable change in the quality of trade associations so that the description of trade associations in the 1950s as understaffed and under-financed was no longer valid. Admittedly, trade associations representing declining industries such as iron and steel, or industries temporarily fallen on hard times such as oil, lost revenue and staff in the 1980s. Most did not.

A third development was a series of attempts to create a more effective 'umbrella' organisation speaking authoritatively for the collective interests of American business. In the mid-1970s, a number of unsuccessful attempts were made to merge the Chamber of Commerce and the National Association of Manufacturers. Although these attempts were unsuccessful, both organisations increased their standing in Washington. Whereas the Chamber improved its reputation largely by becoming a skilled practitioner of 'grass roots lobbying' (mobilising members around the country to put pressure on their legislators to side with the Chamber), the NAM attempted to become a less consistently conservative organisation better able to contribute to specific policy debates. Most promising of all seemed the attempts by large corporations to create an organisation characterized by technical expertise rather than, as with the Chamber and the old NAM, by a commitment to very general conservative causes. The organisation created, the Business Roundtable, rapidly acquired a high standing in Washington. The first chairman of the Business Roundtable, Irving Shapiro of DuPont, became a frequent confidant of President Carter's.

Finally, American business started to fight the war of ideas more vigorously. Most American academics, particularly those involved in the social sciences, are centre-left in their political orientation. Much the same is true of reporters working for network news programmes and quality newspapers such as the *New York Times* or the *Washington Post*. Business executives feared that in consequence the American intelligentsia encouraged the population in general to be more critical of business than they might otherwise have been, and generated a flow of policy proposals or issues damaging to business interests. In the 1970s, business began to fight back by funding such pro-business think tanks as the Heritage Foundation or the American Enterprise Institute.

By the end of the 1970s, American business appeared to be better mobilised politically than ever before. The improved representation of business in Washington led, in the view of many observers, to important defeats for public interest groups and unions even while the Democrats controlled both the White House and the Congress. For example, modest proposals for labour law reform and a consumer advocacy agency were both defeated by a Congress that had been thought to have not only a Democratic but a liberal majority. Even more exciting from business's viewpoint, however, was the election in 1980 of the most explicitly pro-business Administration at least since the 1950s and possibly since the 1920s.

The Impact of the Reagan Administration

When one business executive was asked what he thought about the Reagan Administration, he responded that he thought he had died and gone to heaven.[17] It is easy to see why. The Administration followed clearly anti-union policies, starting by breaking a strike by air traffic controllers and destroying their union and continuing by appointing resolutely pro-management people to agencies regulating labour relations. Strong supporters of business's contention that environmental, health and safety regulations were too strict were appointed to run the agencies responsible for these regulations. In case these appointees proved after all to be insufficiently sympathetic to business, their agencies had their budgets cut, making any growth in their activities impossible, and the agencies were placed under the close supervision of the critical Office of Management and Budget, which is part of the Executive Office of the President. The Administration asked Congress to reduce business taxation; the Congress responded by trying to out-bid the Administration in the generosity of the allowances it offered to business.

The triumphs of business in the early years of the Reagan Administration were considerable. Yet a number of considerations suggest that the political problems of business did not disappear. The public interest groups, which had seen their memberships decline in the 1970s, re-grouped in the 1980s and had some success in attracting new members who were frightened by the threat the Reagan Administration posed to their values. A number of accidents halted the drive to weaken the social regulatory agencies. Scandals or alleged scandals overtook the Director of the Environmental Protection Agency and the Secretary of Labor. The Secretary of the Interior was too indiscreet about his views on racial minorities, Jews and women. In order to cut the Administration's political losses, the top officials involved in these scandals were replaced by moderates more acceptable to Congress and the public interest groups. The vast budget deficits produced by the 1981 tax cuts coupled with the Reagan Administration's appetite for certain types of federal spending (such as defence spending) produced rapid demands for tax increases and tax reforms to make such increases fairer. The 1986 Tax Reform Act in fact increased the tax burden on business considerably, although the opposition of corporate executives was attenuated by vast reductions in tax rates for very highly paid individuals such as themselves.

Above all, business discovered that although the challenges to its *collective* interests had weakened in the 1970s, the imperative for corporations to protect their *individual* interests remained. Changes in the tax system tended to affect corporations differentially. For example, large tax allowances for investments benefited capital-intensive industries. The abolition or reduction of such allowances in return for lower tax rates would therefore set corporations in capital-intensive industries against those in labour-intensive industries. Similarly, while some corporations feared the rising tide of foreign competition, others with a lively export trade or large investments overseas remained attached to free trade.

In consequence, business politics in the 1980s was both active and individualistic. The reduction in the threat of public policies contrary to the collective interests of business consequent upon the election of the Reagan Administration did not result in any reduction in the general level of business political activity in Washington. The quest for federal contracts, tax changes and trade protection which would benefit individual corporations was more vigorous than ever. The drive towards building organisations to defend the *collective* interests of business in contrast all but disappeared. The Business Roundtable became just one of several organisations claiming to represent business in Washington as its novelty and glamour faded. The NAM and the Chamber of Commerce came to differ sharply on a number of issues. The general business organisations, like the trade associations, frequently found themselves immobilised by differences of interest and opinion among member corporations; in American business organisations, individual corporations can often veto a policy commitment by the organisation for fear the corporation will resign and its dues be lost.

The diminished opportunities for organisations representing collective business interests to play a prominent role increased the opportunities for individual corporations to be more prominent politically. Lobbyists for individual corporations supplemented by Washington lawyers or contract lobbyists pressed their cases vigorously on politicians rendered attentive to their clients' needs by ever more numerous PAC contributions. Individual corporations paid what to ordinary Americans were fabulous sums to contract lobbyists thought to be able to reach the appropriate official. Thus TWA paid Michael Deaver, who had left the Reagan White House to make his fortune as a contract lobbyist, $250 000 to make a single phone call to the Secretary of Transportation, Elizabeth Dole. Even President Nixon's disgraced Attorney General, John Mitchell, was able to secure $75 000 from a business that thought that Mitchell could help obtain it a federal contract to build subsidised housing. Former Secretary of the Interior James Watt collected $300 000 from one client. Corporate PACs continued to buy the attention – and possibly the goodwill – of politicians with campaign contributions; the larger the federal contracts received by a corporation, the larger its PAC tended to be. By the end of the 1980s, many Americans wondered where the boundary between corrupt and normal business practices had been drawn.

Indubitably, however, the decade had witnessed a shift away from business politics being routed through business organisations towards greater emphasis on political activity by individual corporations. This did not constitute a return to the situation which had prevailed in the 1950s and early 1960s, however. In the 1950s, individual corporations had been much less actively involved in politics than in the 1980s, while even by the end of the 1980s, general business organisations or trade associations had not been reduced to the same condition of weakness that characterised them earlier. Politics mattered more to most corporations than it had in the 1950s. The early years of the Bush Administration also seemed to promise some return to those issues which unite business by threatening its collective interests. The President's own talk of a 'kinder, gentler society' seemed to hold out hope to critics of business behaviour such as environmentalists. The President's comments almost certainly reflected an upsurge of popular concern about nuclear accidents following Chernobyl, the effect of chlorofluorocarbons on the earth's atmosphere, and a damaging oil spill off Alaska from the Exxon *Valdez*. In contrast to the 1950s, American business remained politically alert and well equipped should any important challenges re-emerge.

Yet in a different sense to their original intent, Schlozman and Tierney's comment on changes in the general American interest group system, 'More of the same', could be applied to business interest groups. As noted earlier, American business has always seemed disorganised by international standards. There is no single organisation which speaks for business authoritatively comparable in status to employers' groups in other democracies. Though much strengthened, business groups in the USA remain fragmented, competitive and lacking in authority.

Regulation

It has been commonplace to note that few industries in the USA have been owned by government. It has been less frequently noted that American government regulated industry more than governments elsewhere.[18] Understanding regulation has been vital to understanding the business–government relationship in the USA. The nature of the regulatory relationship between government and business in the USA has prompted much contradictory theorising. The older theories on regulation were concerned to explain the failure of regulation due to the 'capture' or domination of regulatory agencies by the industry they supposedly controlled. A variety of reasons were advanced to explain the demise of the regulatory agencies. Some stressed the practical and administrative difficulties of operating without the goodwill of the regulated. Regulations are harder to devise if industry is unwilling to share information with the regulators; regulations cannot be enforced effectively unless most firms co-operate voluntarily, for the number of inspectors is never adequate to cover every workplace. Other writers stressed the temptation held out to officials of better-paid jobs in industry in the future in return for their sympathetic treatment of the industry in the present – a system known as the 'revolving door'. Yet others stressed the importance of the fact that regulatory agencies, given independence of the president and Congress by law, could rely on neither for support in conflicts with business. Bernstein summarised these discontents in what is perhaps the single most influential book on the subject.[19] Bernstein argued that regulatory agencies passed through a life cycle of vigorous youth, conciliatory middle age and senility. In youth, the regulatory agency, supported by a political movement which had secured its creation, fought many battles with its industry. In middle age, the decline of the political movement which had created it, and the mounting practical, administrative and legal difficulties of fighting the industry if confronted, induced a more conciliatory attitude in the agency. In old age, the agency succumbed to the steady pressures from its industry, not matched by any pressures on behalf of the public, and adopted pro-industry attitudes.

Ironically, most writing on regulation in the USA in the 1980s was concerned with the problem of 'regulatory unreasonableness'.[20] Regulators in the USA were likely, it was argued, to impose ridiculously costly requirements on industry in return for negligible benefits. Regulators in the USA were also likely to impose these regulations in a harsher, less sensible manner than regulators in countries such as Sweden or Britain. The unreasonableness of regulators in the USA was a function of both culture and law. The culture of the USA is adversarial; individuals assert their rights against each other vigorously, frequently resorting to law to resolve differences, and being less likely to compromise differences (especially with government) than peoples of other countries. Moreover, the emphasis in American law on equal treatment for all inhibits the exercise of sensible discretion by regulatory agencies. Instead, officials of regulatory agencies are more likely to 'go by the book', applying regulations in an arid, uncompromising manner.

The diametrically opposed nature of these two arguments probably reflects the weakness of both. Too much theorising about regulation in the USA overlooks the importance of politics. The theories of regulatory failure referred to a period when there were few powerful critics of business in the USA. The theories of regulatory unreasonableness refer to the period in which the critics of business, particularly in the public-interest groups, were at their strongest. The nature of regulatory legislation, the pressures exerted through the presidency, courts and Congress, differed accordingly. It is important to note in this context how the election of President Reagan emasculated the regulatory agencies which had incurred the wrath of business. The OSHA and EPA reversed policy completely, passing from being regarded as anti- to pro-business in a matter of months, discarding in the process former friends in the unions and environmental protection groups.

The change also reminds us that the nature of regulation can vary tremendously. Calls for 'deregulation' came both from the left and right in American politics. Yet the question 'Who benefits?' draws different answers from agency to agency. The Civil Aeronautics Board (CAB) helped airlines maintain high fares and profits at the expense of the public. The EPA, prior to the election of President Reagan, exerted a substantial downward pressure on business profits because of the vigour with which it pursued environmental protection. Like many aspects of government, regulation is a weapon which can be used to the advantage or disadvantage of different interests. The impact of regulation, therefore, is determined by political conflicts, not by the nature of the process itself.

Industrial Policy

The election and re-election of President Reagan seemed to confirm the commitment of the United States to its traditions of reliance on market mechanisms to secure economic growth. The tentative interest of the Carter Administration, and more explicit advocacy of a more direct role for government in steering economic development of the unsuccessful Democratic candidates for the Presidency in 1984 and 1988 through an industrial policy were apparently crushed by the election returns. Yet a number of commentators continued their advocacy of an industrial policy in the United States and, somewhat surprisingly, signs of interest were detected in President Bush's Commerce Department at the end of the decade.

In the dominant regulatory paradigm of government–business relations, industry and government ideally have an 'arms length' relationship. In practice, a 'revolving door' may allow regulators to take up lucrative posts working for industries they regulate or, as we have discussed, regulatory agencies may be captured. Yet the ideal regulatory relationship in the United States implies distance, policing of industry, and when necessary, punishment to secure compliance in the future. Advocates of industrial policy have argued for replacing this paradigm with one based more on co-operation and concertation between government and industry.

Industrial policies range from those – such as that operated in Japan in the 1950s – in which government, backed with significant legal powers, steers corporations into specified markets or investments to policies such as Sweden's active labour market policy, in which governments facilitate the working of market forces.

It is more or less impossible to imagine the stronger type of directive industrial policy in the United States. Not only would government 'interference' be seen as illegitimate but American political institutions are particularly ill-adapted to the task. A former Speaker of the House of Representatives, Tip O'Neill, was fond of saying that all politics is local. While that saying is an exaggeration even for the United States, it does remind us that American legislators are expected to produce benefits for their districts or states, not just the nation in general. By their nature, industrial policies involve declaring that some industries are tomorrow's winners, and others are tomorrow's losers. In practice, winners and losers are likely to be concentrated in different parts of the country. It is impossible to imagine American legislators from parts of the country in which losers are concentrated voting for euthanasia for those industries so that resources can be switched to tomorrow's winners. In practice, Congress would gradually declare every industry a winner. Those countries which have operated the stronger forms of industrial policy (eg Japan and France in the late 1940s and 1950s) were characterised by weak elected politicians or attenuated party competition and a strong permanent bureaucracy, which could implement industrial policies without much 'interference' from elected politicians. In contrast, in the USA, political competition is considerable, elected politicians are strong, and the permanent bureaucracy is weak. Picking winners and losers would be an impossibly politically charged task.

Yet not all forms of industrial policy are thereby invalidated. It can be argued that all governments have industrial policies in the sense of operating knowingly or unwittingly policies that affect industries. Most tax, trade and environmental policies help some industries and hurt others. Moreover, industrial training, retraining and relocation policies can be designed which reinforce market forces rather than conflict with them. Even such weaker forms of industrial policy would be difficult to establish in the United States. The federal government has little control and experience in running education, training or retraining programmes. Any policy which clearly and predictably had a differential impact on the regions of the country would encounter the forces of localism to which we have referred. If there is to be industrial policy in the United States, it may be possible only at the state, not the national, level.

In spite of all the peculiar difficulties of operating industrial policy in the USA, it can be argued that in a world in which other nations have an industrial policy, the United States has no choice but to follow. If some countries promote the rapid growth of new industries such as semiconductors or high definition television through an industrial policy, then the United States would find its infant industry overwhelmed by foreign competitors before the invisible hand of market forces had time to establish it. The length of time during which the superiority of American science might give its industries a technological lead is diminished by the rapidity of technological diffusion in the modern world; technological innovations are more likely to be copied in months rather than years. It is not surprising therefore that by the end of the 1980s, the United States was attempting to find a way to help and protect infant industries such as semiconductors or high definition television even while the Bush Administration supposedly maintained hostility to industrial policy in principle.

The question which would remain, however, would be the capacity of the American political system to allocate resources rationally. In earlier periods of American history, individual industries had received great help from the state through the imposition of high tariffs on competing imports. Such assistance had been allocated on the basis of the political power of the industry or Congressional manoeuvring – as the Smoot–Hawley tariff in the inter-world-war period illustrated. Might not resources in a modern industrial policy be allocated on a similar, non-rational basis? This fear prompted many commentators to argue against direct assistance to industry. Removing legal barriers to international competitiveness such as the very stringent anti-monopoly laws inhibiting co-operation between American firms might be more effective than providing government aid: this approach was in fact adopted in the semiconductor industry.

State and Local Government

One third of government expenditures are made by state or local governments. In addition, many federal programmes are administered by state or local governments on behalf of the federal government with substantial discretion allowed to the states. State and local government is therefore a natural target for business lobbying. States have their own policies on topics as diverse as employment practices, the permissibility of investments in South Africa by corporations in which the state invests (eg through pension funds) and pollution controls. Even large cities such as New York or Chicago have a similar range of policies. Both cities and states are a valuable source of contracts for a wide variety of businesses.

As we have seen, the fight between those who believed that the USA was ruled by an élite including business and those who believed it was a genuinely pluralist democracy was fought out through studies of cities. Dahl's study of New Haven, *Who Governs?* was particularly influential, although it might be doubted that if there were a power élite in the USA it would care very much who governs New Haven. In general, however, there is a dearth of studies of business's attempts to influence politics at the local or state level. Perhaps the practical difficulties of conducting research in the hundreds of major cities and fifty states discourages scholars.

It has generally been assumed that business enjoys greater advantages at the local or state than federal level. This is thought to be true for a number of institutional and structural reasons. First, state and local governments have in the past had notably weaker institutional capacities than the federal government. Most states have had weaker, less expert bureaucracies than the federal government; legislative staffs were small, legislators were part time, amateur politicians and state executive branches fragmented into numerous autonomous, often conflicting, agencies. There was in general a shortage of the expertise and institutional strength required to confront powerful corporations. Moreover, corporations were further strengthened by the plausibility of threats to move production to other states or cities if confronted with unwelcome policies.[21]

In recent years, however, state government has become a much more vital force in American politics. Although some states, such as New Hampshire, still have legislatures which provide the nation with amusement, most state legislatures are filled with ambitious, younger legislators, eager to make a mark by promoting an issue, and supported by much larger professional staffs to provide policy analysis. The 1970s witnessed a clear improvement in the quality of state governors, and in the degree of control those governors have over their executive branches. Moreover, most states now have modernised tax systems capable of generating sufficient revenue to support a more active role for state governments.

The revival in state government in the United States has both welcome and unwelcome consequences for business. On the positive side, states are extremely active in promoting their economic growth by trying to attract new investment not only through tax concessions but through donating land for development, starting new training programmes to meet the needs of new industries, and making investments in infrastructure such as new roads which will mesh with the needs of corporations.[22] Most American states now have overseas offices charged with attracting investment to the state. Some argue that this activity might be considered the American version of an industrial policy. Individual states can overcome the problem of localism which prevents the creation of a national industrial policy. It is also possible to argue that states have become embroiled in a bidding war with each other which is costly to the nation. If Nissan, for example, plans to build a car plant *somewhere* in the USA, the competition between states to offer the largest tax concessions, low interest loans, free land or other subsidies no matter how rational for the individual state, constitute an unnecessary subsidy from the national perspective. If Nissan would have invested somewhere, it is pointless from the national perspective to offer subsidies to settle anywhere in particular.[23] The bidding war for new investment between the states is obviously, however, very welcome to corporations.

Less welcome to business is the reforming activism evident in the states in the 1980s. As in national politics, issue-orientated state politicians have been building reputations and political careers by looking for problems to solve. The modern state legislator is comparatively young, and is trying to build his or her future political career by claiming credit for solving a real or imagined problem. The activism this produces has been more evident in the 1980s when comparatively little programme innovation was occurring in national politics. Consumer and environmental groups, blocked by the Reagan Administration at the national level, have turned to the state government for action on their concerns, and have often found the new breed of state legislator eager to address their concerns. In the late 1980s, corporations found their interests challenged less at the national level and more at the state level than in the past. This change has posed problems for business. Few corporations are adequately represented in all state capitals, and the quality of trade or general business organisations varies greatly at the state level. Business sometimes loses at the state level, much as it used to at the national level, without realising the danger until it has lost. Moreover, the worst possible outcome for many industries in a conflict over regulation is to have different regulations adopted in different states so that, as has happened, cars which can be sold in Arizona cannot be sold in California. Ironically, corporations have recently discovered the advantages of national regulations, which not only are implemented usually by pro-business, Republican Administrations but also at least offer uniformity of standards across the nation.

In general, however, the fragmentation of authority implicit in American federalism probably still works to the advantage of business. The frantic competition between states for business investment in the 1980s makes any state reluctant to be tagged 'anti business'. Even progressive states such as

Wisconsin have redesigned their tax systems to reduce the level of taxation on corporations, although ironically it may well be the level of taxation falling on individuals that matters more to the corporate executives who make investment decisions. Nation states can be blackmailed by threats from corporations to invest elsewhere if states adopt policies unwelcome to them but it is even easier to blackmail a state that way.

Conclusions

As the continued popularity of the United States for European (particularly British) and Japanese investors reveals, the United States is probably the country in which capitalism is most secure. Unions have never been very strong, and are now much weaker. There is no socialist movement of any significance. The federal system reinforces the structural power of corporations which can threaten to invest only in states with a 'good business climate'.

Yet there are two problems which confront business. The first is that middle-class reform movements such as the consumer and environmental groups have mounted a more effective challenge to business in the United States than in any other country. As we have seen, regulatory agencies created in response to pressures from public interest groups have often been tougher in the USA in their treatment of business than have been similar agencies in countries such as Sweden or Great Britain. The absence of a socialist movement has not prevented the articulation of significant challenges to business in the USA.

The second problem confronting business in the United States is the peculiar difficulty which has existed there in achieving a structured, co-operative relationship between business and government geared to long-term growth. American business is very politically active today, but in a very fragmented manner. Although the American economy performed well overall in the 1980s with comparatively high growth rates and lower unemployment than Europe, the decade also witnessed great concern about whether the USA could retain a competitive manufacturing base. For many observers, the traditional unstructured relationship between government and business was a handicap in achieving American competitiveness. Yet whether the fundamental fragmentation of both American government and business groups could be overcome to produce a more structured relationship remained doubtful.

3

Government and Business in Britain

It is particularly difficult to classify the relationship between business and politics in Great Britain. A whole series of fundamental questions about the relationship between business and politics has no easy answers. These questions include how hostile or supportive is the political culture of capitalism, the degree to which the relationship between business and government is institutionalised, and the character of the 'industrial culture' prescribing what should be the purposes of the government–business relationship. Britain was often said by industrialists and commentators before the advent of the Thatcher Government to have an anti-business culture.[1] Yet the political party closely associated with business, the Conservative Party, has ruled Britain for over half the period since the Second World War. Early comparative studies of interest group politics pointed to the close consultation and partnership which characterised relations between government and economic interests in Britain. Political scientists influenced by neocorporatist theory have often placed Britain extremely low on their scales of how closely government and economic interests are integrated.[2] Other political scientists have argued that the British 'industrial culture' is biased against government becoming involved in detail in making decisions about investment or industrial development.[3] Yet British governments in the last thirty years have spent billions of pounds on assistance to industries, and at times have taken a very detailed interest in industrial restructuring.

Attitudes to Business

Do the British dislike capitalism in general or manufacturing in particular? Militant, even violent, behaviour by striking workers and the rhetoric of the left of the Labour Party sometimes seem to indicate that there is a major constituency for a radical challenge to capitalism in Britain. The version of modern British history favoured by many supporters of Mrs Thatcher is that Britain was drifting into either socialism or chaos or both until resolute action by the Thatcher Government saved the situation. Yet the reality is much more complicated. The bitterest strikes in Britain – such as the coal miners' strike – have generally been directed against government-owned industries. The Labour Party has had a more modest commitment to socialism than the rhetoric of its left wing suggests. The argument – promoted by both Thatcher's admirers and critics – that she created or mobilised support for 'popular capitalism', in which for the first time large numbers of Britons were enthused by capitalism, is at best over-stated and probably wrong.[4] It is important to cut dispassionately through the millenarian assumptions that 'Thatcherism' constituted a major change in British attitudes to capitalism.

Richard Rose has shown that the British give 'two and one half cheers' for the market economy.[5] Socialism produces more favourable responses than capitalism amongst the British in the abstract: socialism evokes more favourable and fewer unfavourable responses as an abstract doctrine than does capitalism. But when the British are asked to make judgements about the real world rather than abstract doctrines, socialism is overwhelmingly rejected, an interesting inversion of the situation in the USA. Only 5 per cent of Rose's sample wanted all industry to be owned and controlled by the government, and only another 13 per cent wanted the government to be involved in the 'day-to-day planning of companies'. A private enterprise system 'with enough government controls to curb abuses' or with 'a minimum of government regulation' attracted the support respectively of 39 per cent and 38 per cent of Rose's sample.

In the USA, the public was much attracted to capitalism in the abstract and favoured stronger government action in practice. In Britain, a substantial proportion of the public (though still a minority) favoured socialism in the abstract, but in more practical terms socialist measures were overwhelmingly rejected.

It is not surprising, therefore, that only intermittently has the Labour Party seemed to promise a break with capitalism. It is true that the Party's Constitution declares in the famous Clause IV that the party is dedicated to taking into public control the means of production, distribution and exchange. Yet in practice Labour governments have nationalised few industries which were not in major financial difficulty; other industries which are, or have been, in public ownership such as electricity generating, broadcasting, or Rolls Royce have been nationalised by *Conservative* governments for similarly pragmatic reasons. Indeed, in spite of the fact that between 1945 and 1979 the Labour Party held power for as long as the Conservatives, Mrs Thatcher inherited a situation in which the proportion of industry owned by the government, or the proportion of gross national product spent by the government, was lower than in other European countries such as France and Italy in which socialist parties had not enjoyed similar electoral success.

For much of its history, the Labour Party has been a coalition of socialists, reformers and union leaders in which pure socialists have been a minority. In the early 1980s, the left wing of the Party seemed to break through to dominance with the help of some of the most important union leaders. The Labour Party changed its constitution and rules in ways which advantaged the left in the selection of the Party leader and Parliamentary candidates. Simultaneously, the Party adopted much more left-wing policies for its 1983 Election Manifesto. The results for the Party were catastrophic. Several well-known politicians on the right wing of the party broke away to form a new political party which, though short-lived, helped lose Labour the 1983 and 1987 elections. The unpopularity of Labour's left-wing policies were a major factor in Labour's share of the vote in 1983 and 1987 plummeting to the lowest levels since the 1920s. By the late

1980s, the Party had resumed the task of trying to convince the electorate that the Party, while seeking to achieve social justice, accepted that capitalism and the market system would remain.

Similarly, the strength and radicalism of British unions is easily over-stated. Unionisation rates in Britain are higher than in the USA, Japan, France and Germany, but lower than in Austria and the Scandinavian countries. As noted above, most of the militant strikes waged by British unions have been in the public, not the private sector. British unions have been more concerned in practice with maintaining traditional wage differentials or working practices than in pressing for the transformation of capitalism. Except for periods such as the late 1970s, the number of days lost per thousand workers due to strike activity in Britain has been about average for western democracies.

The argument that there is an antipathy to manufacturing has been very popular in recent years. Wiener, in a much-debated book, argued that British culture was basically hostile to manufacturing.[6] The British fantasised about country life and country virtues, not urban life and industrial success. The best and brightest in Britain were attracted to the professions, the civil service or possibly finance, but not to industry. A disproportionate share of successful entrepreneurs in Britain has been immigrants creating companies such as Marks and Spencer or ICI. Many British institutions such as the public (private) schools, and Oxford and Cambridge universities, inculcated values even in the sons of successful industrial entrepreneurs more in line with the values of pre-industrial élites than with the demands of modern management. Entrepreneurial success was derided as coarse, vulgar and greedy. The British gentleman did not run a factory with a smoking chimney, noisy machinery and nasty smells; he was ideally a land owner living off rents or investments.

Wiener's portrait of British culture contains much truth. Yet it also leaves important questions unresolved. It might be said that Wiener's perspective is very American. For societies characterised at least as much as Britain by traditional cultures have in fact done very well industrially. Germany, France and especially Japan are not exactly indifferent to traditional values, but have thrived industrially. Traditional values can be used to reward industrial success through honours such as knighthoods or the Queen's Award to Industry which is given to successful exporters. In a wide variety of fields such as car building, aerospace and pharmaceuticals Britain has not lacked innovators but success.

The advent of the Thatcher Government served as a reminder that Britain, the home of liberal economic thought in the early nineteenth century, remained more influenced by it than most European countries. The Thatcher approach of promoting Britain's economic recovery through strengthening market forces has much in common with Reaganomics but has been emulated to only a limited extent in the rest of Europe. The admirers of Mrs Thatcher argue that she has achieved a major change in British culture. Not only has popular support for capitalism been increased according to this view, but the anti-industrial or entrepreneurial values described by Wiener have been eroded. A higher proportion of the British population own stock in corporations than ever before, thanks in large part to the government's privatisation of such formerly government-owned industries as the telephones, natural gas, electricity and British Airways. The number of small businesses has increased considerably. Successful entrepreneurs are more likely to be given honours or appointed to the House of Lords than in the past. The tax system has been changed to encourage initiative and enterprise.

Unfortunately for admirers of the Thatcher Government, these changes have not produced a revolution in popular attitudes. Indeed, surveys indicate that the British are *more* supportive of the welfare state and government assistance to the less well off than when Mrs Thatcher took office.[7] Popular suspicion of the government's privatisation programme increased as the list of industries to be sold off lengthened to include natural monopolies such as the water supply with whose performance the public was basically satisfied. The public seemed ready to forgo tax cuts in order to protect popular services such as the National Health Service from expenditure cuts. In short, just as the radicalism of the British had been over-estimated by socialists in the past, so supporters of Mrs Thatcher over-estimated the cultural change she had brought about in the 1980s. As before, the British response to capitalism was 'Yes, but . . . '

Links to Government

A comparison of Britain and the United States would indicate a much clearer institutionalisation of the relationship between business and government in Britain than in the USA. A number of factors produce this contrast.

First, *functional representation* has been more clearly and generally accepted in Britain than in the USA. That is to say, representation based on occupation or economic interest has been accepted as enjoying a greater legitimacy compared with representation through the electoral system than 'special interests' enjoy in the USA.[8] Government Departments have considered it good and wise practice to consult major interest groups before defining their policies. Indeed, government Departments in Britain have often depended on interest groups for information and technical assistance which the bureaucracy itself lacks. In return, Departments have seen it as part of their duty to act as advocates for interest groups with whom they interact in debates within government.[9]

Second, British economic interests appear to be much more clearly organised than their American counterparts. There is generally one organisation which is clearly the spokesman for the major economic interests in society. That organisation is recognised as the authoritative voice of that interest by top bureaucrats and government ministers. The Confederation of British Industry, for example, generally enjoyed a clear status as the spokesman for industry in the 1960s and 1970s. The fact that the CBI was created by merging three organisations representing business with the assistance and encouragement of a Labour government indicates how widely the belief in functional representation discussed above has been. Both Labour and Conservative governments in the 1960s and 1970s showed such willingness to work closely with the CBI that it became fashionable to suggest that Britain was becoming corporatist. The CBI had regular meetings with government officials and senior ministers to discuss economic policy. The CBI also acquired the right to appoint hundreds of people to government committees including those responsible for policy on health and safety (the Health and Safety Commission) and training (the Manpower Services Commission).

Why, then, have political scientists approaching Britain from a background in neocorporatism argued that the business–government relationship in Britain is comparatively un-institutionalised? A number of considerations lead them to that conclusion.

Although belief in the legitimacy of functional representation is more common in Britain than in the USA, it is still limited. Suggestions in the 1970s that Britain was becoming neocorporatist were seen as cause for alarm in a way that would not have been true in, say, Austria. Suggestions that power is shifting to economic interest groups arouse concern that 'Parliamentary supremacy', meaning in practice the power of elected politicians of the governing party, is threatened.

The Confederation of British Industry also turned out to look more impressive at first sight than on closer examination. Commitments made by the CBI were not seen as binding or particularly authoritative by member companies. The ability of the CBI to influence government policy was less than its members had hoped. The CBI could thus neither deliver the co-operation of corporations to government, nor deliver the co-operation of government to corporations.[10]

Above all, the CBI never really spoke with any authority for the financial sector.[11] The financial sector in fact has had more access to decision makers on its own than manufacturing industry obtains through the CBI. The Governor of the Bank of England, though answerable to the Chancellor of the Exchequer, defined his role in practice as also representing the interests and views of the financial institutions to governments. Governments of both parties tended to listen to the advice because of the strategic location of the financial sector in the British political economy. Links between financial institutions and Conservative MPs have usually been closer than between manufacturing industry and MPs. Not only was the financial sector (the City) one of the few successes in the British economy after the Second World War, but its opinions had tremendous short-term power. If the City thought badly of government policy, huge quantities of British pounds would be sold as the City 'hedged' against what it believed to be the inevitable consequences of poor policy. Pressures on Britain's foreign currency reserves or the value of the pound on the foreign currency exchanges would often bring the government to its senses.

Since the 1970s, the City itself has formalised its links to government.[12] Conventional interest group organisations have developed as the City has found the old, less formal linkages unsatisfactory. There are a number of reasons for this trend. As governments have used monetary policy more, the Bank of England has become clearly an agency of government policy. Moreover, the City itself has changed. Much of the City's success has involved its internationalisation with the arrival of large numbers of foreign financial institutions. The internationalisation of the City was both promoted and signified in the 1980s by the 'Big Bang' of deregulation of financial institutions and trading. Interestingly, although the Department of Trade itself retains significant powers in preventing fraud, most of the regulation of the City, in contrast to the situation in the United States, involves 'self regulation' by financial institutions in which the regulators are representatives of the regulated. This somewhat privileged position is a reminder that although financial institutions and their relationship with government have changed consider- ably, they have by no means been reduced to the point where they enjoy merely the same status as other industries. Finance remains separate and different from the rest of British industry.

A further factor damaging to the status of the CBI was the disorganised state of *trade associations* representing individual industries. Whereas general business organisations in many countries are 'peak' organisations linking strong trade associations, membership of the CBI was often held by individual companies. Trade associations were often poorly developed with small budgets and low quality staffs in competition with similar organisations for the right to represent the same industry.[13] British civil servants found that only a handful of trade associations could give them much practical assistance or useful advice. The CBI's own Devlin enquiry into trade associations showed how unimpressive they were when compared with European counterparts. Large corporations in Britain, like their American counterparts, have moved to open a direct dialogue with government departments, by-passing the trade associations which would form the natural conduit for such talks in many European nations. In the 1980s, in a manner again reminiscent of their American counterparts, many corporations also made increasing use of their *contract lobbyists* who would attempt to promote corporations' interests in Parliament or the bureaucracy. Grant has characterised the British system of government–industry relations as a 'company state' in that government–industry relations are increasingly between government and individual corporations rather than between government and business organisations.[14]

The Industrial Culture

Perhaps because of Thatcher's free market rhetoric, it was common to link Britain with the USA in the 1980s as examples of states which intervened to only a limited extent in specific industries, limiting the role of government to macroeconomic management. This reluctance to intervene was often contrasted unfavourably with the practices of countries such as Japan and France.[15]

The reluctance of British governments to engage in detailed intervention was often seen as a reflection of an industrial culture which was hostile to such policies, and institutional practices which re-enforced the culture. In this view, British economic policy makers continued to subscribe to the scepticism of liberal economic theory about the desirability or wisdom of government trying to be wiser than market forces in allocating resources for investment or production. Moreover, the capacity of the British state to intervene intelligently was thought to be limited. The structure of capital markets in Britain gives government little leverage over the allocation of investment funds. How easily that situation could be changed has been debated,[16] but all participants in the debate would agree that British governments, unlike Japanese or French governments, have lacked the means to promote what they believe to be the industries of the future through making credit easier or cheaper for those industries than for others. Most top bureaucrats in Britain lack the background or training for making detailed industrial decisions. Most politicians share the same weakness. The strength of party competition and the power of elected politicians in Britain makes detailed intervention in industrial or investment decisions easily subject to calculations about what will help the governing party. One of the largest bridges in Britain was built as a result of a promise made by a Minister of Transport in order to win a crucial Parliamentary by-election. There is no reason to believe that other governments would have acted differently. In Britain, as in the United States, politicians and elections shape policy more and more easily than in a country such as Japan with, in effect, only one major political party.[17]

Yet the truth is that British governments have made numerous detailed interventions in industry. Particular products such as *Concorde* have been made as a result of government wishes. Intervention in the day to day running of nationalised industries for social or political reasons has been frequent. As in the United States, defence expenditure accounts for such a large proportion of the orders of certain corporations that their fate is settled by the Ministry of Defence. It is true that British industrial policy has been inconstant and often ineffective. Yet at times British governments of both parties have approached the level of intervention and planning which some political scientists have admired in other countries.

The machinery for neocorporatist consultation was created by the Macmillan Government in 1963. The National Economic Development Council (NEDC) provided a forum for consultation and co-operation between the government, employers, and the Trades Union Congress (TUC). The attempt to move in the direction of the much-admired French system of indicative planning was strengthened by the interest of the 1964–70 Labour government in producing a National Plan to assist the achievement of increased economic growth. Although neither the National Plan nor the Department of Economic Affairs created to supervise its implementation took root, the 1964–70 Labour government continued to favour detailed intervention in industry as exemplified by the creation of the Industrial Reorganisation Corporation (IRC). The IRC promoted mergers and restructuring when it thought these would increase efficiency. Although the Conservative government led by Edward Heath (1970–74) initially favoured a move toward greater reliance on market forces and abolished the IRC, it soon re-equipped itself with powers to make loans or grants to industries and, until blocked by the 1973–74 miners' strike, attempted to move in the direction of neocorporatist collaboration with economic interest groups. That tendency was given added force by the 1974–79 Labour government whose attempts to construct a 'Social Contract' linking government with economic interests were even more serious. As the economic difficulties of British industry mounted in the 1970s, so did government spending on industry.

It is quite incorrect, therefore, to suggest that British government has consistently maintained an 'arm's length' relationship with industry. The situation up until 1979 was rather that governments of both political parties were constantly drawn into close relationships with industries, even though those relationships were neither purposive nor effective. By the late 1970s, British industrial policy was expensive but ineffective, distributing subsidies to many doomed industries in response to political pressures from them.

The Conservative Party and the Thatcher Decade

The British Conservative Party had long been associated with business. Although in the mid-nineteenth century business entrepreneurs felt philosophically and even religiously more comfortable with the Liberal than the Conservative Party, by the twentieth century there was little doubt that the

Conservatives were the party supported by most stockholders and business executives. Yet for many years, the business interest, the Protestant skilled working class especially in Lancashire, imperialists and Unionists in Northern Ireland all have had some influence in the party. Moreover, the Conservative Party has had a shrewd instinct for survival. The need to win a substantial share of the working class vote in order to prosper politically combined with the 'statist' and paternalistic traditions of the landed element within the Party to make it much more accepting of social reform and the welfare state than have been American conservatives.

The rise of Thatcherism within the Conservative Party has been seen as a sign of the triumph of commercial interests within the Party. The Thatcher Government's insistence on self reliance, typified by the advice of one government minister that the unemployed 'get on their bikes' to look for work, sits oddly with the statist and paternalistic traditions of part of the old Party élite. Thatcher's belief in not only the greater efficiency but the higher morality of market systems under direction by the state is equally a major change of emphasis in the traditions of the Party.

Yet the rise of Thatcherism was not only due to a shift in the balance of power among the élites of the Conservative Party. It was also associated with a widespread, pessimistic analysis of the prospects for Britain if there was no radical break with the 'postwar consensus' which had underpinned the welfare state and experiments in government partnership with industry. The postwar consensus had rested upon the practical acceptance by the Labour Party, characteristically masked by a damaging ideological feud about admitting this openly, that the Party accepted the continuation of a fundamentally capitalist economy, and the acceptance by the Conservatives of the welfare state and power of the unions. During the 1950s, the golden years of the postwar consensus, Conservative governments maintained intact the welfare state created by the Attlee Government and took no steps to curb the power of unions even though British industry was manifestly hurt by union excesses. The differences between Labour and the Conservatives were so attenuated that it was common to talk of 'Butskellism' dominating British politics, a term created by fusing the names of the prominent Conservative, R. A. Butler and the Labour leader, Hugh Gaitskell, in order to note the convergence of their ideas.

The years of Butskellism were years of prosperity and full employment during which the British economy grew steadily at a faster rate than usual during the twentieth century. However, the Butskellite years were also the period according to many observers when the *comparative* decline of Britain accelerated. Britain failed to grow at rates comparable to those of its European neighbours so that the trend towards Britain becoming one of the poorest nations of northern Europe was ever more clearly evident. As this trend became clear, Conservative and Labour governments in the 1960s and 1970s attempted to find a relatively painless solution. In the 1960s, the Conservative governments of Harold Macmillan and Sir Alec Douglas-Home followed by the Labour government of Harold Wilson attempted to implement indicative planning on the French model. Growth rates would be accelerated by concerting the plans among government, unions, the different industries, and other economic interests such as farmers. The National Plan published in 1965 was the most complete expression of these endeavours. By 1966, the Plan was a dead letter. The Labour government chose, as would a Conservative government, to place a higher value on defending the value of the pound in foreign exchanges than on implementing the National Plan. Although this judgement seems quixotic from the perspective of the 1990s after such a long period of floating exchange rates, it also reflected the difficulty of engaging in indicative planning in an economy as open as is the British to pressures from the international financial markets. Whether the National Plan would have made any difference to growth rates had there not been a financial crisis causing its abandonment can be doubted. Most studies of French planning indicate that many factors other than the Plan itself, such as the power of government within the financial system, were crucial to the success of French government economic policy.

Another policy technique apparently discredited in the 1960s and 1970s was the attempt to run the economy through a partnership of government, unions, and corporations. This attempt at partnership preceded the National Plan, originating in the creation of the National Economic Development Council (NEDC) by the Macmillan Government. It also survived the demise of the National Plan. As in most countries where such attempts at co-operation between government, unions and business crystallised into neocorporatism, the moves towards co-operation in Britain were driven by the need to reconcile full employment with controlling inflation and maintaining competitiveness. During periods of full employment, wages in Britain have generally risen faster than productivity squeezing the ability of corporations to fund new investment and contributing to inflation. In the absence of regular devaluations of the pound, inflation in turn contributed to the uncompetitiveness of British exports. The attraction of an agreement between government, unions and employers to restrain the rate of increase of wages in return for concessions to unions on other issues was that full employment could be maintained without wages rising at a rate threatening a loss of competitiveness or inflation.

Attractive though such a deal seems to all concerned, in practice it could not be achieved in Britain. The CBI had very little power to commit member corporations to specific courses of action. The TUC had limited power over individual unions, and the leaders of individual unions had limited power to commit their members. Not only were many union leaders ideologically opposed to incomes policies, but most feared that if they were to take too reasonable a stance in formulating incomes policies, they would lose power to local militants within their unions. Finally, governments found their ability to make bargains with domestic economic interests limited by their vulnerability to international financial pressures. All attempts to run incomes policies therefore broke down. When the 1970–74 Conservative government attempted to impose an incomes policy on the unions, it suffered an ignominious defeat at the hands of the miners. Attempting to buttress its position, the Prime Minister, Edward Heath, called an election which he attempted to fight on the issue of whether unions or the elected government ran Britain. Heath lost. Similarly, the defeat of the succeeding Labour government was due above all to the collapse of its Social Contract with the unions, which resulted in a wave of strikes inflicting great hardships on ordinary voters during the so-called 'winter of discontent' in 1978–79.

Thatcherism and Business

The major beneficiary of union militancy was Margaret Thatcher, who gained power with a clear majority in the House of Commons which she could not have obtained by relying solely on an appeal based on the limited popularity of herself or her ideology. Thatcher promised a radical break with the recent past designed to restore Britain's economy. Yet although Britain's recovery was to be achieved through the private sector, 'Thatcherism' was not a dream package of policies for business executives.[18] Certain aspects of Thatcherism were indeed welcome to business executives. The government's step by step but steady programme to curb the power of unions through labour laws requiring a ballot to be held before a strike could be called, and the banning of secondary action (ie strikes to help workers employed by a different corporation) were popular with employers who had so long lacked the strength or courage to defy unions themselves. The government's tax cuts for higher income groups intended to encourage enterprise and initiative were also much appreciated by business executives. But the Thatcher Government also relied initially on the rigorous use of monetary policy to combat inflation. This contributed to a sharp decline in domestic demand and, by boosting the value of the British pound overseas, made British exports even less competitive. Unemployment increased rapidly as corporations scrambled to contain or cut costs in the face of the recession. The industrial power of unions declined, but thousands of employers were also forced into bankruptcy.

The economic strategy of the Thatcher Government had tremendous implications for the relationship between government and economic interests. First, because the government relied on a policy technique over which it had total control (monetary policy) instead of policy techniques which required the co-operation of economic interests (incomes policy), the government was able to reduce considerably the importance of economic interest groups. Both the TUC *and* the CBI found the attention they received from government reduced. This reduction in influence was exemplified by, though not limited to, the government's treatment of the NEDC. First the Prime Minister stopped attending regularly, then the Chancellor of the Exchequer followed suit and finally the frequency of NEDC meetings and the size of its staff were reduced. Consulting economic interests simply mattered less to the Thatcher Government than its Labour or Conservative predecessors. Second, the recession of the early 1980s produced considerable friction between the government and the CBI as many of the CBI's manufacturing members experienced great difficulties attributable at least in part to government policy. In desperation, the Director General of the CBI threatened the Prime Minister with a 'bare knuckle fight' if the government persisted in its policies. In retaliation, a number of corporations loyal to the Prime Minister left the CBI and the Prime Minister herself increased the authority and standing of what had previously been insignificant institutional rivals to the CBI, notably the 'Thatcherite' Institute of Directors.[19]

In brief, if Thatcherism was intended to be a movement to save British capitalism, it was revolution made against the wishes of many leaders of *organisations* representing British capitalists. This the government cheerfully accepted. In its White Paper, *DTI* [the Department of Trade and Industry] *The Department for Enterprise*, the government declared that too much corporatism had been one of the reasons for Britain's economic decline.[20] This odd view – few academic commentators had ever ranked Britain high in the league tables of neocorporatism – was the reason given for a reorganisation of the DTI in order to disrupt relations between the Department and trade associations. The leading authority on business and politics in Britain, Wyn Grant, has concluded that the CBI never recovered its standing with the government after the conflict with Thatcher over economic policy in the early 1980s.[21] Indeed, the CBI was reduced by the late 1980s to complaining that it had been denied what had once been the normal courtesies of consultation for any major interest group on government proposals concerning rates (property taxes). The CBI's complaints were brushed aside. Within government, civil servants learnt that close association with the views of interest groups associated with their Department could be a barrier to promotion into the higher posts as Ministers came to take a closer interest in promotions to higher level civil service posts.

Underlying all these changes was a distrust of capitalists and business organisations in Thatcherism. Although for Thatcherites capitalism is good, capitalists in Britain are often lazy, incompetent and prone to seek rescue from government from the consequences of their own misdeeds. Organisations representing capitalists such as the CBI or trade associations are dominated by business executives who are bureaucratically rather than entrepreneurially minded. In Thatcher's view, business executives should be engaged in making or selling products, not attending committee meetings.

For its part government, while withdrawing from commercial activity by privatising as many industries as possible, had also to promote the efficient working of markets through reforms. One of the most enduring changes brought about by the Thatcher governments is likely to be the selling to private owners of formerly government-owned firms as varied as Associated British Ports, British Telecom, British Airways and the water supply industry. Yet unlike the situation in the United States during the Reagan years, Thatcherian policies were not based on the assumption that all the government needed to do to promote economic success was to do less; the traditional injunction, *laissez-faire*, does not capture fully the spirit of Thatcherism. Measures to reduce the power of unions, encourage initiative through tax reductions for the highest paid, and a major initiative to improve training were all intended to improve the working of the markets. As Polanyi had noted in the 1940s,[22] markets are not spontaneous, self generating social mechanisms; markets must be created by laws and political actions which will break down barriers to their operation. Thatcherism followed in that tradition. Indeed, if necessary the Thatcher Government was quite prepared to expand the powers of the state in order to achieve its objectives of freer markets. Institutions which stood in the way of government policies such as city or county governments and universities found that the government took drastic new powers to force them to comply with the government's will. The Thatcher view of the state was that it should be both smaller in the sense of less involved in business or in collaboration with business, but stronger in the sense of being able to overwhelm opposition to its policies from interest groups or lower level governmental units.

Two obvious questions arise. First, if the Thatcher revolution was partially directed against business organisations, why did the business organisations not rally against her government? Second, how, if business organisations are less respected than previously, are government and business to resolve problems that obviously occur in their daily relations?

There were three major reasons why British business executives did not coalesce in opposition to the government. First, some agreed with the government's analysis of the need for fundamental change in Britain. Certain aspects of Thatcherism – reducing taxes on higher income groups and weakening unions – appealed even to those sceptical about monetary policy. Second, many doubters were deeply committed to the Conservative Party. There was a strong feeling among many executives when the Director General of the CBI issued his 'bare knuckle fight' warning to the government to change its policies that no CBI leader should ever criticise a Conservative government publicly. The shift to the left of the Labour Party in the early 1980s caused many business executives to conclude that any alternative government was likely to be far worse. A few business executives experimented with support for the Social Democrats, but by the mid 1980s it was clear that even in alliance with the Liberals, the Social Democrats had little prospect of forming a government. Third, some businesses thrived. Whereas the government's monetary policies hit British manufacturing corporations very hard in the early 1980s, the high interest rates and high external value of sterling the policies produced had a very beneficial effect on financial institutions. High interest rates generated high profits for banks; a strong pound facilitates massive overseas investment by British financial institutions, which were also aided by the government's abolition of exchange controls. As we have noted above, the financial sector has generally had better links to the Conservative Party than has manufacturing.

If business organisations are suspect, then how are business and government to communicate? The reduction in the standing of business organisations in Britain has been accompanied by an increase in contacts between government and individual corporations. Corporations have built up their own London offices so that they can communicate concerns direct to government rather than operating through a mediating business organisation such as a trade association or the CBI. Corporations have also turned to contract lobbyists, who saw their business expand dramatically in the 1980s, attracting much comment from journalists and political scientists. Ministers and civil servants expressed greater interest in talking to 'real businessmen' than to interest group officials. Britain became increasingly what Grant calls a 'company state' in which government contacts are with individual businesses, not business organisations.

The Permanence of Thatcherism and the Implications of the British Case

British economic policy since the Second World War has been characterised by extreme instability.[23] Not only has economic policy often changed fundamentally when governments have changed, but policies have even changed drastically without a change of government. Until the Thatcher Government, a 'U turn' in economic policy was expected of all governments. Incomes policy typifies British policy instability. Incomes policy was used by the 1945–51 Labour government, abandoned by the Conservatives but reintroduced in the early 1960s, criticised but then strengthened by the 1964–70 Labour government, abandoned by the 1970–74 Heath Government which then met its demise pursuing incomes policy determinedly, abandoned by the 1974–79 Labour government, which then reintroduced incomes policy and again met defeat in 1979 as its policy failed. The Thatcher Government abandoned incomes policy when it abandoned a commitment to full employment. Many similar examples of gyrations in economic policy could be provided, such as the extreme instability of government policies to encourage corporations to move to depressed regions.

It might be assumed that Thatcherism will be but another passing phase in British economic policy, particularly as it is not in step with British public opinion on many issues. Yet most commentators assume that Thatcherism will have enduring consequences. Certain policies will be impossible to rescind either because they are popular (as are the labour law reforms) or because the cost of reversing them would be too great (privatisation). Thatcherism is also likely to have enduring consequences for links between business and government in Britain. Were government policies to become more interventionist, the business organisations such as the CBI could quite quickly increase their staffs to engage in collaboration or consultation with government Departments. But whether the prestige of business organisations could be restored as quickly is doubtful. It is easier to destroy than to build the authority of an interest group. The British civil service, because it is a career civil service, will continue to be staffed and, as they are promoted, increasingly dominated by, people socialised during the Thatcher years into more sceptical attitudes about interest groups than their predecessors displayed. Individual corporations that have built up their own contacts with government Departments are unlikely to hand the representation of their interests back to business organisations.

The reduction in the standing of business organisations is likely to have certain disadvantages. First, as Mancur Olson has argued, it is very difficult for interest group systems characterised by fragmentation to take the long view.[24] When there are many competing interest groups, none can be sure that a sacrifice of its short-term interests to promote its long-term interests will be matched by other interest groups. Second, it remains to be seen whether even giant corporations can match the expertise that a business organisation such as the CBI can bring to consultations with government. Finally, the policy-making process of the European Community continues to give far greater prominence to *organisations* representing economic interests than British practice ever did. Reducing the status of economic interest groups leaves British economic interests with a problem of how to fit into the European policy-making process in a period when the relative importance of decisions made at the Community level has increased and is increasing.

The diminished status of business organisations in Britain prompts a fascinating question for political scientists. In the 1970s, theorists of neocorporatism implied that more institutionalised relations between economic interests and governments were inevitable as economies developed. Britain, and to an even greater degree, the United States, were therefore laggards which might one day catch up with countries such as Norway or Sweden (though a number of pessimists doubted their ability to do so). In the last ten years the links between business and government in Britain have moved in the direction not of being more like Sweden but more like the United States. The reduction in the status of the business umbrella group, the CBI, the continued weakness of trade associations and the increase in political activity by individual corporations – in brief what Grant calls a company state – are all reminiscent of the American model. The growth in the scale of *regulated* – as opposed to nationalised – industries in Britain as telecommunications, gas, water, electricity and other basic industries are privatised seems likely to accentuate this trend. Whether this trend in Britain is characteristic only of what General de Gaulle used to call the Anglo-Saxon countries, or will occur more generally remains to be seen.

4

Germany

The most common and important question about politics in Germany is the extent of the break with traditions, beliefs and practices of German politics which took place in 1945. Most observers believe that West Germany took a massive, permanent step towards democracy when the Federal German Republic was established. It is less clear how fundamental was the transformation of the relationship between business and government. On the one hand, it can be argued that after the Second World War, West Germany embarked on a course characterised by a combination of free market economics and the maintenance of a strong welfare state, a course characterised as *the social market economy*. On the other hand, it can be argued that there were values and traditions too deeply rooted in German history to be eradicated by a mere change of government policy. These tendencies were towards a more organised form of capitalism characterised by corporatist co-operation between business, labour and government. Monopoly or at least high levels of industrial concentration were more common than competition; major features of the domestic economy such as training programmes were run jointly by the unions and employers, while the major banks provided a concertation of investment plans which was achieved in other systems through government lead economic planning. Finally, it can be argued, the re-emergence of older traditions of business–government relations can be seen since the late 1960s in attempts at establishing neocorporatist concertation at the national level accompanied by increasing government subsidies to failing industries.

The crucial question, therefore, is whether or not the social market economy was but a brief episode in the history of the German political economy, or whether its influence persists to this day. In order to address this issue, we must first discuss what the social market economy was meant to be.

At first sight the principles of the social market economy look identical to the principles of *laissez-faire* economics. Government should not intervene in individual industries, nor should they accept responsibility for macro-economic management. The principles of monetarism were popular in West Germany long before they were in Britain and the USA, and Keynes was conversely less popular. The aim of government, apart from providing the general infrastructure for the economy, should be to foster competition, both through attacking monopolies and cartels and through fostering freer international trade. It is important to emphasise that in the German context these were quite novel doctrines. As many writers have noted,[1] German industrialisation, in contrast to British and American experience, was the result of co-operation between highly concentrated industry and the state. In an alliance between the Prussian states, eager for the military might that the industrialisation of Germany would bring, and the industrialists such as Krupp who created the industrial empires, rapid industrialisation took place behind high tariff barriers fostered by government finance. This pattern of close government–industry co-operation continued throughout the Nazi era, although the balance of power between the industrialists and Hitler remains a matter of great historical controversy. The economic principles of the social market economy resonate with the liberal traditions of Britain and the USA. The principles involved a sharp break not only with the protectionism, planning, cartelisation and subjection of economic to nationalist aspirations which had characterised the Nazi era but also with the general pattern of business–government relations in German history.

What, it might be asked, was distinctively 'social' about a social market economy which stressed competition and keeping government at arm's length from the day-to-day operations of industry?[2] The advocates of the social market economy did argue that they saw a major role for government.

Government was to use its power to promote the social market economy by attacking monopoly cartels, etc. Government was also to take action to correct the failings of the market economy, to provide such social services as were necessary to correct poverty, maldistribution of incomes and pollution – evils which would not be corrected through market mechanisms. In a sense, the 'social' part of the social market economy may be the part which was the more fulfilled. The West German welfare state is much more generous than the British variant, let alone the fragmented and incomplete American welfare state.

It is less certain that the social market economy ever displaced the more traditional structure that was rooted in German economic history. Culture, tradition, the political power of business and the desire of the Western allies (particularly the Americans) for rapid recovery tended to subvert the social market economy's stress on competition. Within ten years of Germany's defeat, the very same cartels and giant firms which had been blamed in part for the rise of Hitler were again established. Strong efforts had been made to fragment and localise the banking system, but a series of mergers in the 1950s and 1960s re-established three major banks. Indeed, it has been claimed that this return to concentration merely marked a *de jure* return, as *de facto* the banks had retained the centralised structure they had possessed throughout German history. Similarly, I. G. Farben and Krupp were soon back in their pre-eminent role in the German economy, in spite of the determination of the wartime allies to break up these firms so closely associated with the Nazi régime. Perhaps the greatest political success of the Confederation of German Industries (BDI), to which we shall return later, was the drastic weakening of the laws against cartels and monopolies. Only in foreign trade, with heavy and early cuts in import duties, was the practice of social market economics evident. Even here, however, the principles of social market economics were arguably contravened by the practice in the 1960s and 1970s of leaving the mark drastically undervalued, a policy designed to help German manufacturers both at home and overseas by keeping imports dearer and exports cheaper than they need have been.

Another problematic area is the role of the banks.[3] Although it might be excessive to say that the German banks have supplied the integrative and planning role abjured by government in West Germany, the banks do indeed play a vital role. Unlike British banks, German banks are closely involved with manufacturing industry, supplying a major portion of investment capital in exchange for stocks and seats on the supervisory boards of firms. The Deutsche Bank for example, actually owned 25 per cent of the stock of Mercedes Benz until 1975 when it extended its holding to 56 per cent. In general, banks hold 33 per cent of the seats for non-employees on the supervisory boards of West Germany's 318 largest companies. In turn, the largest companies hold seats on the boards of the banks. German bankers are apparently conscious of having a particular responsibility for the maintenance of the social and economic order, and for the harmonious functioning of the economy *Ordnungsfaktor*.

Whatever the reality, the ideology of the social market economy served several functions. Its stress on decentralisation and competition helped to differentiate West Germany from Nazi Germany, and to reduce the fears of the resurgence of German industry which were bound to arise. Above all, the social market economy provided the centre-right in Germany with an appealing ideology with which to compete against the socialists. The social market economy was established as doctrine by the dominance of the Christian Democrats throughout the 1950s and the first half of the 1960s. But the doctrine of the social market economy also helped achieve this period of centre-right dominance by blunting criticisms from the Social Democrats that the Christian Democrats were heartless conservatives, indifferent to the needs of the poor and dominated by big business. The stress on the free market economy was indeed appealing to German business, while the stress on social responsibility and social programmes helped maintain the Christian Democrats' grip on the working-class Catholic vote vital for their chances of electoral victory.

The General Business Environment

For over two decades after the Second World War, West Germany seemed to offer one of the best environments for business in western Europe. West German politics was dominated by a predominantly conservative, pro-business party, or rather coalition of parties, the Christian Democratic Union (CDU) and the Christian Social Union, essentially its Bavarian counterpart. The CDU/CSU was generally dependent on the support of the Free Democrat Party (FDP) which, because of the modified system of proportional representation in West Germany, proved to be essential to the maintenance of a government majority in the Bundestag. By the end of the 1950s, it was clear that the Social Democratic Party (SPD) also posed no major threat to the capitalist system. In its Bad Godesburg programme (1959) the SPD repudiated traditional calls for the government ownership of industry or even for equality in favour of commitments to pursue 'freedom, justice and solidarity'. In general, the Bad Godesburg programme can be seen as the sort of explicit commitment to seek amelioration of social ills within the framework of a market economy that the leader of the British Labour Party, Hugh Gaitskell, attempted unsuccessfully to have his party make at roughly the same period. Because of the impact of religion and region as well as social class on voting behaviour in West Germany, the political parties have to appeal to a variety of social classes simultaneously. The CDU/CSU has a working class, predominantly Catholic following, which it must cultivate; because the SPD shares the working class vote almost equally with the other major parties, it must also seek support among the middle class.

Business in West Germany therefore benefited in several ways from the political situation compared to business in Britain. First, all major parties accepted the need to maintain successful capitalist corporations as the foundations of national prosperity. Second, the dependence of the two largest parties on the FDP to maintain them in power gave the FDP great leverage in coalition. This leverage allowed the FDP to be a great force for policy stability even if there was a change in the major party dominating the government.

Finally, the parties' need to appeal to more than their 'natural' social class supporters ensured that the extreme polarisation found in British politics in the early 1980s was avoided.

For their part, unions in West Germany have generally been extremely moderate during the period since the Second World War. Union power was curtailed by several factors. The arrival of millions of refugees from eastern Europe including East Germany in the 1940s and 1950s brought in a large pool of skilled labour. Unions, though very strong in certain industries, are in general only moderately strong, organising about 30 per cent of the work force, much higher than the proportion in the USA but much lower than in Britain let alone Norway, Sweden or Austria. The unions themselves, organised largely at the behest of the British into rationally structured, relatively few units, proved more capable of taking a long-term view of their members' interests than unions were in Britain. Competition for members through the 'demarcation disputes' between unions or for higher increases in monetary wages than other unions achieved were avoided in Germany even while they afflicted British industry.

Similarly, since 1947 in the then British occupied zone of Germany, managers were obliged to inform and consult their workers through co-determination councils (*Mitbestimmung*) which the British government continued to resist passionately in the late 1980s. The German economic miracle of the 1950s and early 1960s, when the growth rate of the economy on average exceeded 6 per cent a year, helped convince Germans that hard work and discipline did more to increase living standards than union militancy. As German incomes have gone from about 63 per cent of British incomes in 1951 to about 155 per cent today, it is hard to quarrel with that judgement.

In the 1970s and 1980s, however, a new and, in one case, politically successful critique of capitalism has been articulated in West Germany. The upsurge of the extreme left in the 1970s reflected the appeal of revolutionary, anti-capitalist socialism groups to some young Germans; the head of the employers' organisations was actually murdered by left wing terrorists in 1977. An entirely different movement, the Greens, has been the most successful of the western European environmentalist groups, gaining 5.6 per cent of the popular vote in the 1983 elections and 8.3 per cent in 1987, enough under German electoral law to give them a significant presence in the Bundestag. Though the Greens are ideologically diverse, their policies are generally unwelcome to business, ranging from stricter regulation of business to the transformation of capitalism. As the SPD has also been moving left, and must now worry about electoral competition from the Greens to its left, the ideological climate of German politics was less hospitable to business in the early 1990s than it had been previously even though a conservative government ruled.

Business Organisation

We might expect that as in the United States, what has been until recently a favourable political setting for business would discourage the formation of strong business organisations. In practice, this has not been so. German history has encouraged a comparatively high density of membership for business organisations into clearly structured, authoritative organisations which enjoy a high degree of acceptance as the sole representatives of business in dealings with other groups and with government. Over 70 per cent of all but the smallest-scale employers belong to the appropriate trade association, and the trade associations are in turn affiliated to the German Federation of Industry (BDI). A similar organisation, the National Association of German Employers (BDA) is responsible for labour negotiations.

Several factors explain the high degree of organisation. First, as we shall discuss below, German culture has recognized since the medieval Chambers or *Kammern* the desirability of organising economic interests. Second, the climate for business has not always been as favourable for capitalism as it has seemed since the Second World War. Germany prior to the Nazi regime had a flourishing Communist as well as Socialist Party; even after the Second World War, opinion polls showed higher levels of distrust of managers in West Germany than existed in Britain. Third, the

Federal Republic inherited strong, hierarchically integrated employers' organisations from the Nazi regime, whose corporatist ideology had required their formation.

As in most western democracies, business clearly favours one party more than the others. Business support has gone heavily to the CDU/CSU. In fact, the CDU has received 60 per cent of its funds from business and the ties between CDU and BDI leaders have generally been close since the friendship of the first Chancellor, Konrad Adenauer, and the first postwar leader of the BDI, Fritz Berg.[4] As we have noted, the CDU is more than a pro-business party, with a significant Catholic workers' section. As business has been forced to share power within the CDU with other groups and interests, it has been valuable for it to maintain some links to the FDP, which for most of the postwar period has been firmly in favour of free market policies, perhaps more opposed to moves towards planning than the CDU.

As in all parliamentary systems, most decisions are made within the executive branch rather than in the legislature. The Bundestag with its developed committee system may be more significant than the British House of Commons, but in general it ratifies decisions made within the government it elects. The BDI therefore focuses primarily on government ministries, and in consequence, like its British counterpart the CBI, adopts a non-partisan, technocratic style that it hopes will give it access to officials whichever of the major parties leads the government. As the BDI and trade associations, which are much more lavishly funded than their British counterparts, have the reputation for employing high calibre staff, they have little difficulty in having their views noticed by the bureaucracy. Links to the Ministry of Trade are stronger than links to the Ministry of Finance, which are still stronger than the links to the Ministry of Labour or the Ministry of Agriculture, which naturally are influenced more by other economic interest groups. In 1989, severe criticisms were made of the Ministry of Trade because of its failure to regulate exports by German corporations effectively in deference to their wishes. One result was the export to Libya of plants capable of manufacturing poison gas, a capability with which it seemed unwise to equip Libya's unstable leader.

The Evolution of Policy from Social Market to Neocorporatism?

As the economic miracle ran out of steam, so did pressures increase for a new approach to economic policy. These pressures were also associated with the end of the period of Christian Democratic dominance. The 'Grand Coalition', in which the Social Democrats made their entry into the government of the Federal Republic in partnership with the Christian Democrats, made moves towards increased government planning, so popular at that time in Europe because of the apparent success of the French example. By its very nature, the Grand Coalition was more difficult to co-ordinate than previous governments. There had been a growing awareness in the previous Christian Democratic government, however, that the capacity of the Chancellor's office to co-ordinate the work of the different ministries was inadequate. Ministries had a clear tendency – as in so many countries shown at its most extreme by the Agriculture Ministry – to develop 'clientelistic' relations with the beneficiaries of the programmes they administered. The coal industry, too, was highly subsidised by an indulgent parent ministry. Such pressures for greater co-ordination from within government combined with the concern aroused by the decline of the economic miracle to push the Coalition towards greater planning.

The Grand Coalition of the SPD and the CDU/CSU which governed West Germany from 1966–69 introduced the most visible attempt at making economic policy in a neocorporatist style that has been seen in the history of the Federal Republic. Acting on what it was hoped would be widely accepted as impartial economic advice, the federal government, the Lander and representatives of the 'social partners', the unions and the representatives of employers, would concert their actions in a manner which would ensure growth, full employment, and avoid inflation or deficits in the balance of payments.[5]

The average level of unionisation in West Germany (about 30 per cent of the workforce) might not seem sufficient to prompt neocorporatist developments. However, unionisation levels are higher in crucial export industries. Moreover, other factors in German culture provided a basis for experiments with neocorporatism. There was a long-standing belief in *organised* capitalism, for example, which pre-dated and survived Erhart's social market economy. Cartels or even monopolies had never been regarded with the same suspicion in Germany as in Britain or the USA. The industrialisation of Germany, which occurred later than in Britain or the USA, had been accomplished by relatively few large corporations encouraged by the state, not by the spontaneous actions of numerous entrepreneurs. Acceptance of the idea that people should be represented on the basis of their occupations and that the guilds representing those occupations should regulate the conduct of their members can be traced back to medieval Germany. Catholic social thought in Germany, as in much of continental Europe, had promoted a middle way between socialism and capitalism through corporatist compromises between economic interests and the state. The acceptance of functional representation was therefore more solidly grounded in West Germany than in Britain. Unions and employers had experience of working together on the supervisory boards required for all large corporations and in administering industrial training. Extending this partnership to the national level seemed a logical step to take. Finally, the basis of the entire strategy of the SPD particularly after acceptance of the Godesburg programme (see below) was to promote the interests of ordinary Germans within the framework of capitalism. The institutionalisation of co-operation between labour, government and the state in the late 1960s expressed this strategy. It is not accidental that the moves towards neocorporatism followed the entry of the SPD into government for the first time in the history of the Federal Republic.

Full scale institutionalised neocorporatism lasted only briefly, however. The formal meetings of governments and the 'social partners' were held only in the late 1960s and early 1970s. Thereafter, however, informal consultations were held in the so-called Bungalow Meetings at the Chancellor's residence in Bonn. Particularly during the Chancellorship of Helmut Schmidt (1974–82), the government continued to attempt to achieve agreements with unions and employers on desirable directions for economic policy. Arguably this process allowed West Germany to cope with the 'oil shocks' of the 1970s better than countries such as Britain or the United States which lacked such effective consultative procedures. Informal consultations continued after the switch of government to a coalition led by the CDU/CSU's Chancellor Kohl.

It is surprising, however, that not only did the more formal neocorporatism of the late 1960s and early 1970s fail to become established, but that the informal neocorporatism of the Bungalow talks also faded in significance in the 1980s. As in other countries which have experimented with neocorporatism, the practice was strained by issues extending beyond those normally covered in social partnership discussions. The pressure from unions, for expanded rights for workers in co-determination councils of corporations, and determined resistance from employers was a strain on social partnership. The German economic miracle also faded in the 1970s and 1980s. As growth rates faltered, automatic increases in wages based on economic successes diminished. Union militancy rose as workers attempted to improve their living standards through industrial strength instead of growth. Disagreements about how to combat rising unemployment also strained relations. In the early 1980s the unions launched a major drive for a shorter working week in order to share work. The unemployment rate climbed, however, to levels not witnessed since the Second World War before falling back as the international economy recovered. Finally, German employers became more nervous about the degree to which they were vulnerable to competition from Asia and, as complete removal of trade barriers within the European Community in 1992 drew near, from countries such as Britain, Spain and Portugal with lower wages and less generous, so less costly, welfare states.

There were also longer term limitations on the development of neocorporatism in West Germany. West German peak organisations do not have the full authority that they seem to enjoy at first sight. Unions in the 1970s proved unwilling to follow the lead of the DGB in the 1970s and fully accept limitations on wage increases which had been negotiated on their behalf. The BDI was also not immune to challenges to its authority. As early as the 1950s its then leader, Berg, had been rebuffed openly and vigorously by large firms that wished, contrary to Berg's policies, to make trade deals with eastern Europe. Though the separation of the BDI and BDA has mattered little (prior to his murder by terrorists Hans Martin Schleyer was president of both organisations), the separation of the two organisations is clumsy when so many political issues that arise, and are therefore matters for the BDI, concern industrial relations, supposedly the responsibility of the BDA; co-determination and incomes policies are two examples.

The federal government itself has limited ability to make neocorporatist bargains. Tax revenue has been divided between the federal government and the Länder according to a complicated and relatively inflexible formula. The ability of the federal government to engage in Keynesian manipulation of taxation – or aggregate government spending – would have been severely restricted by the federal character of the West German state; in practice Keynesian economics had limited appeal to German policy makers. Monetary policy, however, was also outside the direct control of the federal government. The central bank, the Bundesbank, is among the most insulated from political control of central banks. Finally, the character of German electoral politics has limited the ability of governments to engage in bargaining with interest groups because explicit or implicit bargains between political parties are so important within government. Most West German governments are coalitions between the FDP and one of the larger parties; even the ties between the CDU and CSU have been strained at times. Clientelism has been a strong influence in the executive branch, too. Major interests such as farmers or – as the Christian parties also have a working-class following – workers expect 'their' ministry to be loyal to them whether the SPD or CDU/CSU dominates the government. In practice, therefore, *intra*-government bargaining might be too prevalent to allow the government to bargain as a unit with the social partners. Perhaps the limited development of formalised neocorporatism in West Germany is not so surprising.

In spite of recent difficulties, social partnership is not dead. German employers and unions continue to maintain generally collaborative relations within which realistic judgements are made about the ability of the social partners to meet each other's demands.[6] If the SPD returns to power in the near future, it will attempt to strengthen neocorporatist practices and extend their coverage to other spheres of economic and social policy. However, increasing concerns about maintaining the competitiveness of German industry would discourage employers and the CDU/CSU from making such an extension, while the increased strength of the left within unions and the SPD will make social partnership harder to operate in the future.

Future Prospects

In the late 1960s, *Modell Deutschland* seemed to be an exemplar for western Europe of how to achieve economic growth. The rapid rise in real incomes, low inflation and success in exporting which characterised the German economy contrasted vividly with Britain's dismal record. Perhaps the model was never fully understood. The role of banks as organisers of German capitalism was generally underestimated by those looking for a triumph of less-structured free enterprise. The trends towards neocorporatism were evident by the mid 1960s. None the less, the German economy was clearly established as the most powerful in western Europe.

The 1980s left a number of questions about the German economy. The decade witnessed high levels of unemployment and although West Germany continued to run high trade surpluses with the rest of Europe, concerns about the competitiveness of the high-wage, high-welfare-state-benefit German economy mounted. Pressures from Japanese business, moving into many high-value, high-skill industries previously dominated by Germany such as optical and electronics equipment increased. Concerns have been expressed about the willingness of German banks, previously praised for their support to older industries, to support the new 'high-tech' industries of the future characterised by lower capital values than, say, steel. The creation of a single European market in 1992 will expose German industry to increased competition from low-wage economies such as Spain, and Britain, where efficiently managed Japanese car plants could threaten their German competitors. Other member nations of the European Community offered business less strict regulations than prevail in West Germany. Economists noted that although West Germany subsidised failing industries less than Britain or France, the commitment to allow market forces to operate had been attenuated by the growth of such subsidies during the economically troubled 1980s. Simultaneously, the willingness of workers, unions and environmentalists to subordinate their interests to the success of German industry seemed to decline in the 1970s and 1980s.

The German economy remained very strong using a very highly skilled work force, effective management and industrial peace to maintain a high standard of living. Whether such success could be maintained in the future was unclear. A widespread feeling in the late 1970s that the German economy was faltering inevitably raised questions about the structure of the German political economy. However, in the late 1980s, the German political economy seemed to perform comparatively strongly again, reviving confidence in *Modell Deutschland*. The tearing down of the Berlin Wall in 1989 seemed to open the way to the reunification of Germany. A united Germany would be an economic super power dominating Europe. West Germany in case would probably be the largest single economic beneficiary of the end of the isolation of Eastern Europe in general.

5

Italy

In 1987, many people in Britain were astounded, and many Italians delighted, by claims that Italian *per capita* income had surpassed British. Italian commentators declared 1987 the year of *il sorpasso*, the overtaking. Whether or not the claim that Italian *per capita* GNP had exceeded British can be debated. Not only does the calculation depend on either volatile foreign exchange rates or questionable attempts to calculate purchasing power equivalents, but it also depends on attempts to calculate the size of the underground (ie not declared for taxation) economy. The Italian claim to have overtaken Britain in fact resulted from a recalculation raising even higher the scale of economic activity hidden from their tax authorities. Clearly, the scale of cheating on taxes is hard to estimate in both Britain and Italy. More important than the relative and certainly close positions of Italy and Britain in the league tables of economic well-being was the indubitable success of the Italian economy. A country loved or derided by many foreigners had joined the ranks of the largest, wealthiest economies.

The Italian economic success is more puzzling and, like Italian politics, more complicated than other examples we have discussed. Those who believe that only private ownership of industry produces economic success can point to the role of corporations such as Fiat or Zanussi, supplier of domestic appliances to many European consumers, in Italy's success. The areas where such internationally successful corporations operate have been called the 'first Italy' in contrast to the less economically developed 'second Italy' of the south or *mezzogiorno*. Smaller-scale enterprise has become more important in the 1980s, constituting, according to some, a 'third Italy'[1] of highly efficient, commercially outstanding firms utilising relatively small factories usually located in smaller cities away from traditional manufacturing areas. Benetton started as a celebrated example of such smaller scale enterprise.

Yet Italy has also attracted academic attention because of the vast scale of public ownership. Initially as a result of rescue operations to maintain bankrupt corporations in the 1930s (a process repeated in the 1970s), the Italian state acquired ownership of a vast array of corporations. The stock of most of these corporations and about sixty banks was vested in a holding company, *Istituto per la Ricostruzione Industriale*. Separate holding companies covered the oil and allied industries (*Ente Nazionale Idrocarburi* – ENI) and steel (*Ente Participazione Finanza Manifatturiera*).[2] Publicly owned enterprise accounted for about 60 per cent of manufacturing output in the postwar period. Although Italians across the political spectrum have become aware of such problems of public enterprise as tendencies to make heavy losses and patronage, the public enterprise have also played a role in modernising Italy. The meshing of such a large public sector – and one used so blatantly to generate patronage – with a thriving capitalist economy is not the least of the puzzles of the Italian political economy.

A further enigma is the role of the state. Italian government is much more stable than one would suppose from the fluctuations of Italian politics. As in the French Fourth Republic, frequent changes in government often mask continuity as the same person continues to hold the same ministerial portfolio under different Prime Ministers. Yet no one would expect the Italian state to play the same sort of leadership role as its French or Japanese equivalent. It is true that the Italian state has considerable leverage over the financial sector through the Bank of Italy. But this leverage has been used not to direct economic development but to deal with the state's own financial problems such as the need to finance a massive budget deficit equivalent to 15 per cent of GNP. (The very high Italian savings rate makes this easier to achieve than might be supposed.) The executive branch is deeply divided not only because of the permanent need to form coalitions between numerous parties in Parliament, to form a government with a (temporary) Parliamentary majority, but because the bureaucracy is also divided. Individual ministries have their own purposes, objectives and *clientela* of interest groups with which they work.[3] The bureaucracy, seen as a desirable career primarily in Southern Italy, lacks the general prestige to lead the political economy in a manner comparable to the Japanese or French. Laws and regulations are ignored to an infamous degree in the country as a whole, a fact that helps to explain the extraordinary number of times cases have been brought against Italy in the European Court. The Italian state lacks the ability to enforce agreements it has made with its European partners. Indeed, Italian officials often welcome decisions made at the European level even against the wishes of the Italian government because officials know that the policy in question, though wise, could not be decided upon and enforced by the weak Italian state.

It might be argued that the inability of the Italian state to enforce law and regulations effectively has contributed to the success of Italian capitalism. Italian businesses have not in practice been as burdened with taxes and regulations as the law in theory would suggest. Yet the Italian state has also played a more direct role in facilitating development. The development of Fiat as one of Europe's largest car manufacturers might not have been possible without the protection afforded Fiat from foreign competition. A celebrated and ironical example is the agreement between Italy and Japan to limit auto exports to each other to extremely low levels. The agreement, made initially at the behest of the Japanese to protect their own auto industry, has been maintained eagerly since by Italy so that Japanese auto exports to Italy are very low indeed. Italy has continued to resist the Japanese auto industry by refusing to accept as British cars manufactured in Britain (and hence within the European Community) by Japanese corporations with at least 80 per cent local content; such cars, if counted as British and hence made in the European Community, could not in theory be excluded from Italy.

The state-owned enterprises have also contributed to the growth of the private sector. For example, the postwar head of

Fiat, Pietro Valletta, accepted the desirability of continued state ownership of the steel industry. A state-owned industry could secure the capital necessary to expand sufficiently to supply Fiat with the steel it would need for its own expansion better than could a privatised steel industry.[4] Given the domination of Italian capital markets by the state-owned industry, Valletta was almost certainly correct. Thus the state, through state-owned industries, has often assisted the private sector. In general, state-owned industries have managed in such a way as to be complementary to, rather than competitive with, private corporations. Thus for nearly all of its history as a state-owned firm (prior to its privatisation in 1983), Alfa Romeo concentrated on high-cost, high-performance cars leaving the mass-production field for Fiat.

The Italian economy has therefore been shaped by a complex interplay between large-scale and dynamic corporations such as Olivetti or Fiat, smaller-scale firms that were once regarded as predominantly old-fashioned but now in the 'third Italy' are also very successful and innovative, and the very large public sector, plagued with political problems but also vital in the rise of industrial Italy.

The Political Context

Italian business has flourished in a political context that would make most British or American executives tremble. Italy has the distinction of possessing the largest Communist party in western Europe, a party that could still gain 27 per cent of the vote by the end of the 1980s. One reason for the success of the Party is its moderation. The PCI was the bedrock of Eurocommunist tendencies that sought to combine Communism with democracy. By the end of the 1980s the PCI accepted continued membership in NATO, some privatisation of state-owned industries and was contemplating changing its name to demonstrate its moderation. In short, the PCI was a little to the right of the British Labour Party. It had not always been so. No matter how deep the roots of Italian Eurocommunism may be – and the Party claims its current doctrines stretch back to the thought of Gramsci before the Second World War

– prior to the 1960s, the PCI could not be regarded as anything other than a threat to the continuation of capitalism, and, in the view of many Italians, of democracy.

The PCI's move to the right has contributed greatly to the increased stability of Italian capitalism. Yet as the PCI moved towards accepting a share of responsibility for governing the present socio-economic system, new threats to business arose on the left. The most dramatic though numerically smallest of these groups were the *Brigada Rosa*, the terrorist Red Brigades. Unions also became much of a problem. During the period from 1945 to the late 1960s, Italian unions had been among the weakest in Europe. Divided politically during the Cold War years, organising a small proportion of a work force often new to industry because it had just left southern farms, unions at first constituted a minimal problem for business. Things changed after the year of student revolt, 1968, a revolt that in Italy spread into the factories. The turbulent 1970s witnessed as noted above the highest strike rate in advanced European countries, much higher even than Britain's strike rate. Labour militancy was sufficiently great in Italy in the 1970s to increase real wages much more than underlying increases in productivity producing extremely high unit labour costs for Italian industry.[5] In the 1980s business in Italy fought back – as it did elsewhere – but the entire period since the Second World War was a period in which it had been challenged in some way or other, electorally or industrially, from the left.

The most obvious bulwark for business against the threat from the left was the Christian Democratic Party (the CD). Yet even here there were problems. In the first place, the Christian Democratic Party was primarily a *Catholic* not a conservative party. The continued ability to capture working class votes has been vital to the CD, reinforcing tendencies in Catholic social thought stressing the need to ameliorate the negative consequences of capitalism for workers. Thus the Italian welfare state has expanded steadily even though the left in Italy has never been anything more than a part – usually a small part – of coalitions. Christian Democratic governments have taken a number of steps that have been most unwelcome to private-owned business, such as nationalising the electricity industry in 1962. Moreover, the CD aspires to being a 'catchall' party, embracing all interests in society. Though business is of great importance to the CD, other interest groups such as farmers are also of significance.

The final problem that the CD poses for private business is that CD politicians have a symbiotic relationship with *nationalised* industries. In general, the public sector corporations experienced increasing politicisation from the 1950s until the early 1980s. Managers in IRI, ENI or EFIM were expected to provide more jobs for CD politicians to dispense as patronage. The widespread acceptance that nationalised industries had social obligations stretching beyond making a profit paved the way for CD politicians to use their investment programmes to reward areas that voted CD. It is not even just that the CD as a whole uses the nationalised industries to build support. The CD is a highly fragmented party that consisted by the late 1980s of five significant factions, the left wing Sinistra, the Andreottiani (after their leader, Andreotti), the Grande Centro, Forze Nuove and the Fanfaniani (led by Amintore Fanfani). Patronage supports the factions, even though some hope that their influence will soon fade. The patronage is supplied through nationalised industries. In return, the government meets or approves the requirements of the industries, such as issuing government-backed bonds.

Relations between private business and the CD have therefore been unstable. For most of the postwar period business has supported the CD. Indeed, business has been the CD's largest source of funds. But the largest of the business organisations, Confindustria, was never really integrated into the community or kinship of the CD, and thus never achieved what Lapalombara terms a *parentela* relationship. In 1953, the leaders of Confindustria cut off funds to the CD because the party did not nominate a sufficient number of candidates supported by business.[6] Some leading industrialists argued that business should support a more purely pro-business party such as the Liberals. A political action organisation, Confintesa, was formed to support candidates and parties supported by Confindustria. However, after what was regarded as an inept performance by Confintesa, the strategy was quietly dropped. In the mid to late 1970s, Confindustria's

leadership was taken over by Agnelli, the head of Fiat. As part
of a general shakeup of the organisation, Agnelli favoured a
distancing of Confindustria from the CD. Agnelli himself
favoured an alliance with the Radicals, and political strategy
based on bringing into policy making and government the
widest possible range of groups and parties. This strategy
conflicted with the CD's futile attempts during the 1970s to
maintain its hegemony over Italian politics, dominating
government and providing the Prime Minster for every
coalition government.[7] In particular, Agnelli's strategy
implied an opening not only to the Socialists but, informally,
to the Communists as well. In the 1980s, conservatives in the
Confindustria reoriented the Party's strategy back to its
traditional path of alliance with the CD. Thus the relationship
between private business and the CD has been unstable and
varied.

Business Organisations

The leading organisation representing private employers in
Italy is Confindustria. Although Confindustria recruits only a
minority of all Italian businesses (Lapalombara estimated
80 000 out of 680 000 in the 1950s),[8] it recruits the over-
whelming number of those employing twenty or more people.
   In his magisterial study of Italian interest groups,
Lapalombara identified Confindustria as the leading example
of the type of alliance between an interest group and the
bureaucracy he termed *clientela*. Confindustria enjoyed a
permanent alliance with the Ministry of Industry and
Commerce. Confindustria needed this alliance in order to
ensure that laws and regulations targeted on business were
acceptable. The Ministry would also act as Confindustria's
voice within government. For its part, the Ministry needed the
technical assistance of Confindustria. The Italian bureaucracy
has generally lacked, even disdained, technical or statistical
knowledge; it is, after all, dominated by southern Italians in
search of a gentlemanly profession not a meritocracy. In
consequence, as one bureaucrat told Lapalombara, 'Not a
single ministry . . . has at its disposal . . . the number of

technicians and research facilities Confindustria has organised in this postwar period.'[9] The *clientela* relationship rested on several factors.

The first was the political acceptability of the interest group, guaranteed in part by the usual if unstable alliance of Confindustria with the CD. The second factor, easily achieved for business, was a feeling that the interest group spoke for an important sector of Italian society. The third factor was the ability of interest groups to supply technical information. The final factor was that the interest group enjoys a monopoly in its field. In the case of Confindustria both the interest group and the bureaucracy worked to maintain this monopoly. Confindustria, according to officials of Confapi (the Italian Confederation of Small Business) would refuse to make agreements with government when they were included in meetings or on committees. Lapalombara found the officials of the Ministry of Industry and Commerce would 'go to some distance to support and reinforce' the status of Confindustria. Because Confindustria enjoyed a monopoly in representing the general interests of business, it was the forum in which the great issues of business politics were resolved in the 1950s. An important example was the debate about whether the Italian economy should be, as in the Fascist period, relatively sheltered from trade, or should aim more adventurously at larger growth in the context of integration into the world economy. Finally, business groups could win the favour of bureaucrats by asking them to address prestigious gatherings or by giving them *bustarella* (graft, literally a little envelope).

Lapalombara wrote before the term neocorporatism was popularised. However, the *clientela* relationship clearly involved elements reminiscent of neocorporatism. The co-operation between bureaucrats and Confindustria and the reinforcement of Confindustria's status by the bureaucracy would be familiar in neocorporatist nations. In contrast to the situation in many countries, the relationship between Confindustria and government became *less* rather than more neocorporatist in the 1960s and 1970s. Several factors undermined the status of the organisation. In the first place, Confindustria, as noted earlier had always been challenged by

Confapi, arguing that it alone represented smaller businesses. Similarly, Confindustria had been dependent on the goodwill of the bureaucrats to prevent individual corporations such as Fiat from dealing direct with government instead of through Confindustria. Perhaps because of the evolving political situation as the dominance of the CD diminished, the bureaucracy ceased to provide as much protection for Confindustria. In the third place, as we have noted earlier, the relationship between CD and nationalised industries became more organic as the CD used patronage from the nationalised industries to prop up its support. The nationalised industries have their own representative organisation. Finally, to an important degree that perhaps Lapalombara understated, the links between the Ministry of Industry and Commerce and Confindustria when his research was conducted in the 1950s represented a continuance (though declining) of the relationship created under Fascism when corporatism was official doctrine.

Challenges to Confindustria and broader changes in Italian politics have eroded its standing since the 1950s but Confindustria remains one of the most developed business organisations in western democracies, and perhaps the most important interest group in Italy.

The Future

In the 1980s, Italian business moved in the direction of greater distance from politics or government. Several factors contributed to this development. The success of major Italian enterprises such as Fiat and Zanussi made their futures dependent on their ability to compete throughout the European Community and indeed internationally. Increasing competitive pressures strengthened the need for efficiency. Competition from Asia became more vigorous; even if Italian consumers were not allowed to buy Japanese cars, Fiat customers in other countries could. Fiat's withdrawal from the American market in the 1980s indicated the strength of the pressures it was facing. The achievement of a single European market in 1992 will add further to competitive pressures.

Italian industry has faced two major difficulties in adapting to increased international competition. The first was that in the nationalised industries the gradual increase in politicisation, in order to serve the interests of the CD through patronage in the 1960s and 1970s, diminished the competitiveness of those industries. Under the original so-called IRI formula, managers of specific corporations owned by state holding companies such as IRI to some degree were insulated from political pressure; the state holding company stood between the management of the specific corporation and the government. That insulation was gradually stripped away. The increase in the losses of nationalised industries and decreased competitiveness were important results. Public corporations also suffered from the major problem to hit private corporations – the rapid increase in unit labour costs that occurred in the 1970s to which we have referred earlier.

A number of developments have helped Italian industry escape from these problems. First, privatisation has restored some of the autonomy of the managers of state-owned corporations. Selling off entire corporations (such as Alfa Romeo) or some of the stock in corporations owned by the state has provided IRI or individual corporations with funds that could be used for investment instead of government-supplied funds that would have had political strings attached. This tendency has been strengthened by the ability of managers to borrow externally. The rise of the Italian economy and increased foreign understanding of it allowed both public and private firms to escape government's financial controls by obtaining loans overseas.

Second, the decline of the CD, visible in earlier periods, reached a point that really mattered. The divorce and abortion referenda illustrated the diminished hold of Catholicism on Italy;[10] the (by Italian standards) long tenure of the Socialist Prime Minister, Bertino Craxi, demonstrated the slackening of the CD's grip on government itself. The decline of the CD allowed public corporations to more easily resist pressures to be suppliers of patronage or pork barrel for the CD.

Third, the Italian government and Bank of Italy have followed restrictive macroeconomic policies which have produced very high unemployment. In the late 1980s, Italian unemployment was still over 16 per cent of the work force. In consequence, the power of unions declined. Italian wages and prices rose at an unusually slow pace by Italian standards, still faster than German or Japanese but slower than British increases. In consequence, some competitiveness was restored.

Finally, the dynamic smaller firms of the 'new Italy' such as Benetton escaped many of the problems of Italian industry. Such firms often operate in areas in which unions are weak. Firms in the 'third Italy' are often also in practice and sometimes by design less supervised to ensure their compliance with regulations or tax laws than are larger corporations.

In the 1950s, the Italian economy benefited from its late start. A supply of cheap labour especially from the south allowed its corporations to compete vigorously with European rivals. By the 1980s, the Italian economy had caught up with most of its European neighbours. Yet in so doing, the Italian economy had come to share in some of the general problems of European industries. In particular, Italian corporations were threatened with loss of competitiveness. Steel mills built in the south to boost the local economy and to take advantage of cheap labour could not compete with South Korea. Yet it is improbable that Italian success will end. The confused Italian political economy allows flexibility for adaptation even if no one points the way forward as clearly as in Japan or France. The skills of Italian engineers and designers also continue to provide products that consumers around the world want. As in politics so in the political economy, Italy may confuse observers yet still work.

6

The Neocorporatist Nations

The Historic Compromise

The British often believe they have (and are believed by other people to have) unusually powerful unions and employers' associations. It is certainly the case that, by almost any measure, British unions are stronger than American. Yet British unions in turn can be outmatched by their counterparts in many European countries, a fact their insular leaders often overlook. In Norway, Sweden and Austria, for example, the proportion of the workforce belonging to unions is over 80 per cent, a far higher proportion than in Britain. Nor is the strength of working-class movements confined solely to the industrial sector. In the European countries in which the unions are strongest, not surprisingly, the Social Democratic Party has also fared well. The classic example is of course Sweden, where the Social Democrats have dominated government since the early 1930s, forming the government continuously from 1936 to 1976. The combination of strong unions and almost continuous Social Democratic rule might fill the British or American businessman with despair.

How can capitalism survive in such an environment? In practice, the neocorporatist countries such as Austria, Sweden, Norway and the Netherlands have prospered.[1] Austria, for example, passed from being one of the poorest to one of the richest West European countries between the end of the Second World War and the 1970s.[2] Sweden, too, exemplifies a high-income economy, matching the USA in terms of real income *per capita*. The number of working days lost per 1000 workers due to strikes has also been low in the neocorporatist countries, while levels of productivity have

113

been very high. In short, in spite of the apparent strength of working-class movements, the neocorporatist countries have sustained highly successful capitalist economies, providing a congenial setting for business activity: a most successful compromise has been struck between capital and highly-organised labour.

Definitions of Neocorporatism

One of the liveliest topics in comparative politics since the mid-1970s has been neocorporatism. The topic is of considerable importance for the study of the relationship between business and politics. Does neocorporatism offer a successful alternative mode of linking government and economic interests, particularly business? Or is neocorporatism a relationship between government and economic interests that can exist in only a limited number of countries? This chapter considers a number of questions including what is neocorporatism, where it is found, what the conditions are for its existence, what the economic record has been of countries where neocorporatism is practised and what the future holds for neocorporatism.

As we have seen in Chapter 1, neocorporatism is a system of interest intermediation in which organisations representing the major interests in society – in practice business, labour and frequently farmers enjoy –a monopoly of representation which is recognised and encouraged by the state.[3] The interest groups involved in neocorporatist relations are given excellent opportunities to influence public policy; indeed, the economic interest groups involved in such relations are often able to engage in something more like bargaining than consultation in their dealings with government. At least in certain policy areas, the government will not act in a way that is unacceptable to the major economic interest groups. For their part, the economic interest groups accept a responsibility to help government *implement* policies, often acting to free government from the obligation to do something itself. Interest groups may help government by running training programmes, by promoting exports or by encouraging compliance with government regulations or policies to protect the environment or safety or health. One of the most important obligations of interest groups in countries in which neocorporatism has been strongest has been to implement incomes policies designed to avoid inflation or the loss of competitiveness in foreign trade.

Although this definition covers the core of neocorporatism, many questions remain. The first is the problem of what issues are covered in neocorporatism. Neocorporatism generally covers economic issues. But the nature of bargaining between interest groups and government in neocorporatist systems has been such that the scope of bargaining widens. Typically, unions have agreed to restrain wage demands in return for increases in the 'social wage' of government expenditures on welfare, retirement pensions, health care, education and other domestic policies that unions believe will benefit those they represent.[4] If we believe that an entire political system is neocorporatist, we should have to demonstrate that the most, or at least the most important, issues are made through neocorporatist discussions between government and economic interests. Such a claim should ideally also show that discussions between government and interest groups are more important than the impact of other parts of the political system such as political parties, the bureaucracy, elections, or legislatures.

It is very hard if not impossible to substantiate such claims for many policy areas in most democracies. At most, industrial or economic policy is made in a neocorporatist manner while other issues such as foreign policy are handled in a different manner. In consequence political scientists attracted to the concept of neocorporatism have modified their arguments in a number of ways. One way is to accept that only certain issues are handled in a neocorporatist manner in any country. However, the issues handled within a neocorporatist framework might be seen as the central or crucial problem of the modern state – managing the political economy. A second response is to argue that we should look for neocorporatist relations at a different level; failing to find neocorporatist relations linking government as a whole with organisations representing employers in general and a labour union federation, we should look instead at the level of the individual industry. Neocorporatist relations linking a section of a government department, a particular union and a trade association representing employers might flourish where no such relations exist at the national level. Such a situation would be termed 'meso-level corporatism'. Unfortunately, it is a less interesting finding than neocorporatism offered initially, leaving unanswered the questions of whether meso-level neocorporatist relations are typical or atypical of the entire economy, and how the relations between different industries are managed. Finally, we can understand neocorporatism to be not an absolute situation but a continuum; countries are more or less neocorporatist. Even the most-neocorporatist countries will have some policy issues that are handled in a non-neocorporatist manner; even the least-neocorporatist countries will handle some issues in somewhat neocorporatist style. This is the approach used in this chapter.

Where is Neocorporatism?

To say that neocorporatism is a continuum and that some countries are more and others less neocorporatist requires us to say which are the most-neocorporatist countries. In fact, there is a general consensus that the most-neocorporatist countries are Sweden, Norway, Austria and the Netherlands.[5] Denmark follows somewhere close behind. Katzenstein adds Switzerland to the list.[6] As we have seen, West Germany and Great Britain passed through periods in which they seemed more interested in neocorporatist approaches to economic policy, and in certain policy areas, such as health and safety at work in Britain[7] or industrial training in West Germany, neocorporatist influences are evident to this day. The least-neocorporatist of the western democracies is generally agreed to be the United States, though even here some have claimed that the politics of certain industries (for example the dairy industry) can be seen as neocorporatist.

Why are Some Countries more Neocorporatist than Others?

It is difficult to explain why some countries are more neocorporatist than others in a way which does not simply re-describe neocorporatism. A number of obvious explanations might also be seen as characteristics of neocorporatism.

Interest group structure might be seen as either a characteristic or a cause of neocorporatism. On the one hand, it is characteristic of neocorporatist systems that there are organisations representing economic interests that have a virtual monopoly on the claim to do so. On the other hand, the existence of strong interest groups certainly facilitates the creation of neocorporatist systems. It is much easier for a government to bargain with labour and business if each is represented by a single organisation than if there are several organisations competing for the title. It is much easier for comprehensive interest groups to make compromises on their members' short term interests than if there are numerous interest groups; if there are numerous groups, none can be sure that a concession they make on their short-term interests in order to promote their long-term interests (eg forgoing a pay increase in order to maintain competitiveness or avoid inflation) will be matched by other groups.[8] Political scientists debate whether neocorporatist systems can be created in countries where there already exist strong, monopolistic interest groups or whether strong, monopolistic interest groups can be created by the state.

The degree to which the state can create suitable interest groups where none previously existed or can help monopolistic interest groups depends in large part on the character of the state. States that are sufficiently centralised and hierarchical to be able to control which interest groups have access to policy making and which do not are more likely to create neocorporatism than states which do not. Thus one factor that would impede any attempt to build neocorporatism in the United States is the fragmentation characteristic of the state; just because the White House might want to help the Business Roundtable establish itself as the dominant business group would be no reason for other Executive branch Departments, the committees of the House and Senate or individual legislators to follow suit. Centralised systems of government are more able to create centralised interest group systems. On the other hand, the potential power of centralised systems of government to influence interest groups adversely is a powerful incentive for economic interests to unite in their defence; in purely constitutional terms, a Labour government in Britain or a social democratic government in Norway could do more to hurt business interests than could any American administration which would have to overcome resistance in the very independent legislature and courts.

Finally, *political culture* again both describes and helps to explain neocorporatism. One characteristic of all the most-neocorporatist countries is an emphasis on compromise in their current political cultures. In Sweden, the emphasis on the value of compromise is manifest in a long legislative process during which disagreement can be minimised. Legislation is usually preceded by Royal Commissions that, unlike their British counterparts, act as forums in which interest groups and government can compromise as well as search out the facts. After the government announces its proposals, it is common to follow the *remiss* procedure in which they are forwarded to all major interest groups for comment. Even during debates in the Storting, amendments are accepted much more readily than in Britain. Modern Austria (the second Austrian republic) has emphasised the value of compromise between socialists and non-socialists because of the role that violent confrontation and civil war between left and right played in the downfall of the first republic; well before the Nazi takeover in the *Anschluss* Chancellor Dollfuss had waged bloody conflict against strongholds of the Socialists. Modern Austrian leaders realised that they could secure the withdrawal of Soviet troops (in 1955) and maintain the independence of Austria thereafter only by compromising with each other. Compromises included long periods of coalition government (*Konkordanzdemokratie*) between the Socialist Party and its main rival the Ostereiche Volks Partei (OVP). Even posts within government were shared out on the basis of bureaucrats' partisan affiliation in the *proportz* system. Finally, the Netherlands has a well-earned reputation for compromise reflecting the need to accommodate an almost equally balanced Catholic and Protestant population; the Netherlands is therefore seen by Lijpart as a *consociational*[9] state in which potentially profound divisions are accommodated.

Is willingness to compromise therefore a precondition for the existence of neocorporatism? Not only is willingness to compromise a characteristic commonly found in all the most neocorporatist countries, but its absence might also help explain why certain countries are not more neocorporatist. Britain, for example, might have failed to become more neocorporatist because of the unusually adversarial style of its politics; the government proposes and the opposition responds simply by opposing to an unusual degree by the standards of western democracies.

A further characteristic of the political cultures of neocorporatist countries is acceptance of the legitimacy of functional representation – representation on the basis of one's occupation or economic interest by an interest group rather than one's opinions by an elected politician. Sometimes – as in Austria – it is possible to see in this acceptance of functional representation an unbroken tradition stretching back to the middle ages and the establishment of Chambers to represent occupations or trades. Indeed, the Austrian legal system continues this tradition by giving interest group leaders *legal* powers over their followers to a degree that their counterparts in Britain or the USA would find surprising. Austrian employers' organisations might forbid members to give more than a certain percentage pay increase, or union leaders might forbid a strike. In contrast, one of the factors limiting the growth of neocorporatism in the United States is widespread suspicion of 'special interests' and profound mistrust of secret bargaining between interest groups and government officials. Such secret bargaining is a common feature of neocorporatist policy making.

Unfortunately, however, it is again difficult to distinguish causes and characteristics. Willingness to compromise and acceptance of functional representation may facilitate neocorporatism but they can also be seen as characteristic of it. It is hard to imagine how a neocorporatist system could function without a widespread willingness to compromise or acceptance of functional representation. We might instead be attracted to describing the most-neocorporatist countries as countries in which highly institutionalised solutions to class conflict have been developed. For the most neocorporatist countries generally combine high levels of working class mobilisation, as demonstrated by the proportion of the work force who vote Socialist or join unions, with great dependence on foreign trade. In Sweden, for example, over 80 per cent of the work force belongs to a union and the Social Democrats have dominated politics and government since the 1930s with only limited interruption. Yet the very high Swedish standard of living can be maintained only if the large Swedish corporations (such as Saab or Volvo) remain successful exporters. Neocorporatism is therefore a way to combine strong unions and support for such social democratic objectives as full employment and the welfare state with high degrees of dependence on foreign trade.

It might be easy to forget in a discussion of neocorporatist interest group structure that the most-neocorporatist nations have all been nations with unusually strong social democratic parties. The strength of the social democrats in Austria, Sweden, Norway and similarly neocorporatist states increased the need for employers to reach a bargain with the representatives of organised labour in the unions and the state that would protect their own competitiveness in international markets. Neocorporatism provided the frame-work for such bargaining. The erosion of the strength of the political parties in Austria and the social democrats in Norway raised doubts about whether neocorporatism would survive without strong social democratic parties.

The Performance of Neocorporatist Countries

Neocorporatist practices would surely not have attracted the degree of academic attention they have received were the most-neocorporatist countries thought to be merely unusually small (at least in terms of population), and ethnically homogeneous countries. In practice neocorporatist countries have been the objects of much theorising because they seemed to have solved the problems of managing the economy unusually effectively. In the later 1970s in particular, neocorporatist countries on balance had less inflation, less unemployment, fewer strikes and, reflecting the greater 'governability' of such countries, smaller government deficits than most advanced democracies. It was plausible to argue that in what Schmitter had said to be 'still the Century of Corporatism', larger countries and economies would follow the lead of the most-neocorporatist countries and imitate their methods for governing the economy.

Why should neocorporatism work? The most obvious reason is incomes policy. Agreement between unions, employers and government on desirable levels of wage increases allows government to operate the economy at stable levels of full employment. Policies that contain inflation at the expense of curtailing economic growth (such as high interest rates) need not be used, and investment can be planned without worry that the economy will alternate between stronger growth and government-mandated recession characteristic of the British economy. Strikes can be avoided both through negotiation, and through the feelings generated by 'social partnership' that all interests are being given some consideration. Economic policy is not seen as biased in favour of the more affluent. Adjustments to economic change can also be made more rapidly if government, employers and unions recognize their necessity and work to reduce the hardship they cause. Sweden has avoided both strikes to prevent modernisation and the resulting high levels of unemployment common in Britain because government, unions and industries have worked together in 'active labour market' policies to facilitate the retraining and, when necessary, relocation of workers who lose their jobs through changes in demand or technology. Finally, neocorporatism allows many of the benefits of indicative planning to be achieved even though as formal a structure as that in France is not employed. Close consultation between government and business or between different businesses with the strong employers' organisations helps corporations identify future possibilities and move to exploit them.

Threats to Neocorporatism

If neocorporatism has so many advantages, why was it perceived as losing ground? A number of different factors were seen as threatening the continuance of neocorporatism in countries where it was strong and making unlikely the anticipated extensions of neocorporatist practices in countries such as West Germany or Britain which had shown some interest in them.

One threat came from doubts about the *fiscal viability* of neocorporatism. As we noted earlier, bargaining between employers and unions on wage restraint was often aided by government promises to increase social expenditures benefiting workers indirectly. In the 1980s, however, widespread protests against tax levels occurred even in Norway and Denmark. Rapid gains in support by new, anti-tax parties in Sweden seemed to signal an end to tolerance of the growth in the proportion of GNP spent by government. In Austria, too, the government was threatened fiscally by a very large deficit in its accounts of over 100 billion Austrian schillings, prompting the Socialist Chancellor Sinowatz, prior to his retirement, to argue that Austrian social policy now had to be guided by what was practical rather than by what was desirable. In more- as well as less-neocorporatist countries, citizens seemed unwilling to pay the taxes that would finance the increase in social expenditures that would grease the wheel of neocorporatist bargaining. Governments were constrained by the threat or reality of deficits.

A second threat to neocorporatism came from *class decomposition*. Neocorporatism rested on the belief that there was one major divide in society, between employers and employees. Such a division, though possibly profound, could be compromised. The neocorporatist vision of societies dominated by two interests that could forge agreements with government was threatened in the 1980s by the fragmentation of interests. Some industries did well throughout the 1980s; others, such as shipbuilding in almost every European country, were devastated. Nearly all the developed countries reduced steel production, while the service sectors expanded. In short, success and failure were distributed sufficiently unequally among employers and workers to accentuate potential conflicts of interest not between but among the 'social partners'. In Sweden, for example, the annual, economy-wide wage bargain between the union federation (the LO) and the Swedish Employers Federation that had been at the heart of neocorporatism was not made for most of the 1980s. Certain industries and unions – notably the Metalworkers – concluded that they could promote their interests better outside an economy-wide framework than inside it. Some saw in this emergence of narrower self interest an irony. The very success of neocorporatist systems had produced standards of living that were so high that they encouraged 'class decomposition'. The affluent worker no longer felt the same sort of solidarity with other workers that had allowed unions to speak with one voice to employers and government.

A further factor threatening neocorporatism was the regained intellectual confidence in markets in the 1980s. After the deep recession of the early 1980s, the American economy displayed a capacity to grow and generate new jobs that was much admired, even envied, in Europe. Whereas the more organised capitalism of neocorporatist countries had seemed to facilitate change in the 1970s, the less-organised capitalism of the United States seemed better able to cope with change in the 1980s. The apparent economic successes of President Reagan and Prime Minister Thatcher gave credence to their arguments that allowing market forces to operate without government or neocorporatist committees getting in the way maximised growth. However, the triumph of the 'neoconservative' faith in markets in the 1980s was not merely based on pragmatism. It also reflected a strengthening in the acceptance of the *moral* legitimacy of market forces that was felt even in neoconservative countries. In Austria, something of a revival in liberal thought threatened both the *proportz* system of allocating government posts and the legitimacy of neocorporatist bargaining. Although modest by Thatcherian standards, a programme of privatising part of the vast Austrian nationalised sector was undertaken.

Further, a number of *issues* arose that could not be contained within the neocorporatist framework. The most famous of these was the conflict in Sweden over the creation of wage earner funds linked to unions that would acquire increasing proportions of the stock of Swedish corporations. Although in the end the issue was compromised, conflict was sufficiently intense to impede the normal operation of neocorporatism. In Austria environmental issues, especially debates about building a hydroelectric power project in a sensitive environmental location on the Danube, reminded politicians of the increasing importance of interests (here environmentalists) not part of the neocorporatist system. In Norway, the issue of whether or not the country should join the European Community broke apart neocorporatist alliances.

Finally, and probably most importantly, it ceased to be the case that neocorporatist economic systems performed noticeably better than others. We have noted earlier the massive public debt in Austria – equivalent to 5 per cent of GNP – that represented the continued need for government expenditures and subsidies to the large nationalised sector to grease the machinery of neocorporatism. Unemployment also rose in Austria to the unusually high level of 5.2 per cent by 1986, low by the standards of the worst of the years of recession in the United States, Britain or even West Germany, but regarded as serious in Austria. Perhaps most importantly, the growth rates in neocorporatist countries such as Sweden or Norway were very disappointing throughout the 1980s. Austria averaged less than 2 per cent growth per annum throughout the 1980s. The neocorporatist countries had achieved a more even performance than, for example, the United States, failing to achieve the same growth rates of the United States at its strongest but also avoiding the worst levels of inflation or unemployment in the USA or Britain in the 1980s.

Is there anything inherent in neocorporatism that might produce comparatively poor economic performances in the future? Two criticisms are often made. The first is that the high levels of government expenditure, particularly on the welfare that neocorporatist bargaining encourages, reduce competitiveness. The second is that neocorporatist economies will be characterised by greater 'rigidities' than less-neocorporatist countries such as the USA. Neither criticism is conclusive. Many of the costs of the welfare state are costs that society would presumably have to pay in some form even if the welfare state did not exist. So long as voters are prepared to pay sufficient tax to finance the welfare state, it need not reduce competitiveness. Take health care as an example. Health care costs are a significant element of the total costs of any welfare state. It is true that taxes to finance health care contribute to the total costs of corporations. Yet in the United States health care costs for health insurance for employees are a major cost for employers; Mr Lee Iacocca of Chrysler has argued that major corporations should support national health insurance in order to rid themselves of the costs of health insurance that add up to $600 to the cost of an American car. In short, private sector alternatives to the welfare state can reduce competitiveness as much as taxes to support the welfare state.

Neither is it clear that neocorporatism builds in rigidities to economies that must, like all others, adapt ever more quickly to changes in demand and technology. It is true that Austria has faced the same difficulty that faced Britain in connection with its nationalised industries; painful adaptation can always be avoided so long as the government is willing to foot the bill for large losses in the industries it owns. Yet Sweden, where the Social Democrats have avoided extensive nationalisation, has proved as adaptive to change as any economy. The active labour market policy might be seen as sharing the costs of adaptation more widely than in countries such as the USA, where the costs of change fall almost entirely on those in declining industries. But the main effect of an active labour market policy is to facilitate change by retraining workers and assisting movement from depressed to prospering regions. It is arguable that the general sense of fairness and security that neocorporatist systems encourage among their citizens also facilitates change by reducing the fear that any change in technology or employment will result in long-term unemployment and loss of income.

The Future of Neocorporatism

In the mid 1970s it was plausible to argue that neocorporatist practices would spread into larger numbers of countries. Admittedly some authorities such as Lehmbruch[10] doubted that neocorporatism could be adopted easily in countries where it did not already exist; neocorporatism was produced by long term influences that could not be short-circuited. However, the performance of the most-neocorporatist countries certainly seemed admirable. In the 1980s, the most-neocorporatist countries fared less well economically while intellectual tides turned against organised capitalism in favour of greater reliance on market forces. Indeed, it became plausible to argue that neocorporatist practices were doomed even where they seemed most entrenched. The ability of unions to operate neocorporatist systems was threatened by *class decomposition*. As more-affluent workers ceased to think of themselves as part of a wider working class, so the ability of union federations to agree to an economy-wide policy of wage restraint declined. Workers in successful industries were less likely to forgo wage increases in order to benefit colleagues in declining industries. Governments were less able to supply increases in the social wage to facilitate neocorporatist bargaining because of tax revolts and needs to reduce national debt. Corporations, faced with more severe international competition, would demand a move away from neocorporatist bargaining so that they could change production costs, techniques and content more rapidly. Interests not represented in neocorporatist arrangements would press for changes in policymaking processes that would give them greater influence.

It would be reacting too much to short-term trends to think that neocorporatism will disappear even if it is on the defensive. Political economies do not change overnight. Many of the factors promoting neocorporatism, such as political culture, change relatively slowly. The habits ingrained in policy makers during decades of neocorporatism about how to make good public policy will not be eradicated overnight. Public law – particularly in Austria – will continue to give special status to the interest groups most involved in neocorporatism. Above all, the most-neocorporatist countries, in spite of an upsurge of conservatism in the 1970s and 1980s, remain countries in which social democracy and unions are unusually strong. Yet the most-neocorporatist countries are also highly dependent on trade and open to influences from world markets. It is hard to imagine any alternative to neocorporatism that could solve equally well the problem of reconciling the challenges to free market capitalism that unions and social democrats inevitably pose with the need of countries such as Sweden to be successful, competitive trading nations. Lehmbruch has reminded us that neocorporatist arrangements were very resilient in the face of the challenges of the 1980s.[11] We can anticipate their survival throughout the 1990s.

7

Government and Industry in France

Dangers for Capitalism

The survival of private enterprise in France seemed to many problematic immediately after the Second World War. The radical sentiments stirred by the war throughout Europe and, after the German attack on the Soviet Union, the prominent role of the Communist Party in the Resistance carried support for the French Communist Party (PCF) to new heights. The PCF gained 28.6 per cent of the vote in the November 1946 elections, apparently demonstrating the existence of a strong radical challenge to the capitalist order. Moreover, many French voters believed that French industrialists had been guilty of collaboration with the Germans during the Occupation, while much of the Right had been discredited in the years up to the fall of France. The *Comité National du Patronat Français* (CNPF) commissioned an opinion poll after the war on attitudes to private employers; its results were so bad from the employers' point of view that the results of the poll were suppressed.

Whatever the extent of collaboration by French employers in war-time, there was a strong argument to be made that French industrialists had failed their country before the Second World War. French industry in the inter-war period was notorious for its conservative and uncompetitive practices. Sheltering from foreign competition behind the highest tariff barriers in Europe, French employers further reduced the need to modernise or change by forming cartels to divide the domestic market between them. The employers no doubt in part merely reflected the conservatism of French society as a whole. France, prior to the Second World War, was a nation which was resistant to change. Just under one third of the population were still involved in a peasant agriculture which constituted a way of life rather than an industry. Although the politics of the peasantry could be quite radical, with peasants in some regions such as the Dordogne or the Languedoc supporting Socialist or Communist candidates, the peasantry in all regions was more eager to defend its way of life than to adapt to commercial pressures.[1] French industry also impressed observers by its small scale, backwardness and lack of competitiveness. On the eve of the creation of the European Economic Community, even a politician noted in general for attempts to modernise France, Pierre Mendès-France, expressed grave doubts about the ability of French industry to survive *European* competition. Thus the entire French economy seemed to be characterised by pessimism and conservatism. The role of the state in such a society was to hold the ring between different interests, most of which sought the aid of the state through protection or subsidies from the pressures of modern economics. Rather like Britain in the 1970s, France before the Second World War impressed observers as a land rich in natural resources which, because of its 'blocked society' of cautious, defensive interest groups, failed to realise its potential.

The economic resurgence of France is perhaps the greatest economic success story of postwar Europe. Whereas West Germany recaptured an industrial leadership which it had enjoyed before the Second World War, France became a leading industrial power to a degree it had never previously approached. During the *trente glorieuses*, the thirty glorious years of rapid growth when the growth rate exceeded 6 per cent a year on average, France surged past Britain in terms of *per capita* real income. A study in the 1970s by the American Hudson Institute forecast that France would become the richest country in Europe except for Sweden.[2] The 1980s cast this judgement into doubt, as French growth rates fell back to low levels. The low growth rate of the French economy in the 1980s reflected the international recession and the failure of the policies of the 1981–86 Socialist government. It also temporarily revived doubts about the suitability of the French economy to withstand international competition. However, by the early 1990s, the performance of the French economy was once again improving. Moreover, by the late 1980s, a remarkable change appeared to have taken place in French intellectual life. For most of modern French history, the weight of intellectual opinion was on the left. Thinkers such as Sartre were much more critical of capitalism and the pre-eminent capitalist nation, the United States, than of Stalinism and the Soviet Union. In the 1980s, much of the intelligentsia was disillusioned with socialism. Solzhenitsyn's *Gulag Archipelago* had a profound impact on an intelligentsia which had closed its eyes to Stalin's murders. The view that socialism led necessarily to both tyranny and economic inefficiency was more intellectually fashionable than ever. The bicentennial of the French Revolution in 1989 was marked by debates about whether there was a direct link between the tactics of the once-revered Jacobins and the tyranny of the Gulags. In consequence, French capitalism seemed on the verge of an acceptance and intellectual respectability it had long lacked.[3]

How had the remarkable transformation in the respectability of capitalism in France come about? Obviously, the dramatic success of the French economy since the Second World War helped. Other factors were at work. The PCF after 1947, with the exception of the early years of the Mitterand Presidency, was 'ghettoised'. Tainted by expansion of Soviet power in Europe – often, as in Czechoslovakia, at the expense of democracy – and by its slavish devotion to Soviet foreign policy, the PCF steadily lost ground in the electorate. The PCF's share of the vote fell back to around one-fifth of the electorate by 1968, and then declined even further in the late 1970s to 16.2 per cent in 1981. Moreover, until the rejuvenated Socialist Party was prepared to deal from a position of strength, with the Communist Party forming a coalition with it in 1980 which captured the presidency and Parliament, other political parties were not prepared to deal with the PCF. Writing of his post-war government, de Gaulle remarked that he could not give the Foreign Ministry to a Communist minister for fear of endangering France, and he could not give the Ministry of the Interior to a Communist either since it guarded the Foreign Ministry. The Communist seizures of power in Eastern Europe in the 1940s naturally strengthened such fears of the PCF, perhaps the Communist Party most obedient to Moscow outside Eastern Europe. In consequence, the Left was split between democratic socialists and a PCF which was beyond the pale.

The divisions of the Left in France are all the more important because of their consequences for French unions. Unions in France are not strong in general. Only 20 per cent of the workforce can be regarded as members of unions in the British or American sense of paying dues regularly in order to hold a union card. This weakness is accentuated by the split between Communist, Socialist and the formerly Catholic affiliated *Force Ouvrière*. The distrust of the Communist Party which impeded co-operation between Socialists and Communists politically weakened the chances of co-operation between the unions industrially. In consequence, French managers have not had to worry about the institutionalised power of labour at the factory level which has confronted British managers. This is not to say that industrial relations in France have always been smooth. On the contrary, French labour has periodically displayed a potential for almost revolutionary action rarely matched in Europe. In 1968, the protests of students in Paris unleashed a wave of strikes and factory occupations which rocked the Republic; only after de Gaulle had secretly visited French troops in Germany to assure himself of their loyalty and availability to suppress insurrection did he recover his nerve. But, as in similar circumstances in the 1930s, though workers made considerable immediate gains (for example, in wage increases), there was no translation of this semi-revolutionary upheaval into institutionalised union power.

Although capitalism has survived and flourished in France, an unusually large sector of state-owned industry was created. Even prior to the capture of the Presidency and a majority in the National Assembly in 1981 by a coalition of Socialists and Communists that, under the leadership of President Mitterrand, was intent on a large-scale programme of nationalisation, the proportion of industry owned by the state was unusually large in France. The proportion of the economy controlled by state-owned firms was about double the proportion in Britain or Italy. The Mitterrand government took into ownership thirty-six private banks (many of the larger banks were already in state ownership) and eleven large industrial conglomerates. The range of industries owned by the state was impressive, including not only industries often owned by government in other nations such as gas, electricity, the railways and the major airline, but a large auto manufacturer and major companies in the chemical and steel industries. The nationalised corporations have themselves acquired a number of private companies which have not been officially nationalised though they are ultimately government-owned. (One example, ironically, was for a time the American Motors Corporation in the staunchly anti-nationalisation USA).

In the mid 1980s, the post-war consensus in favour of a large-scale publicly-owned sector disappeared under the impact of the upsurge in support of free market economics noted above and of opposition to what some thought was the excessive nationalisation programme of the Left in the early 1980s. A modest programme of privatisation was started by the non-Socialist Prime Minister, Jacques Chirac, during a period of 'cohabitation' when the Socialists controlled the Presidency and the Right the National Assembly. However, privatisation in France never seemed likely to reach the proportion it did in Britain. The large scale of the public sector in France had an importance in implementing economic policy to which we shall return below. It should be noted immediately, however, that the nationalised industries have been operated in a much more purely commercial manner than in, for example, Britain. The managers of state industries are expected to maximise profits, and their own pay is influenced by their success in doing so. No one has suggested that pay, manning levels or working conditions are better in state-owned Renault than in private-sector Citroen car plants.

We should also note that the social order in France, as in other capitalist democracies, has been strengthened by the growth of the welfare state. In most respects, the French welfare state is more generous than the British, let alone the

American. The French welfare state and large nationalised sector might be seen as constituting a slightly greater compromise between socialism and capitalism than we have encountered in the USA, Britain or West Germany. However, as we have seen, the compromise has been very effective economically.

Organisation of Business

French culture is not as favourably disposed to interest groups as is American or even British culture. The very term 'interest group' is used by civil servants as a term of opprobrium. An interest group to them is necessarily a self-interested group whose claims detract from the public good. The public, too, has often been thought of as having an ambivalent attitude to interest group activity. De Tocqueville argued that the French had two conflicting attitudes towards authority, one supporting authoritarian rule by distant rulers, the other inclining them to revolt against their rulers.[4] Neither practice is conducive to the growth of institutionalised interest groups.

At first glance, however, French industry seems highly organised politically. The *Comité National du Patronat Français* (CNPF) provides an umbrella organisation for the collective interests of French employers. As Suzanne Berger notes, however, the CNPF has constantly faced challenges from other groups speaking for those who think that the CNPF is dominated by large corporations or by the government.[5] In the 1950s the CNPF was criticised by the right-wing populists (the Poujadists) for neglecting the interests of small business, a criticism continued for most of the last thirty years by the Confédération Général des Petites et Moyennes Enterprises (CGPME). In the 1970s, this criticism was renewed by the Comité d'Information et Défense – Union Nationale des Travailleurs Indépendants (CID – UNAFI) and then in the 1980s by the Syndicat National du Patronat Moderne et Indépendant (SNPMI). It was the leader of the SNPMI, Gérard Deuil, who referred to the Council of the Patronat as the 'nationalised council of the French patronat', a sneer which contained some truth as many of the largest corporations in the Patronat are nationalised. However, the CNPF has ridden out such criticisms while its challengers, including the SNPMI – have faded. An important reason for the triumph of the CNPF has been the support and encouragement of the French state. Just as the French state looked for and encouraged an interest group representing farmers with which it could work in modernising agriculture, so the French state has built up and encouraged the CNPF to be its partner in industrial modernisation. In 1969, the CNPF was reorganised at the encouragement of government so as to increase the power and autonomy of its leaders. As the frequency of challenges to the status of the CNPF makes clear, partnership with government has come at the cost of alienating sectors of the business community; Hayward reports, however, that though the CNPF is most trusted by large, Paris-based corporations, smaller, provincial firms are still more likely than not to believe that the CNPF represents their interests.[6]

The CNPF is a federation of trade associations. Indeed, trade associations themselves play a vital role in representing business. It has been calculated that only one-fortieth of expenditure on representing business in France goes to the CNPF. As in Britain, the quality of trade associations varies considerably. There has been a tendency, however, for the trade associations to increase in strength *vis-a-vis* individual firms. Zysman reports, for example, that the proportion of seats held on consultative committees by trade associations, as opposed to individual firms, has increased considerably.[7] Some of the trade associations have developed only because of the deliberate or accidental support of the state. The Vichy régime obliged firms to belong to trade chambers, thus accustoming them to paying subscriptions.[8] The fact that France has had what Hayward has called a 'semi-permanent' incomes policy has encouraged firms to join interest groups in the quest for extra leverage with government on matters of crucial concern to any enterprise.[9] The Chambre Syndicale de la Siderurgie Français (CSSF), the trade association for the steel industry, in contrast to the trade associations in less-organised industries, has a history going back to the mid-nineteenth century. The CSSF is so powerful *vis-a-vis* individual firms that it guides their strategies and arranges joint borrowing. Apart from representing the industry to the National Assembly and executive, the CSSF provides its members with extensive services, including comparative cost studies, centralised purchasing of inputs and research.

The style of trade associations and the CNPF is generally technocratic. Wilson quotes one of the trade association leaders he interviewed as arguing for a technocratic approach: 'We try to avoid political discussion because this tends to become polemic rather than produce constructive debate.[10] There is a tendency for trade associations to have a dual leadership: a president who is popular with (or at least acceptable to) the membership and a more technically-minded director-general.[11] Many of the directors-general of trade associations are examples of a more general phenomenon in France known as *pantouflage*, the process of civil servants taking jobs in organisations and firms they have dealt with. The presence of these technicians in the highest posts of trade associations is an indication of the closeness of the ties between trade associations and government departments. Hayward reports that the closeness of trade associations to the relevant ministry is so great that divisions within trade associations more or less correspond to divisions within the ministry.[12]

The Theory and Reality of French Planning

There has been considerable controversy among scholars over the nature of French planning. In part this controversy exists because of the considerable gap between the theory and reality of planning in France. In theory the Plan is the guiding document for French economic policy, it is produced in a highly participatory process through which the Commissariat Général du Plan consults a wide range of economic and social groups, and it merely *indicates* (or is *indicative* of) future lines of economic development. In practice, all of these features can be debated.

It is clear that the Plan has not been the only or even the main influence on French economic policy. Considerable friction has existed between the Commissariat Général du Plan, operating out of the Prime Minister's office, and the Ministry of Finance which has often seen the Plan as a threat to its power. At times of economic or financial crisis, the Ministry of Finance has led governments into measures which involve clear departures from policies on which the Plan is based. This is not to say that the Plan was ignored totally. Ministries opposing Finance and supporting economic policies emphasising growth would use the Plan as one of their weapons. However, the Plan itself did not command the loyalty of every government department – the Ministry of Finance being a regular critic with its officials boasting that they did not even have a copy of the Plan in their offices – and was therefore susceptible to the usual vagaries of bureaucratic politics. Conflicts over issues to do with the Plan between different Ministries often continued as if the Plan had not been issued. For their part, individual corporations have also departed from the Plan when it has suited their interests to do so. MacArthur and Scott argued that the Plan was not a significant influence on the decision making of individual corporations about investment.[13] As we shall see, that is not to say that the *government* was not a major influence, but it is to say that the Plan was not as influential as might be supposed.

The process of producing the Plan was also less participatory than it seemed. In particular, although the Plan seemed to invite neocorporatist consultation between government, business and unions, unions were never effective actors in the process. As we have noted, French unions are weak (organising permanently less than 20 per cent of the work force) and fragmented by religious and political divisions. The unwillingness of the communist-dominated union, the Confédération Général des Travailleurs (CGT), to help make the existing socio-economic system work made it less than useful as a partner in the planning process; the Socialist rival to the CGT, the CFDT, was inhibited by competition from the CGT from seeming to be too co-opted. In the 1970s, a third union grouping, the Force Ouvrières (FO), was given government assistance in return for assuming some of the obligations of partnership with government that the French state expects from favoured interest groups.

However, for most of the period, unions were poorly represented in the planning process. The Mitterrand government started out determined to involve groups such as unions more in the planning process. However, the collapse of the Mitterrand government's attempts to implement more left-wing economic policies in the early 1980s ended the importance of these reforms. In general, the comments of MacArthur and Scott that the planning process was in effect 'a close partnership between business and the state'[14] are fully justified. Similarly, Cohen concluded that 'The *économie concertée* is a partnership of big business, the state, and, in theory though not in practice, the trade unions'.[15]

Was the Plan indicative? The theory of indicative planning is that growth will be achieved if industries, unions and government understand each others' objectives and problems. 'Bottle necks', which might result from, say, inadequate supplies of steel to meet the needs of auto or agricultural machinery producers, can be avoided if steel producers know in advance what demand they will be asked to meet. Economic targets will be more readily achieved if economic actors indicate their plans to each other and try to coordinate them.[16] In practice the Plan was both weaker and stronger than indicative planning seems. As we have noted, if the Plan was taken literally then neither corporations nor government departments were bound to it, and neither government policy nor the investment plans of individual corporations fully reflected it.

Yet on the other hand, provided the Plan was understood in a wider sense as a reflection of government industrial policy, it was much more than indicative. For to use a common metaphor, French government stopped functioning as the brake upon economic development and became instead its motor. Planning was but a part of the drive that government provided. The process of formulating the Plan might have achieved some of the benefits of coordination that its advocates believe indicative planning generally achieves. The Plans themselves may have spread optimism needed to overcome the pessimism which dominated pre-Second-World-War France. And the Plans helped mobilise patriotic sentiment around the cause of economic growth. French governments, pursuing traditional goals of power and influence for their nations, realised that successful industrial performance was essential to achieving those goals. It was de Gaulle who made that point most explicitly,[17] arguing that in the contemporary world, the glory of France depended on the strength of its economy. Stanley Hoffman brought out vividly the transformation of the role of the French state. Whereas the state had expressed, protected and guaranteed a conservative static social order by granting concessions to special interest groups, it now took the lead towards greater efficiency. 'When the watchdog became a greyhound, those holding the leash had to learn to run.'[18]

French industrial policy has also not been dosed with the nostrums of classical economics. Instead of focusing on short-term profitability or regarding as axiomatically correct the decisions of the market, it has taken a much more structural view of French industry. The goal has been to ensure that France is represented in the industries of the future (space, aircraft, cars), generally by two firms. The classic example is the car industry where France, represented by the privately-owned Talbot–Peugeot and the state-owned Renault, has become one of the world's leading car manufacturers in the same period as the British car industry collapsed. The government views large firms with favour, and often gives small business the feeling that it is regarded as outmoded. The French thus do not follow the anti-monopoly practices common in the USA. On the contrary, industrial giants capable of competing in international markets are the goal.

The government has at its disposal a number of weapons for use in the pursuit of industrial policy goals. First, whatever the theory of GATT or the EEC, the French civil service has managed to impede the import of goods threatening the French industry. The Japanese car and video cassette recorders found that major administrative barriers were put in their way, unlike the situation in Britain or the USA where civil servants faithfully honoured free-trade rules. Second, the large nationalised sector of French industry joins with government itself to provide a sizeable protected market for French industry. It is inconceivable that the French air force or the government-owned airline Air France would buy military or civilian planes from the USA if a French alternative was available; the same cannot be said of the British Royal Air Force (or, when it was a state-owned airline, British Airways – which, in fact, had a strong attachment to the American planemaker, Boeing). Finally, the French government, even before the nationalisation of banks in the 1980s, had at its disposal considerable investment funds through government-controlled savings banks such as the *Caisse des Depôts*. Funds from these banks would be made available on favourable terms of interest to firms undertaking investments of which the government approved (and, of course, denied to those who did not). Government has thus had a variety of practical measures available to it to assist in the implementation of its plans for the development of French industry. Zysman emphasises the importance of the structure of the French financial system in giving government powers that made its industrial policy much more than a statement of aspirations.[19] In Zysman's view, it is government control of the allocation of credit and ability to grant credit at different interest rates that has given it real leverage.

Why has Industrial Policy been Institutionalised in France?

Although the importance of the Plan can be debated, the importance in general of government in leading France from the middle ranks to the vanguard of the European economy cannot be denied. We must explain, therefore, why the French state has been able to play regularly a leadership role that the British, American or even German states have not.[20]

One potential explanation is Zysman's, based on the structure of financial systems. Some countries have financial systems that funnel funds through government-controlled or -influenced banks to industries, and government control can be used to promote growth. Other nations have financial systems less easily controlled by government and in which investment is typically funded from the internal resources of corporations. Two problems arise with this explanation. First, government influence can be used unwisely as well as wisely. Mistakes can be made by government officials as well as entrepreneurs about what is the optimal investment decision. Governments can intervene not to promote growth but to rescue 'lame duck' industries with limited prospects of commercial success. Second, as Cox has argued, financial systems are not eternally fixed, but could be changed were there the political will to do so. While the nature of the French financial system is important, we need to consider other factors as well to explain the strength of French industrial policy.[21]

One factor of great importance is differing ideology between France on the one hand and Britain and the United States on the other. In the first place, faith in the ability of market forces to allocate investment funds optimally has, at least until now, been weaker in France than in the USA or Britain. A separate but related ideological factor has been the greater faith in the state in France than in Anglo-American democracies. As Peter Hall shows, French governments have been able to evoke a tradition of regarding the state as a servant or guarantor of the long term public interest, that which citizens pursuing what Rousseau termed the 'General Will' would favour, that has found little support in British or American intellectual life. The market is seen as less intelligent and the state as wiser than in Anglo-American thought.[22] The argument that the state needs to promote economic growth is therefore more readily accepted.

A second factor of great importance has been the character of the French bureaucracy. The senior bureaucracy in France has been much better suited than bureaucracies in Britain or the USA to playing a leadership role in the economy. At its highest levels the French bureaucracy has been disproportionately – and overwhelmingly – recruited from the École Polytechnique and the École Normal d'Administration (ENA). The most successful graduates of these bodies are admitted to the *Grands Corps* of the civil service, such as *Ponts et Chaussés*, handling civil engineering and the Inspectorate of Finances. The fact that the top civil servants are recruited from the Polytechnique and ENA has a number of important consequences. First, their élite status prepares (and predisposes) them for a leadership role in French society, particularly in economic matters. Second, the nature of their education increases their willingness – unlike the top British civil service – to take an interest in the details of individual firms and industries, and not just in macroeconomic policy. Finally, graduates of the Polytechnique are bonded together by a loyalty to each other and familiarity with their fellow graduates who so often occupy the top positions in French society.[23]

For it is the case that the graduates of the Polytechnique and ENA occupy the crucial positions in business as well as government. The process of *pantouflage* results in the movement of the very highest civil servants from government into the management of private firms, particularly the largest of the private firms. Vincent Wright reports that of the 560 firms employing more than 1000 workers, a majority were headed by a graduate of the École Polytechnique and almost all had ex-civil servants on their Boards of Directors.[24] Whereas such moves are feared in the USA and Britain as extending the influence of business into government, *pantouflage* is welcomed in France as a means of extending the influence of government into large-scale businesses. Suleiman has drawn attention to the increasing percentage of the graduates of the École Polytechnique who resign from public service immediately after graduating and enter private industry without a civil service career.[25] But even these graduates remain a resource for the state, tied to their more numerous colleagues in the civil service by a common education and friendships. Thus, as befits its role in co-ordinating government and industry, the cohesive élite of the French civil service spans both the civil service and the highest posts in private industry.

A third factor facilitating industrial policy in France has been the insulation from politics which the bureaucracy has often enjoyed. A great danger in industrial policy is that resources will be directed as a result of political pressure into declining industries with few future prospects instead of into industries with great future promise. After all, even declining industries tend to be stronger politically because of the voters they employ or the interest groups they deploy than industries which, though they will be strong in the future, employ few people and have weak interest groups today. The natural tendency, if political factors predominate, is for politicians to direct government resources into declining industries, a tendency visible in Britain in the 1970s. For most of the period after the Second World War, this tendency was held in check in France by factors which minimised the impact of electoral competition. Under the Fourth Republic, the impact of political pressures was attenuated by the extreme instability of governments. The preoccupation of governments with the difficulties of building and maintaining majority coalitions in the Assembly left little time for making a deep impact on public policy, even though it is true that many ministers kept the same post in a different government. In contrast, the civil servants who had acquired (particularly at the ENA) a strong sense of mission had long term goals and lengthy tenure of office in which to achieve them.

The constitution of the Fifth Republic was designed to strengthen the executive branch. The government was led (until the Mitterrand–Chirac cohabitation of the mid-1980s) by the President, who was elected for seven years. The power of the National Assembly was reduced substantially, and the President was given a variety of means to by-pass it, such as national referenda. Until 1973, the Presidency of the Fifth Republic was held by Gaullists, and for the remainder of the 1970s by the leader of their allies, the Independent Republicans. Only from the late 1970s onwards could we say that there has been effective party competition for the Presidency. As we might expect, this period has also seen a move towards greater use of industrial policy for electoral rather than economic purposes. Government aid to declining industries rose in the late 1970s and even faster in the early 1980s; the Socialists liked to argue that there were no declining industries, only declining technologies. As we shall see in Japan, the limited importance of electoral politics is probably essential for the maintenance of an industrial policy that emphasises economic growth rather than winning votes for the government.

The dramatic changes of policy by the Socialists in the early 1980s, in the direction of greater acceptance of market forces, ended the tendency for rescuing lame ducks to dominate industrial policy. For most of the period since the Second

World War, French industrial policy has emphasised long-term growth over short-term rescues for declining firms. Concessions have been made where necessary to interests, as the extensive and expensive subsidies to agriculture attest. In general, however, French industrial policy has made clear and resolute decisions ranging from the build up of the atomic power industry to the location of maritime development areas around new ports at Dunkirk and Fos. Not every decision has been wise – the British were right, at least commercially, to argue against building the Anglo-French supersonic airliner, Concorde. But the overall effect of industrial policy on France has been immensely positive.

Conclusions

Whether French governments can play as direct a role in leading the economy in the future as in the past remains to be seen. The increased openness of the French economy within the integrated market of post-1992 Europe and in the world more generally diminishes the opportunities for national economic planning or industrial policies. French imports and exports are now equivalent to about 20 per cent of gross national product. Not only officials of the European Community watch carefully for subsidies to French industries; the United States has exerted strong pressure against any subsidies to concerns which compete with American firms, such as the collaborative European Airbus Industrie in which France has the major stake. The ability of French governments to maintain competitiveness as they did in most of the period since 1945, by frequent and drastic devaluations of the franc, has been limited by French membership of the European Monetary System (EMS). It was the 1981–86 Socialist government that pointed out to its electorate the *de facto* integration of the French and German economies; in consequence, the government warned, tendencies towards higher inflation in France than in Germany had to be defeated. After the rapid demise of attempts in the early Mitterrand Presidency to achieve a more socialist and democratic form of planning, French industrial policy has shifted towards an emphasis on competitiveness. The slow growth, high unemployment and inflation of the 1980s have shown that the French economy is not immune to the problems of mature European economies. The weight of opinion behind greater reliance on market forces in economic policy is greater than before. With the total removal of barriers to trade within the European Community in 1992 looming, the challenge for France as for Britain and West Germany is the maintenance of competitiveness.

The French example also points to the difficulty of conceptualising business–government relations purely in terms of power. Did French industry have power over the French state, or vice-versa? Certainly business was able to obtain special privileges from government, but government also steered industry in the directions it favoured. In a successful quest for increased power, prestige and wealth for France, a governmental technocracy which also reached into the large-scale private firms produced economic growth which might not have materialised if the private sector had been left to its own devices. It is traditional in Britain and the USA to think of government and industry as two separate areas which press upon each other but remain distant. Obviously in France the 'distinctness' of government and industry has not been preserved. On the contrary, French government involved itself in the details of French industrial life, not to contain or alter commercial priorities (for example, by imposing regulations to protect the environment), but by exhorting and assisting French industry to exploit commercial opportunities. Peter Hall argues that the practice of planning in France reduced the distinctiveness of the state as government and corporations became more integrated. Hall also notes, however, that so extensive had the influence of the state become in many corporations that their managers noticed little difference when they were formally nationalised by the Mitterrand government.[26] Some Marxists might argue that the pattern of government-led capitalist development illustrates the dominance of both state and industry by the bourgeoisie. A more plausible interpretation which might find favour with different types of Marxists would be that the state's interests in a strong French economy and the capitalist's interests in profits coincided. The success of the state in educating French entrepreneurs into being more successful served both their interests.

8

Japan

The magnitude of Japan's economic success is enormous. A nation of 117 million people living in crowded islands endowed with few natural resources has become the second largest economy in the world, less than half a century after being defeated and devastated in the Second World War. Japanese wages have increased in money terms from levels comparable with third world countries to levels comparable with the United States. It is true that because of the high cost of living in Japan, real incomes when adjusted to take account of differences in price levels are still significantly higher in the USA. But the constant, almost remorseless economic progress of Japan suggests that in the foreseeable future the Japanese people will enjoy one of the very highest standards of living in the world. Consumers around the world have become accustomed to relying on Japanese corporations for a wide range of goods. Many American or British people drive to and from work in a Japanese car, use a Japanese microwave oven to prepare part of their dinner and spend the evening watching a movie on a Japanese television or VCR. In less than forty years, Japanese goods have passed from being regarded as inferior and unreliable to being regarded as the epitome of quality. As the economy has progressed, Japanese corporations have moved up the hierarchy of industrial sophistication from cheap textiles to supercomputers. As Japanese wealth has increased, Japanese banks have become among the largest in the world. Once-powerful industrial nations such as Britain have been delighted to host Japanese factories hoping that corporations such as Nissan or Toyota will revive industries in which domestic corporations have failed.

The essential challenge posed by Japan to academics and policy advisers is to understand this extraordinary economic success. Understanding the Japanese phenomenon is crucial for foreign policy makers in other countries. Is Japan fundamentally a free market country, albeit an unusually successful one? If it is, Japan's huge balance of payments surpluses, which seemed so threatening to its trading partners in the 1980s, may be cured by its citizens starting to spend their greater wealth more freely on imports. Perhaps, however, there is a distinctive Japanese model of the political economy which, while seeming to have most of the characteristics of a capitalist market economy, is fundamentally a country managed in such a way that its domestic markets will never be truly open to foreign competitors.[1] Leaders of poorer nations must also consider whether the Japanese model of economic development is one that other countries can emulate[2] or was due to certain factors or characteristics that only Japan possesses.

Academic analysts also wish to appropriate the Japanese success story to support their own favourite theory of how countries make economic progress. A number of different approaches, all with some plausibility, have been advanced to explain Japanese success.

The first approach to explaining Japanese success stresses the contribution of Japanese culture. The Japanese worker views his (women are not considered a normal part of the work force) corporation somewhat as a loyal peasant regarded a feudal lord. The worker supplies hard work, diligence, loyalty and obedience demonstrated by willingness to sing with gusto the corporation's anthem; the corporation, acting as the modern equivalent of the feudal lord, provides housing, health care and the promise of lifetime employment. Japanese workers show unusual willingness to defer gratification, accepting a lower standard of living than the country could provide in the cause of long-term Japanese economic success, and saving a very high proportion of their incomes. Workers rarely join unions – only one quarter of the work force is unionised – and if they do, often join a company union which is committed to the success of its corporation. The number of days lost to strikes is, of course, extremely low. Even following major scandals, such as the Recruit affair in 1989 that included the involvement of many leading figures in the Liberal Democratic Party that has ruled Japan since the Allies restored civilian government, support for the Socialist Party remained low. The Japanese remained hardworking, loyal, obedient workers and citizens.

Admirers of the Japanese system see many advantages that other countries might wish to emulate if they could. Apart from the extraordinary success of the economy, Japan is a relatively tranquil country with low crime, and even few legal disputes. Income differentials are unusually low. Japanese corporations encourage loyalty by having managers wear the same uniforms as workers and eat in the same canteens. Japanese high school students study hard, and learn more than their American or British counterparts.

Yet the cultural explanation of Japanese success is not entirely convincing. There have been periods – such as the late 1940s – of intense labour unrest in Japan. Protests over the visits of American warships thought to carry nuclear weapons or the building of the new Tokyo airport at Narissa can develop into furious pitched battles that exceed in violence British football riots or militant protests in the USA. The famed lifetime employment system benefits only one-quarter to one-third of the work force. A large number of workers are employed by subcontractors of the large corporations that offer few benefits and little security. The Japanese manager may eat in the same canteen and receive wages that are a much smaller multiple of the salary of the average worker than are the vast wages paid to American executives of the average American wage. Yet status differences in Japan are acutely important, and non-wage remuneration to executives (e.g. expense account dining or foreign travel for the executive and family) is considerable. Japanese culture, even if it did promote high economic performance, may have other disadvantages; for example, some writers see in Japanese culture a degree of nationalism that verges on racism. Postwar Japanese history and society is also too complicated to ascribe Japanese success solely to Japanese culture.

A second approach sees Japan's success as a vivid demonstration of the importance of free markets and capitalism for economic success. In this view, Japan succeeded because of the vision of its entrepreneurs who, even when discouraged by government (as was Honda), have had the vision and tenacity to achieve success at home and abroad. The Japanese government, unlike governments in many third world nations, has had the intelligence not to impede enriching free-market forces. Other east Asian countries that have followed this example (the 'Four Tigers' of Singapore, Taiwan, South Korea and Hong Kong) have started to enjoy similar success.

Although there are indeed examples of Japanese corporations that have succeeded contrary to the expectations of government experts, most authorities on Japan regard the free-market interpretation of its success as fundamentally and wildly incorrect. The Japanese economy, most historians would agree, has never been a free-market economy in which numerous firms have competed free and equally. On the contrary, ever since Japan started its drive to catch up with the west after the Meiji restoration, its economy has been dominated by a small number of very large corporations that have been helped, licensed and supported by government. Even many of the numerous small-scale subcontractors are in fact dominated by a single giant corporation to which they supply their product and from which they often receive raw materials and working capital.

The dominant view of Japanese economic development is probably that is has been *government led*.[3] Government leadership has fostered economic development through the financial system and through a form of partnership with business, that might be likened to indicative planning without formal consultation, the participation of interests other than business or a published document. There is widespread agreement that business and government in Japan have co-operated closely. The characterisation of that close co-operation has varied from the much resented label 'Japan Inc.', that suggests that the entire political system and economy of Japan is put at the disposal of large corporations, to interpretations that have seemed to suggest that a few key bureaucrats in the Ministry of International Trade and Industry (MITI) have controlled the development of the entire Japanese economy. The truth is of course much more complicated.

The Organisation of Business and its Political Situation

There is no doubt that Japanese business is highly organised. Trade associations representing individual industries are generally well staffed, and are accepted as partners in policy making by government departments. Indeed, trade associations sometimes act on behalf of government, saving the government time, resources, and official sanction for policies it accepts in practice more than in theory. For example, the Japanese 'voluntary' agreement not to sell as many cars as they could in Britain has been made and implemented not by government but by the trade association representing Japanese automobile manufacturers. The trade association also divides up the total quota between its members. The Ministry of International Trade and Industry (MITI) is organised so that its divisions parallel major trade associations such as the Japan Steel League, the Electrical Manufacturing Federation and the Automobile Industry Association.

Trade associations and major corporations all belong to the *Keidanren*, the Federation of Economic Organisations. Although there are other significant organisations representing business, such as the Japan Chamber of Commerce and Industry, there is no doubt the Keidanren is regarded as the authoritative voice of business. The relationship between the Keidanren and MITI is extremely close. Top officials of both organisations share a common educational background and consult very regularly. To facilitate co-operation, Keidanren is organised in a way which mirrors MITI. Keidanren recruits retiring civil servants from MITI and there are even exchanges of junior level officials between the Ministry and the Keidanren. The Keidanren, like trade associations, is fully accepted as a partner in both policy making and policy implementation. The Keidanren has negotiated trade agreements with Communist countries and helped organise a project in Brazil that involved a number of Japanese corporations. The Keidanren's links are primarily to the bureaucracy. But leaders of the Keidanren such as Taizo Ishikaza are prominent public figures in Japan in a way that their counterparts in most democracies are not. Moreover, as we shall see, the links of the Keidanren and other business leaders to the Liberal Democratic Party are extremely close.

As we noted in chapter 1, it has been common to link the strength of business groups to the strength of the challenge confronting them. Japan is an exception to this generalisation. The forces confronting business are weak. Unions, as we have noted, recruit at best 25 per cent of the work force, and are divided politically. The Japanese Socialist Party receives a small and declining share of the vote. The primary reason for business organisations in Japan is not to defend business interests but to co-operate with the state. Indeed as we shall see, if the travails of the LDP in the late 1980s were to weaken its position profoundly the most serious questions would be raised about the entire Japanese political economy.

The Organisation of the State

All observers agree that the Japanese state has attempted to steer industrial policy; most think that it has succeeded. But who wields power within the state?

Formally Japan is a parliamentary democracy more or less on the British model with the Emperor functioning as a more or less powerless constitutional monarch. However, Japan has yet to pass that hallmark of democracy, a peaceful transfer of power from one party to another; one party, the Liberal Democratic Party, has completely dominated Japan since the restoration of sovereignty to Japan by the allies, forming all the governments and possessing a majority (though of varying size) in the Diet. The Liberal Democratic Party is a somewhat unusual party. Although closely allied with the business community, it has a limited ideology based on nationalism of varying degrees of intensity, support for private ownership of business, acceptance of a role for government in steering economic development and concessions to whatever further demands for government action seem irresistible. Japan is the only industrialised democracy with a less-developed welfare state than the USA; environmental controls were adopted in the 1970s only after the need for them was demonstrated by a series of appalling disasters such as large-scale mercury poisoning caused by eating fish from heavily polluted waters.

Yet ideology is not central to the LDP. It is a highly fragmented party with factions playing a major role in its affairs. Factions, as well as the party as a whole, raise money from business; factions expect turns in choosing the leader of the LDP (and thus the Prime Minister). In order to accommodate bargaining between factions, Japanese Prime Ministers serve for very short periods, generally about two years, which helps to explain why they are among the weakest democratic chief executives. But the factions, like the party, are not particularly ideological. Observers note limited ideological conflict or even difference of emphasis between the factions. Nor are they, as in old-style American political parties, based on regions. Certainly patronage is the lifeblood of the LDP, linking faction leaders to followers and LDP members of the Diet to their constituents. The constituencies of powerful politicians such as former Prime Minister and faction leader Tanaka are crowded with public projects, such as highways clearly too large for the traffic they carry. Adherence to a faction leader appears to reflect the LDP Diet member's assessment of what will serve his interests rather than any permanent relationship between factions and constituency.

The patronage which is the lifeblood of the LDP, its factions and its members of the Diet is expensive. Even ordinary constituents expect what by the standards of other countries are expensive gifts or gestures from their legislator. It has been calculated that, in spite of the weakness of party competition in Japan, Japanese politicians with half the population spend on average twice as much as do American politicians in a comparable period. Scandal is therefore endemic as politicians scramble for funds largely from business. The Lockheed scandal in the 1970s and the Recruit scandal in the 1980s were both reflections of a much more widespread pattern of business executives and LDP politicians exchanging favours.

Both were followed by prosecutions, moral outrage and little fundamental reform.

If the LDP needs business to provide the funds which its practices require, the party also serves a valuable function for business. The dominance of the LDP has ensured that a political climate generally favourable to large corporations has been maintained. Moreover, with the notable exception of the farmers, the absence of party competition has enabled the state to act in a manner conducive to economic growth without having to worry much about the political consequences. A large literature in political science focuses on how and why governments take economically irrational steps to bolster their political strength. Japanese governments have little need to worry about losing power in the Diet.

Japanese ministers are not, however, the clearly dominant policy makers that their British namesakes are. The balance of power between senior civil servants and ministers is tilted much more in favour of the permanent civil servants in Japan than in Britain. The unusually forceful prime ministerships of Tanaka Kakuei (1972–74) and especially Yasuhiro Nakasone (1983–87) seemed to call this view into question. However, the retirement of Nakasone was generally seen as marking a return to business as usual. It has been common to view Japanese government as government by the permanent bureaucracy, though as we shall see, this view is simplistic.

Not surprisingly, the senior bureaucracy is prestigious and to some degree cohesive. As in France, a career in the senior civil service has been seen as one of the most desirable careers a bright young person can follow. Also as in France, entrants to the civil service are the intellectual élite of their generation, selected from a very limited number of very prestigious universities, notably the Imperial University of Tokyo, Todai. Unlike the situation in France, however, the rigorously selected undergraduates of Todai are not given a particularly rigorous training at university, and there is no equivalent of the *Grands Corps*. Friendships formed at Todai do, however, sill help to bind to each other members of the Japanese élite of the civil service, industry, important pressure groups and the LDP.

One further similarity with France exists. Civil servants who have reached the top or close to the top of their profession move out to posts in industry or in politics, running for office as LDP candidates and sometimes subsequently becoming ministers. The move out of the civil service, reflecting the diminution of prestige involved in moving from the top civil service to top management, is known as the 'descent from heaven'. As in France, former civil servants are likely to carry with them a general orientation to support the policies and viewpoint of their former colleagues. The danger that what in Washington would be called 'the revolving door' would corrupt government is not seen as important in Japan; former civil servants extend the reach of government when they move into private sector jobs rather than the private sector extending its reach by recruiting from the public sector. The 'descent from heaven' is, however, a structural necessity for the civil service. Convention requires that when a member of an entering class of the civil service reaches the most senior post possible, his class mates must resign. There is therefore a constant flow of retiring bureaucrats for whom work must be found.

What constrains the power of the bureaucracy? In the first place, bureaucrats need politicians to perform certain tasks that they cannot. Such tasks include the mobilisation of popular consent and the representation of agencies in the Diet. A second limitation is that the bureaucracy is not entirely cohesive. Important disputes separate government Departments. The Ministry of Finance has fought numerous battles with MITI over the years. In the 1980s, MITI's prestige was dented by its failure to defeat a move by the Ministry of Posts and Telecommunications to be the sponsoring agency for much of the electronics industry. Conflicts between bureaucrats therefore act as important checks on the collective power of the bureaucracy.

The image of an all-directing Japanese state therefore needs much qualification. It has been argued by van Wolferen that nobody is fully in charge of the Japanese state. Politicians are generally too weak *vis-à-vis* the bureaucracy and too preoccupied with their own contests for power to make a deep impact on public policy. The bureaucracy, however, needs the co-operation of the LDP to save it from the interference of other politicians and is itself too divided to provide cohesive rule. Whether van Wolferen's interpretation is accurate or merely a valuable corrective to earlier views of the Japanese political system will be debated by Japanese scholars for some time to come.

The Nature of Industrial Policy

Two basic questions about Japanese industrial policy have yet to receive a definitive answer. The first question is what has been the form of industrial policy; how is industrial policy expressed and implemented? The second question is how important has been industrial policy in causing the dramatic increase in Japanese income and wealth.

One reason why it has been difficult to determine the nature of Japanese industrial policy is that it has been changing. There is little doubt that as Chalmers Johnson describes,[4] MITI's powers to direct industrial development were much greater in the past than more recently. In the 1950s, MITI had authority to permit or ban imports of technology, to permit or ban foreign corporations to set up plants in Japan (a power it used to exclude American auto companies until the infant domestic industry was established) and to allocate quotas of imported raw material (e.g. iron ore) to corporations. These very extensive powers gave way, especially after Japan joined the General Agreement on Tariffs and Trade (GATT), to a more informal and elusive system.[5]

After formal controls were abandoned, MITI continued to give importance guidance on how Japanese industry should develop. MITI's authority stemmed partly from the general high regard for bureaucracy in Japanese culture – a belief that bureaucracies have the ability to analyse trends and therefore predict the future better than individual entrepreneurs. But MITI's authority rested on more than political culture.

In the first place, Japanese corporations continued to need more licences and permits to conduct their business than their American or British counterparts. Most forms of economic activity require permits. Moreover, MITI officials, very knowledgeable about individual corporations, often know of breaches of regulations or potentially embarrassing scandals that they can cover up or publicise according to the corporation's degree of 'voluntary' co-operation with MITI's plans. Government officials like to pretend that they rely on 'voluntary' co-operation; the reality is that they have veiled forms of coercion available to them.

In the second place, as Zysman[6] emphasises, the Japanese financial system, like the French, is a system in which government can operate through the banks to direct investment funds towards or away from industries or corporations, depending on both the government's views of their potential and the willingness of corporations to co-operate with the government's plans. Japanese corporations operate with what by American or British standards are massive levels of external indebtedness to finance growth. The funds are provided by banks which take a close interest in the fate of large corporations, rarely if ever allowing them to go bankrupt but occasionally intervening to reorganise failing concerns. The banks in turn are driven into dependency on the Bank of Japan for their funds (or the Ministry of Posts and Telecommunications which controls post office savings banks) because much of the massive level of Japanese savings goes initially to government financial institutions. Thus corporations were dependent on banks, and banks were dependent on government. Government policy therefore was more than a general statement of goals that corporations could decide to honour or ignore.

None the less, the capacity of MITI or the government in general is probably less now than it was in the 1950s. There are celebrated examples of corporations that have defied MITI's views and have succeeded; MITI wanted far fewer automobile companies than now exist in Japan yet one of the firms that refused to comply with MITI's plans, Honda, has thrived. The ability of government to deploy its full power over corporations through the financial system is limited by intra-governmental conflicts between the Ministry of Finance, MITI and the Ministry of Posts and Telecommunications. Above all, as Samuels has argued,[7] it would be incorrect to see MITI as trying to thwart or block market forces. The general character of Japanese industrial policy has been to anticipate, reinforce and quicken market forces rather than fight against them. The logic of MITI's policies is intended to be in line with what market forces would produce, but to produce the outcome faster and more efficiently. Japanese corporations will be ready positioned to exploit new possibilities (e.g. microchips, VCRs) to which corporations in countries with less assertive industrial policies will respond through market forces alone, too late to prevent Japanese domination of the industry.

Managing Change

One of the many impressive characteristics of the Japanese economy has been its ability to shift from decline to expanding sectors and from industries suited to low-wage economies to industries suited to high-wage economies. The management of industrial change offers instructive examples of the strengths and limits of the power of government in Japan to manage industrial change.

Inevitably, industries do go into irreversible decline in Japan; as the wage rate in Japan increases and the labour-intensive industries become more vulnerable to competition from places such as Taiwan or South Korea, such declines may become all the more common. Japan has had to contend since 1973 with the particular problem of paying much higher energy costs when she has no indigenous energy reserves. This again has called into question the viability of formerly strong industries. Eight industries were designated as being in decline in the 1980s – aluminium, cardboard, cotton and wool spinning, electric furnace, steel ferrosilicon, fertilisers, ship-building and synthetic fibres. The contrasting fates of these industries illustrates the implausibility of regarding Japan as a homogeneous undifferentiated system.

Declining industries have been assisted by the 1978 Depressed Industries Act. Industries designated under the Act are eligible for government financial assistance and can be exempted from the Anti-Monopoly Law, bequeathed to Japan by the Occupation Administration. The use of the Act has varied from industry to industry. The Act worked most smoothly in the case of shipbuilding. Japan was hit hard by the decline in world demand for ships, particularly super-tankers. The Ministry of Transport arranged a limit on domestic production in line with the trade association (the Shipbuilders Association of Japan). After nineteen companies went bankrupt, the Ministry of Transport succeeded in persuading companies to agree to a 35 per cent cut in capacity. A Shipbuilding Rationalisation Council made up of academics, businessmen, bankers, journalists, and union officials supervised the process, which was, however, planned primarily by the trade association and the ministry. Every effort was made to avoid redundancies, including cutting executives' salaries, dividends, and transferring workers to other jobs, either in a subsidiary or (with the help of the bank) to a job in a supplier's or customer's factory. The banks also helped by rescheduling debt and accepting a moratorium on loan repayments.

The aluminium industry was hit badly by the increase in energy costs. Yet in spite of the obvious danger, the aluminium smelters were unable to arrange a reduction in production. One reason for this is that the aluminium smelters are part of very large companies such as Mitsubishi. Only after several years of heavy losses could MITI arrange a reduction in the scale of the industry, with one entire plant being shipped to South Africa. A similar, and so far even less tractable, problem developed in the electric steel-generating industry. The industry's trade association has proposed that the large firms pay the small firms to go out of business, but the largest firm – the Tokyo Steel Manufacturing Company – refused to comply. It is symptomatic of the changes in Japan that MITI lacked the power to compel obedience, something unthinkable in the 1960s. Indeed, by 1984 the Fair Trade Commission (the anti-monopoly agency) was pressing hard for MITI to lose even more of its powers to suspend or limit competition. None the less, Japan retained (through MITI and its trade associations) a capacity to manage the processes of industrial change in excess of that of Britain or the USA. Increasing competition, particularly from other Asian countries, might make that capacity all the more useful.

The reasons for the ability to contain the inevitable pressures to use government grants to resist change rather than to foster development are fairly apparent. The very success of the Japanese economy reduces pressures; the fear of unemployment is much reduced if an economy is growing. Guarantees of lifetime employment make a similar contribution. Though being shifted to an entirely different part of Japan by a large firm may not be particularly appealing, it is much less alarming than lifetime unemployment. The political system itself, however, also contains pressures. The fact that the Liberal Democrats have been in power continuously since 1948 reduces the importance of inter-party competition. The main motive of the American and British political systems in advantaging geographically-concentrated special interests is reduced in importance by the fact that the Opposition parties, Buddhist or Socialist, have little chance of forming a government. Moreover, the fact that the power of politicians relative to the power of bureaucrats is lower than in Britain or the USA again reduces the power of interests to press for protection. Even if the politicians are inclined to 'give in' to firms or workers seeking government assistance for doomed industries, the civil servants in ministries such as MITI are not. In consequence, the civil servants allow the politicians to make incremental changes in their plans in order to accommodate political deals, but do not facilitate the adoption of policies detrimental to long-term growth or efficiency. The power of the bureaucrat necessarily reduces the power of the politician to bid for votes. It is interesting to note in this context that Japan has also proved particularly resistant to the 'political business cycle'. Whereas there are good grounds to believe that on at least some occasions British and American governments have changed economic policy in order to pick up votes, Japanese fiscal and monetary policies have shown very little variation which can be attributed to electoral pressures. The weakness of party competition and politicians in general would again seem to provide an explanation.

The Impact of Policy

Industrial policy is not the only reason for Japanese success. As we have noted at the start of this chapter, a number of competing explanations have been provided for Japan's success, stressing the qualities of its work force, its entrepreneurs or the willingness of the population to save and invest. It would be difficult or impossible to produce an economic model that would permit precise comparison of the relative importance of these factors and of industrial policy. Yet at minimum, the Japanese example should give pause to those in Britain or the USA who assume that government intervention in the economy serves to reduce economic growth. The Japanese example shows that active industrial policy is at least compatible with economic success. Most Japanese officials would argue that an able government agency such as MITI has greater ability than a single corporation to predict future commercial opportunities. What is commercially attractive for a corporation today may not yield what for a country is the industrial ideal situation of tomorrow. It may have been attractive for Japanese corporations to manufacture American or Italian cars under licence in the 1950s; such a practice would have inhibited the rise of the brilliantly successful Japanese auto industry. Moreover, in a world characterised by international competition and rapid diffusion of technologies, the commercial prize will generally go to the country that can produce and market a new product the fastest. That country is more likely to be one such as Japan in which a government agency can identify commercial trends and organise banks and corporations to meet them rapidly, while preventing foreign competition from undermining its infant industry through *de facto* import controls. It is less likely to be a country such as the USA that waits for market forces to operate. By the time market forces operate in America, Japanese corporations will have been organised to meet the demand with high-quality attractively-priced products.

The Exportability of the Japanese Model

If the Japanese model offers real advantages for international trade competition, how easily might it be copied by other countries?

Many countries could create an agency modelled on MITI. There is little in the training of Japanese civil servants that would make them more technically or economically proficient than their counterparts in European countries or the USA. The senior Japanese civil servant has little training to compare with the French administrative élite.

Yet there are a number of important features of the Japanese political economy that countries could not, or might not wish to emulate. First, as Zysman has shown,[8] the Japanese financial system is structured in such a way that it gives government real leverage over corporations. Government influence over corporations through the allocation and pricing of credit gives the Japanese authorities power that their British or American counterparts lack. Similarly, MITI's authority has been buttressed by a history of extensive government controls that have socialised corporate executives into habits of complying with government requests; this socialisation is reinforced by the continuing reality of a need for government licences and permits beyond that needed in other countries, and that can be given or denied by bureaucrats with a discretion that gives them important power over business.

Second, the history of Japan has endowed the bureaucracy with a degree of prestige that is unmatched in other countries. Whereas for Americans or the British bureaucracy conjures up images of delay, waste and confusion, for the Japanese bureaucracy stands for intelligence and disinterested pursuit of national interest. It is politicians who are corrupt and grubby; civil servants promote the national interest.

Finally, Japan has solved the perennial problem of how to prevent an active industrial policy being captured by industries trying to avoid economic decline by minimising the impact of electoral politics. The LDP does need to make concessions to local interest and, above all, the farmers, in order to maintain itself in power. But there is no likelihood in the foreseeable future of a government being elected based on a party other than the LDP; a really poor showing by the LDP in an election might result in some of the independent members of the Diet being brought into the government, but it would not result in a party such as the Socialists forming a government. Moreover, as we have seen, Japanese bureaucrats are much more powerful vis-à-vis their political 'masters' than in Britain or the USA. In a sense, Japan has created a political economy capable of implementing a purposive industrial economy by minimising democracy within a shell of Parliamentary government. Whether, as Fallows suggests, the Japanese are happy with this situation or, as van Wolferen argues, the Japanese would prefer 'the system' to change is uncertain. Certainly policies which would have benefited Japanese industry such as keeping down the value of the Yen and discouraging imports have hurt the interests of ordinary consumers. It might be agreed by British or American citizens that making their political system more like Japan's would be a high price to pay for more successful industrial policies.

9

The Multinationals – Companies without Governments?

The Transnational Company

One of the more dramatic developments of this century has been the expansion of companies across national boundaries. Today's motorist can drive in Europe or the USA without abandoning his or her favourite brand of petrol; the company that has franchised and supplied the petrol station might well be one of the 'Seven Sisters' of the oil industry which has extracted the petroleum from the ground in Saudi Arabia, the north slope of Alaska, or the North Sea, has transported it to a refinery it owns and operates in a consumer country and has organised its sale to the ordinary motorist. The car which the motorist drives may well be a car produced by a company which is itself manufactured in Europe but whose head-quarters is in the USA. Numerous of our motorist's other needs may be supplied by similarly 'crossnational' companies. The soap in which the motorist washed before leaving the house, the word processor which the motorist uses at work, and the films watched for entertainment in the evening may all be manufactured by companies whose headquarters are in one country but which have manufacturing capacity in others.

It is not surprising, therefore, that the multinationals, as they are called, are seen as one of the major features of the current world economy. Multinationals, precisely because of their importance in daily life and obvious size, can also seem threatening or even frightening. It has been calculated that the turnover of the ten largest multinationals is greater than the entire gross national product of 80 nations. This fact alone has been sufficient to convince many observers that multinationals are more powerful than governments, able to stride the globe arrogantly, bending countries to their wills. Before determining whether multinationals are as powerful as this suggests, or, as their officers would suggest, are tremendously vulnerable precisely because they come under the authority of so many governments, an attempt to clarify terms and issues should be made.

The first term which causes difficulty is 'multinational' itself. There are some firms which are genuinely multinational in that they are owned by stockholders in several countries, but they are comparatively few in number; Royal Dutch Shell and Unilever are two examples of firms which, unusually, are based in two countries (Britain and the Netherlands). Most of the multinationals are, in fact, companies which are based and owned in one country but which have branches in other countries; profits, unless reinvested, are repatriated to the home country. Even banks – which after all deal in that eminently transportable product, money – are usually still British or American banks which have branches in other countries, rather than being owned by stockholders in all the countries in which they have interests. Precisely because few giant firms are genuinely multinational, a number of authorities, including the United Nations agencies, are in favour of using a different term, the *transnational* corporation. Transnational corporations are corporations which derive a substantial part of their revenues by operating in more than one country. Even this definition leaves problems, however. The question of what proportion of its revenue a corporation should derive from more than one country in order to qualify as transnational can be debated, and there is no one correct answer. The usual figure chosen, perhaps arbitrarily, is 60 per cent. Again, it might be argued that a truly transnational company should operated in at least several countries. It might also be argued that whatever the terminological difficulties, in practice we all know the phenomenon that we are talking about; only the boundaries are in dispute.

Moreover, the term 'multinational' is so firmly established in popular usage that it seems futile to attempt to displace it.

Economic impact

Multinationals have been attacked frequently, and yet also (less frequently) praised. The lines of attack on multinationals are that they are too powerful and damaging to the economies of countries in which they operate and even the countries in which they originate. Their defenders argue that the multinationals can, in the spirit of Adam Smith's 'invisible hand', diffuse technologies around the world and contribute to development while seeking only to make a profit. We shall begin with the case against the multinationals.

The very size of multinationals which we have mentioned above is not in itself proof of their power. Some connection has to be shown between their undoubtedly considerable financial resources and their ability to reach their goals in dealings with governments for us to say that they have power. A variety of such linkages have been suggested.

The most obvious is that the international structure of the multinational makes it extremely easy for it to redistribute resources. A major oil company will at any time be holding the currencies of numerous countries, as it both makes payments to host governments for the crude oil it extracts and receives, further down the line, payments from consumers. In between, the company may be making payments of an oil tanker bought in South Korea and drilling platforms built in Britain. The shrewd company treasurer not only can, but should, play the currency markets to the advantage of his or her firm. If there are rumours that the British pound will decline in value, it is only prudent for the company to delay transferring money currently held in, say, US dollars to Britain, as the price of our imaginary drilling platform will be less once the pound has fallen against the dollar. Without any particular wish to exert pressure on the British government, the multinational may thus have contributed to its problems. As left-wing governments are more likely than right-wing governments to favour policies which will arouse unease in the international currency markets (which British or French socialist government has not faced a run on its currency?), politicians may be excused for feeling less than reassured by arguments that multinationals are simply behaving rationally in timing their currency movements to their best advantage.

In the last analysis, of course, multinationals cannot delay indefinitely their currency movements. Perhaps more serious in the long term for countries in which they operate is that multinationals embody to the highest degree the privileged position of business that Lindblom described. In an extreme case, a multinational may actually decide that the policies of a country, or the strength of its unions, are such that the multinational will pull out, closing or selling its plants. More likely is the possibility that a multinational will more gradually reposition itself, concentrating investment in countries which provide the most congenial policies, lowest wages or highest productivity. The Ford Motor Company, for example, has manufacturing capacity in the USA, Canada, Britain, Belgium, West Germany and Spain, amongst other countries. Such a spread of manufacturing capacity enables the multinational to respond to purely economic or commercial considerations, or to exert very obvious and direct pressure on a host government for changes in policy to its advantage. A somewhat crude example involved the Chrysler Corporation, which in addition to the subsidies it obtained from the US government received major payments from the British government in return for keeping open the company's plants in Britain. The British government, fearing that closure of the plants would add to rising unemployment, felt that it had no option but to pay up. Ironically, a few years later the Chrysler Corporation sold its plants in Britain to the French company, Peugeot. Less crude (and perhaps less precise) pressures on politicians help to account for decisions such as the rapid shelving of proposals during the 1974–79 Labour Government for a measure of worker participation lest Britain be thought an even less desirable place to invest than it was already.

The ability of multinationals to relocate should not be exaggerated. It so happens that the majority of the known oil reserves in the world are in the Middle East and the Middle

East's reserves are unusually easy and cheap to extract. Although Alaska and the North Sea may be more attractive politically, they are not as easy environments in which to operate in terms of the engineering required. The copper reserves of Chile operated by Kennecott cannot be moved outside the country; the diamond or gold mines of South Africa have no counterparts which can be developed as easily outside the Soviet Union. Multinationals, particularly in the extractive industries, must often grin and bear conditions which they dislike because, until alternatives are developed, no substitutes are available. The oil industry is perhaps the most interesting to watch in this respect. For obvious reasons – including the tendency of more radical Arab governments to impose more onerous conditions and taxes on multinationals – the oil companies have been prepared to develop other sources of supply. Their ability to move towards production in politically safer environments is limited by the differential costs of production. It has been argued, however, that the oil companies' greatest problems arise when they wish to operate in politically unstable regions where no régime lasts long enough for them to make a lasting deal. Such problems may have prevented serious explorations of possible oil reserves in Africa, and suggests that one of the greatest gains for multinationals from the colonial era may have been the stability of colonial régimes.

The abilities to move funds and redirect investment are not the only powers enjoyed by multinationals. One of the crucial resources enjoyed by multinationals is *knowledge*. The multinational companies often do not bring the majority of the capital needed to a branch they create in a country; the majority of funds may well be raised locally. The major contribution of the multinational to the local enterprise may be knowledge, knowledge that may range from the secret formula for making Coca Cola to life-saving drugs. The oil companies again provide an example. The 'Seven Sisters', the giant firms that dominate the oil industry, have been able to survive the more radical countries because they have more knowledge or skills, at their disposal in oil extraction than could be readily available to the governments themselves. It has been quite common for oil companies to see their assets nationalised only to be immediately re-employed by the nationalising government as its agent, receiving a commission on the oil extracted and sold instead of a profit. Oil companies are also more experienced and better placed to organise the raising of investment funds than are many governments, which have in some cases vowed to drive them out of their countries. When exploration and development of the British North Sea oil fields began, the British government of the day, while giving some of the reserves to a government-owned corporation, was delighted by the positive impact on the British balance of payments of the movement into Britain by the multinational oil companies of funds to finance development. This ability to raise finances may again provide a powerful inducement for governments to make a deal with a multinational they publicly attack. Governments as far apart as Norway and Bahrain have for such reasons entrusted most of the development of their reserves to multinationals.

The powers of the multinationals which we have described so far are considerable, and yet might be said to be the inevitable consequence of the existence of multinational firms. The executives of multinational companies could not ignore factors such as government policies in making investment decisions without what might be seen as quite scandalous disregard for the interests of their shareholders. More controversial, however, is the question of the extent to which multinationals engage in what might be widely regarded as illicit interference in the politics of the countries in which they operate. Obviously no one could object to a multinational joining the trade associations and the employers' organisation of a country in which it operates. There is no reason why the Ford Motor Company in Britain should be barred from joining the CBI. Yet there are a number of disturbing examples, from Europe as well as Africa and Asia, of multinationals exerting political pressure which crosses the boundaries of acceptability. Lockheed paid bribes around the world and, even worse, multinationals operating in Chile used a wide variety of weapons to attack the constitutionally elected, if minority, government of Salvador Allende. Money was given to Opposition parties, an economic blockade of Chile was organised, and multinationals urged both domestic dissidents and the government of the USA to assassinate or overthrow Allende.[1]

The activities of multinationals in Chile remind us of a further point. We noted earlier that the term 'multinational' could be misleading because most firms are firmly based in one country. The government of that parent country will be asked to assist in cases in which the interests of the multinational are attacked. The American multinationals operating in Chile soon asked the American government to unleash the Central Intelligence Agency (CIA) against the Allende government once that government's threat to expropriate their assets, in return for what they regarded as inadequate compensation, became clear. The American government tightened the screws on Chile by using its influence in international financial institutions to block loans; the CIA, which had long been the primary source of funds for the pro-business parties in Chile, encouraged plots against the government – on one occasion supplying revolvers for an abortive assassination attempt on General Schneider, the Chief of Staff, whose attachment to constitutional government was a major barrier to the military coup which ultimately occurred.[2]

The destruction of constitutional government in Chile, brought about by internal as well as external forces, is a particularly painful example of intervention. It is not, unfortunately, unique. The government in Guatemala was also overthrown with considerable American help, in part because it was a threat to the interests of United Fruit which has large investments there. One is reminded of the comment of US Marine General Smedley D. Butler in 1931 as he looked back on his career:

I helped make Mexico safe for American oil interests in 1914. I helped make Haiti and Cuba a decent place for the National City Bank boys to collect revenues in. I helped purify Nicaragua for the International banking house of Brown Brothers . . . I made Honduras 'right' for American fruit companies. Looking back on it, I might have given Al Capone a few hints.[3]

It is a great advantage for multinationals that, though they may invoke the assistance of the government of the parent country, they may also keep their distance from it. Firms which are thought to be domestically owned stir up less nationalist resentment. Really powerful firms such as the oil companies may prefer to rely upon their technical and financial power rather than the military or domestic pressure of 'their' government in dealings with countries in which they wish to operate. It is certainly the case that multinationals are often devoid of feelings of loyalty to the home country. When British Prime Minister Edward Heath told the head of British Petroleum (BP) during the first oil crisis (1973) that he was counting on BP to make supplying Britain its first priority, he was told to think again. Both BP and Shell, in spite of their British connections, were active in supplying the rebel régime in what was then Rhodesia with oil, thus undermining the sanctions which British government were trying to impose upon Rhodesia. This is given added irony by the fact that BP was a company in which the government had a major – almost a majority – shareholding.

Multinationals and the Third World

Particular concern has been expressed about the relationship between multinationals and Third World countries. The term 'Third World' is, of course, ambiguous and broad. Countries such as Argentina certainly resent being bracketed with Chad, and whether there are worthwhile analogies to be drawn between Latin American and African countries may indeed be doubted. Yet a number of common problems do arise for the less-developed countries in dealing with multinationals which exacerbate the criticisms of multinationals which we have encountered. Less-developed countries are likely to be particularly short of capital, and by definition desperately in need of generating employment and economic growth. Such countries are therefore even less able to bargain successfully with multinational companies than are the developed countries. Developing countries are also less able to use the normal government weapons to restrain their power. Few developing countries have a civil service of sufficient size and skill to monitor the activities of multinationals, or to impose the environmental or safety standards which would be regarded as essential in developed countries. The dreadful disaster in Bhopal, India, following the escape of poisonous gas from a Union Carbide Factory in the town demonstrated vividly the tolerance of lower safety standards in the Third World. Local cultures in many less-developed countries and poor pay for officials or lack of accountability for leaders combine to make bribery endemic, a practice which multinationals can follow without financial embarrassment.

The host government may thus be totally incapable or unwilling to control the activities of multinationals. Even an honest government in a less-developed country may suffer from a chronic inability to collect information, except such information as the multinational chooses to give it. Efforts to tax multinationals have been impeded by their ability to transfer goods at unrealistic prices between branches in different countries so as to minimise tax – a practice that the civil service of a very advanced country would have difficulty checking. An extremely high 'price' may be paid by a subsidiary to a parent company for machinery or a process supplied by it, thus reducing the taxable profits of the subsidiary. Alternatively, goods from the subsidiary may be sold at an inflated price to the parent company in order to minimise its taxable earnings. Both strategies may be combined by using as an intermediary a third branch of the company located in a country such as Panama with low corporate taxation, the subsidiary buying and selling from other branches of the multinational at artificial prices. Such manipulations, beyond the capacity of most Third World civil services to check, may make meaningless the profit figures declared by a multinational.

A further criticism of multinationals, all the more important for involving no allegation of conspiracy or malevolence, is that they distort the development of Third World countries. Such criticisms focus on allegations that multinationals deploy inappropriate technology in the Third World. Third World countries generally have a chronic over-supply of labour. If multinationals deploy technologies in the Third World which are capital-intensive but which use little labour, they are bringing to the Third World country a technology which is inappropriate to its needs. Developing a new, more labour-intensive technology may be uncongenial or unprofitable for the multinational; moreover, the multinational's workers, and particularly its manager, may come to be not only a commercial but a social intrusion into the life of the country. The Western-trained and Western-oriented élite fostered by the multinational will look to the advanced countries when they are looking for a home for their savings, for luxury goods, or for a university to which to send their children. All of these practices may have a most deleterious effect on the usually precarious balance of payments of the developing country, and contribute to its usual chronic shortage of foreign exchange. Multinationals, in short, may act as agents to spread 'dependency' upon developed countries.

Finally, multinationals are criticised for remitting profits from developing countries to the home country. Countries already short of capital must thus endure a further flow back to the developed world. Ironically, multinationals will be criticised in the developed world for exporting capital and jobs to the Third World, slowing growth and reducing the number of jobs in the home country. Thus no one may be satisfied.

The Case for Multinationals

So far we have considered only the case for the prosecution against multinationals. Naturally, the multinationals think that much can be said on their behalf.

As their critics have contended, multinationals can be instruments of technological diffusion. Certainly such technological diffusion may be conducted in a manner not conducive to the interests of the recipient country, but it is easy to make a contrary argument. It is not good economic sense for a multinational to substitute capital for labour if suitable labour is available. Company profits, as well as the recipient country, would suffer. Nor is it obvious that critics of the multinationals would be satisfied if they restricted the Third World to simple technologies. It is noticeable that India, to the despair of many international advisory bodies, has been determined to conduct advanced research on atomic power and space programmes rather than concentrating exclusively on schemes which would have a high demand for manpower. Moreover, it is by no means proven that multinationals do impose overly advanced technologies on Third World countries; practice almost certainly varies considerably from firm to firm. Theorising on the practices and consequences of multinationals runs far ahead of empirical research.

It might also be noted that, contrary to the arguments of the 'dependency' theorists, multinationals have not been a complete barrier to development in the past. Much of Sweden's economic development was carried out earlier this century by multinationals; Canada combines a high standard of living with extensive domination of its economy by American firms, a domination which does indeed cause problems but which has not been crippling. One might doubt, too, whether the Latin American students and academics who flock to London or Paris are there because of the activities of a British or French multinational.

Both critics and friends of multinationals have been forced to concede in recent years that the extent of the impact of multinationals on capital movements has been exaggerated. Multinationals have often argued that they fulfil a useful social purpose by distributing capital to the Third World. In practice, it seems that multinationals bring little capital into countries; most subsidiaries of multinationals are apparently created by organising capital, much of it local, rather than by bringing in *tranche* of funds from the parent company. Whether the repatriation of profits made with these funds is justified depends on one's point of view. Such profits can be termed surplus value in Marxist terminology, or rewards for entrepreneurship in more conventional economics.

Perhaps the most useful contribution made by multinationals is the one which could not be fulfilled by any democratically-elected government and is often wildly unpopular in the parent country. This is the function of transferring to developing countries the production of goods which require large quantities of low-cost labour. Low-cost labour is one commodity which less-developed countries possess in abundance. If developing countries are ever to progress economically, they must be allowed to capitalise on this 'natural advantage' by making textiles or assembling electrical equipment for sale in the more prosperous countries. Such an 'export' of jobs would not be tolerated willingly by elected governments, but can be arranged – barring effective protectionist measures – by multinationals. In the last analysis it may be, too, that the prospects for a developing country turn more on whether its local entrepreneurs and middle class have the character of the Korean, Taiwanese and Singapore, or whether they have the aversion to trade and commerce found in many Latin American countries.

It may also be that the significance of multinationals for the Third World has been exaggerated. Multinationals are largely a phenomenon of the developed world. In the years since the Second World War Europe, not the Third World continent, has been the favourite investment area for American multinationals, and European firms such as Volkswagen have been expanding into the USA. The activities of multinationals do indeed pose problems for the governments of developed countries, but those problems are more manageable for them than for their Third World hosts. Developed countries have stronger governments, better equipped with skilled bureaucracies than are Third World countries. Moreover, the exchange of multinationals which now characterises the relations between most of the developed world is less likely to result in exploitation than when a country is only a host for, not a source of, multinationals.

Multinationals themselves have changed in ways that might soften the criticisms of some their critics. At one time the term 'multinational' was often seen as a synonym for 'American'. Most multinational corporations were in fact American corporations with overseas subsidiaries. In fact, there had always been some conspicuous exceptions to this generalisation such as Nestlé, Unilever or Royal Dutch Shell. In recent decades, the 'exceptions' to the expectation that multinationals are in fact American corporations have increased. Japanese corporations such as Nissan, Toyota and Sony have opened plants in Britain. Most of the major Japanese car producers now have manufacturing plants in the United

States. Indeed, American politicians have started to express concern about the amount of foreign investment in the United States, investment that is in fact more likely to come from Britain or the Netherlands than from Japan. Thus American politicians have come to echo – in reverse – the concerns of French observers such as Jacques Servan Schreiber who worried in the later 1960s about *le défi américain*, the American challenge.

Even when multinationals remain in effect American-based corporations, there are signs that they are less likely to operate as American corporations. Multinationals with headquarters in the USA have been increasing rapidly their investment outside the home country. Many of the more advanced forms of manufacturing are conducted outside the USA, a reversal of the tradition of foreign subsidiaries sending their semi-finished or simpler products to plants in the home country for completion. Executives of multinationals based in the USA have claimed that in the next recession they will treat all their plants equally in deciding which to close down and not discriminate in favour of those in the USA. Were multi-nationals to keep this promise it would meet an important criticism of such corporations – that their foreign plants are the first to be closed down in a contraction. Again, however, not all American politicians are pleased by such a promise of impartiality from what they still see as 'their' corporations.[4]

One final development that made multinationals seem more desirable was the debt crisis. Following the 'oil shocks' of the 1970s, OPEC countries deposited large amounts of money in the United States and, to a lesser degree, Europe.[5] Although the advanced economies suffered from the large and sudden increase in the price of oil, the developing countries suffered even more. Their ability to pay the increased costs of fuel imports was minimal, was export earnings came from other primary commodities (e.g. coffee) for which demand was static and prices hard to change. In order to avoid a massive crisis in the Third World that might have caused a deep world wide recession, banks in the USA and Europe were encouraged to lend generously to Third World countries. American and European banks therefore received OPEC deposits and 'recycled' them into loans to the Third World and some Eastern-bloc nations, such as Poland. In practice, the loans were wasted. The loans were spent on ineffective projects, corruption, and the purchasing of the goodwill of the populace through short-term increases in living standards. Naturally, the borrowing countries were unable to repay their debts, threatening a collapse in the western banks that had made the loans throughout the 1980s. Sometimes, as happened with the Continental Illinois Bank, governments had to step in to rescue banks from collapse caused by these bad debts.

The 'debt crisis' of the 1980s cast the multinationals in a more favourable light. If loans were squandered by Third World countries themselves, then investment conducted by profit-seeking multinationals would be more effective. Multinationals were less likely to commit money to corruption, buying political favours or building prestige projects of dubious economic advantage. In brief, multinationals might do a better job of building economies than the countries in which they invested.

Controlling the Multinationals

It remains the case that multinationals are not susceptible to control by any one national government. Problems of control which overwhelm the governments of less-developed nations are not fully solved by developed countries. A country which sets it face against multinationals (as France did with American car firms in the 1960s) risks losing them to a neighbour, such as Belgium, who exports their products to the resistant country. Japan excluded American car firms while developing its own car industry in the 1950s, but whether any country could follow suit in the liberalised trade atmosphere of the 1980s may be doubted. Even Japan is under heavy pressure to allow in not only foreign goods but also foreign capital as it liberalises its restrictions.

Organisations linking nations offer some prospect of increasing controls over the multinationals. One of the most exciting developments as Europe entered the 1990s was the commitment by the members of the European Community to secure a truly integrated European market by 1992. This move was designed to rescue the European Community from the condition referred to as 'eurosclerosis', the alleged tendency of the welfare states of the Community to grow less rapidly than the USA. The total abolition of tariffs within the Community had long since been achieved. But, it was argued, the differences in regulations, law and practices in areas such as government contracting had prevented the merger of the economies of the twelve member nations into a single economic unit. Achieving a single market throughout the European Community would offer corporations from the member states a domestic economy larger and wealthier than any in the world, including the USA. At the same time, the increase in 'domestic' competition would encourage corporations within the Community to increase investment, productivity and competitiveness, thus curing 'eurosclerosis'.

'1992', as the creation of a single market is referred to, has profound implications for the European political economy. The attempt to secure truly equal competition between corporations from member nations has involved a vast harmonisation of company law. The incomplete process of harmonisation raises acute questions about whether corporations will see their powers reduced or increased. On the one hand, corporations in some countries might feel that their powers were threatened by moves to bring the rights of workers up to the levels prevailing in, for example, West Germany. The British Prime Minister, Mrs Thatcher, determinedly resisted moves to increase the rights of workers, a process called giving 1992 'a social dimension' by Jacques Delors, then President of the European Commission, as threatening to introduce socialism through the back door. Thatcher declared that she had not rolled back the frontiers of the state at the national level only to see them expanded at the European. Moreover, precisely because 1992 involves a strengthening of supranational power, the ability of corporations to play off one nation state in the Community against another in the quest for special treatment would be reduced as Community controls over subsidies by member states increase.

In another respect, however, 1992 offered corporations tremendous advantages in dealing with governments and workers. 1992 will not create a nation state, let alone a centralised nation state. Major areas of public policy affecting business have been left in the hands of nation governments. Thus levels of welfare, retirement and unemployment benefits, together with the levels of taxation needed to support such policies, have been left to the governments of the nation states. Further, member nations of the Community have been obliged to extend mutual recognition to the company law or regulations imposed on corporations in their home nation. In practice these provisions will encourage corporations to move to or invest in member countries within the European Community with the least onerous policies. Thus Volkswagen will be tempted to escape the high wages, taxes and generous welfare state of West Germany by investing in Spain or Portugal. Japanese auto companies will be attracted to Britain with its comparatively low wages and less generous welfare state than in many other member states of the Community. And, in a process referred to as 'becoming the Delaware of Europe', Luxembourg will attract corporations to make it their headquarters by regulating them much less strictly than most member nations. Landlocked Luxembourg will begin to be a centre for the European shipping companies.

The integration of the European market seems to offer the opportunity to control multinationals better. The fact that 1992 did not have much of the 'social dimension' sought by Delors and feared by Thatcher strengthened the position of corporations. Corporations could now shop around even more than before within the Community for a country that would treat them generously or the least onerously without losing access to the markets.

Conclusions

It would be idle to pretend that diversification of further development of regional blocks such as the European Community will solve all the problems of the multinationals' influence in world affairs. The threat to political control and autonomy becomes apparent when posed by the simple fact that the ten largest multinationals have turnovers in excess of the total GNPs of 80 nations. But multinationals are not in practice regarded as all bad; both the British Government and Labour MPs from areas where the factory might be located begged Nissan Motors of Japan to locate in Britain, strengthening its development into being a multinational. Indeed, it might well be that protectionist pressures will encourage more and more firms to become multinationals, setting up manufacturing plants inside trading blocks, such as the EC, which might erect barriers against them. If the multinational is to become more and more common, an increase in empirical research, perhaps at the expense of theorising, would be welcome. As Vernon argues,[6] generalisations about multinationals are dangerous. Different firms, different countries and even different government agencies create different situations. At the very moment that the CIA was operating on behalf of United Fruit in Guatemala, the Justice Department's Antitrust Division was trying to break up the company! Research on individual companies will not be easy; they are more secretive than governments. Yet the flow of accusation and counter-accusation discussed above can be avoided only by theoretically conscious research.[7]

10

Conclusions

If any one theme has emerged from the previous chapters it is that there is no single pattern to the relationship between business and politics in the countries we have surveyed. The major differences we have observed are in the degree to which links between business and government are organised and institutionalised into contacts between organisations representing employers, in particular industries or in general, and government. We have noted great differences in the degree to which employers band together forming united, cohesive organisations with high prestige among employers and in society in general. In particular, in some countries, governments have accepted and encouraged specific employers' organisations to be their partners in seeking economic growth or prosperity, while in other countries, employers' organisations have been mere interest groups whose views are politely received by government, but have been accorded no special status. The advanced, industrialised democracies covered in this book occupy different points on a spectrum that represents the degree to which there is a set of integrated, authoritative organisations representing employers in individual industries, or in the economy as a whole, that have been accepted as partners by government. The spectrum has ranged from the United States, where a number of different organisations claim to represent employers and trade associations representing specific industries have been accorded no great status, through Britain, West Germany, Italy, the necorporatist nations, France and Japan, where the employers are highly organised and accepted as partners by government.

Two questions which arise in this book are why organisations are better organised in some countries than in others, and why governments in some countries seek a closer relationship with those organisations than in others.

The most obvious explanation for why employers are better organised in some countries than in others is the degree to which employers are challenged. Unions and socialist movements have been the major single challenge. Strong union movements in Austria and Scandinavian countries are faced by strong employers' organisations. As Truman led us to expect, the more challenged an interest group is, the more likely it is to organise.[1] Britain fits this generalisation to a mixed degree. The CBI has been a body accorded significant prestige as a representative of manufacturing industry; however, trade associations have been comparatively under-developed in Britain and as we have seen, the CBI has also been unable to speak authoritatively for finance. In recent years, the CBI has been losing ground to the Institute of Directors, closer in its approach to the Thatcher government. In the United States, the challenge to employers from unions was never particularly strong, and has been fading since the 1950s so that currently only about 17 per cent of the work force is unionised. However, challenges to what employers perceived to be their interests by public interest groups in the late 1960s and early 1970s did indeed produce a marked increase in political activity by business. The growth in business PACs, the business lobby in Washington and the formation of the Business Roundtable all testified to the growth of corporate political activism. Admittedly the American business community remained fragmented so that there was still no single body that spoke for general business interests and trade associations retained only modest significance. However, as Truman would have predicted, increased political challenge to business had indeed produced more political activity by business.

A number of countries, at least at first sight, seem to contradict the generalisation that challenges to business encourage the development of business organisations. West Germany, Japan, Italy and France might all be ranked highly in terms of having authoritative, well established employers' organisations. The BDI in West Germany, the Keidanren in Japan, Confindustria in Italy and the Patronat in France are all weighty organisations. Yet all are countries in which unions are either of modest strength (as in West Germany) or strikingly weak in terms of the proportion of the work force they recruit. It can be argued that appearances are illusory or that past history, rather than the current situation, is important in shaping interest group systems. In both France and Italy, the strength of militant unionism can surge while permanent union membership lags. For example, 1968 witnessed what by international standards was great turmoil in Italian and French industrial relations even though union membership on paper was comparatively low. Japanese labour relations, regarded today as a model of stability, were disturbed and even violent in the late 1940s. It can also be argued that the degree of challenge capitalism has faced historically in Italy, France and even Germany from socialist or Communist movements rather than unions has been high, and sufficient to prompt employers to develop habits of organising. Yet it would be misleading to suggest that a simple model of challenge leading to business response is adequate. Challenges to business do indeed help to explain the development of business organisations, but other factors are undoubtedly at work.

The character of the state in which business groups are implanted is of considerable significance. The state shapes the character of business groups in a variety of ways. First, the state to some degree structures all groups in society through laws and legal customs. In the Anglo-American tradition, organisations are allowed unless forbidden by the state for specific reasons (e.g. criminal law). According to Stepan,[2] in countries with Roman law traditions, the assumption is that organisations need permission or licensing from the state in order to have legitimacy, a practice more likely to result in the establishment of authoritative and monopolistic groups than the *laissez-faire* Anglo-American approach. States are also arenas in which interests such as business contend for power. As we have argued earlier, the character of the state as a political arena helps shape the character of interest groups including business operating within it. The more fragmented the state, the easier it is for numerous interest groups to exist and maintain a degree of influence. The more cohesive the state, the more it is able to require interest groups to coalesce in order to aggregate their demands before presenting them to the government for decision. It is significant that the country we have examined that has the most fragmented system of government, the United States, is the country that also has the most fragmented interest group system. Finally, states as actors have sought out interest groups to serve as aids or partners in economic development. Business and other interest groups not only supply government with advice and information but share in the difficulties and costs of governance. This tendency, as we shall discuss, has been at its strongest in Japan and France. The more state authorities intervene actively in an economy to promote economic growth, the more need they are likely to have of interest groups to help them. The more state authorities need interest group help, the more likely they are to build up the authority of interest groups through techniques as varied as supplying cash subsidies (as in France) or restricting access to the favoured group (as in Japan). In short, the more economically activist is a government, the more it will build up interest groups to help it.

Two other factors either facilitating or inhibiting interest group development are the political culture and economic structure of a nation. To some degree, we have touched indirectly on this factor above. Countries in which capitalism is most deeply entrenched and respected have been countries in which challenges to employers are unusually weak; in consequence, there have been fewer incentives for employers to unite to defend collective interests. Yet in no country has business been unchallenged. Thus it has been common to cite the United States as the example of the country in which capitalism is unquestioned as a system. Yet capitalists have not in consequence escaped challenge or scrutiny. In practice, employers in the United States have experienced more severe confrontations with regulatory agencies charged with defending the environment or safety and health than have their counterparts in countries such as Sweden or Britain in which capitalism is more questioned in theory. It was perhaps true that employers in the USA had little need to be politically active in the 1950s; now they have.

Political culture exerts another influence, however. The degree to which what Beer called in the British context 'functional representation'[3] is accepted varies from country to country. The extreme cases of acceptance of functional representation are of course the neo-corporatist countries. It is widely accepted in Austria that the leaders of the unions and employers' organisations should have more opportunity to influence the conduct of economic policy than the vast majority of elected politicians. Such a view would not be entirely accepted in Britain itself, in spite of the fact that, as Beer noted, functional representation was an important component in the British political system and culture. Many Britons were deeply concerned when commentators in the 1970s told them that government was paying more attention to the views of major economic interest groups than to the views of MPs. In Norway or Austria such concerns would have been seen as irrational; partnership between government and the major economic groups is merely a fact of life, a process that enables better policy to be made and ensures social harmony. Representation through major economic groups was an effective and legitimate means for the representation of the individual citizen.

The British are in this, as in so much else, a halfway house between the USA and Europe. If the British are uneasy and uncertain about functional representation, Americans are unambiguously hostile. The very idea that the major economic interests could exert great influence on policy behind closed doors – greater influence than a member of Congress – would be cause for deep concern. 'Big unions' and 'big business' are targets of popular criticism, not bases of representation.

Economic Structure

We might suppose that the greater the degree of industrial concentration, the easier employers will find it to unite to protect their common interests. If there are only a handful of major corporations dominating the economy, as in Sweden or as used to be the case in Italy, then it may be easier to organise an employers' interest group than in an economy in which industrial concentration is less. As Olson argued, the more numerous the potential members of an interest group, the harder it is for them to be sure that everyone will follow their example and pay the costs of joining the interest group.

At first sight, this seems a plausible view. The less concentrated, more competitive character of the American economy might be seen as a reason for the slow and limited development of its employers' associations. In contrast, the more highly-concentrated economies such as Britain or Japan do indeed seem to have stronger employers' organisations. Yet the consequences of industrial concentration are more problematic than this suggests. The presence of very large firms may actually impede the creation of strong, authoritative employers' organisations, precisely because the large firm has the resources to make contact with the government and to engage in lobbying itself. It is the smaller firm that needs the services of the employers' organisation. Dominant firms such as ICI have indeed been seen as one factor in Britain limiting the authority of trade associations, they are large enough to talk directly to government.

A less obvious factor of some importance is the relationship between the *financial* institutions and *manufacturing* companies of a country. If, as in Britain, the two sectors are distinct, it will be difficult to create an organisation which will speak for both. British banks have in fact kept their distance from manufacturing companies, and from the interest groups such as the CBI which represent them. Indeed, the separation of financial and manufacturing interests in Britain has been a major constraint on the political power – as well as commercial success – of manufacturing companies.

The absence of financial companies from the CBI weakened its authority, while the separate interests of the financial institutions were often more influential than the views of manufacturing industry. Partly in consequence, British governments have usually followed policies (such as on the exchange rate) which were much more advantageous to financial institutions than to manufacturers.

Three further economic factors have a considerable impact on the business–government relationship. The first is the degree to which an economy is involved in *international trade*. In economies which are extensively involved in international trade the capacity of governments to plan the economy is reduced. As the French and Japanese examples indicate, as economies become more involved in foreign trade, governments become less able to influence economic development, for both customers and suppliers are beyond their jurisdiction. It is striking that as the French economy became less self-contained and more involved in trade, the Five-year Plans, so much a feature of post-war France, became less and less meaningful. Similarly, the internationalising of the Japanese economy (or at least sales of Japanese goods) has diminished the leadership role of the Ministry of International Trade and Industry (MITI). Moreover, the need to achieve in the long term equilibrium in the balance of payments will make even a left-wing government attentive to the needs of major exporters or producers of import substitutes. Both the Mitterrand Government in France and successive Labour Governments in Britain have been driven in part by such exigencies to listen very carefully to business.

A further economic factor of some significance is the degree to which government itself is the major *customer* of business.[4] This is not quite the same as the question more commonly posed of the percentage of GNP to which government expenditures are equivalent. It is quite possible for a government's budget to be equivalent to a high percentage of the GNP without the government itself being the major customer. Transfer payments such as social security or old age pensions may simply shift money from one set of citizens to another, with government merely acting as the intermediary. On the other hand, government can also be a major customer, purchasing a high proportion of the output of the defence, aircraft and construction industries for its own use. To the degree that government itself is a major final consumer, individual firms will be 'politicised', realising that lobbying and political pressure are an inherent part of the company's life. Even while the organisations to defend the collective interests of American business were weak in the 1950s, individual firms seeking defence contracts were used to wage vigorous, often highly-visible contests for a contract to build a war plane. Defence contractors were aware that politics could be as important as design in winning a contract.

The final, and arguably most important, economic factor influencing the nature of business–government relations is the degree to which government engages in *economic planning*. If a country generally operates incomes policies, its government will have a compelling need to consult authoritative representatives of both unions and employers on the drafting and implementation of that policy. If governments decide that the economic performance of their economies would be improved by indicative planning, they will also need to strengthen the mechanisms for consulting employers. Planning also involves constant detailed dialogue between government and employers (and as in Austria or Sweden where they are strong enough, unions). Participation in planning will also change the skills needed by an employers' organisation; political skills will be less important than technocratic skills such as economic analysis and forecasting. Planning thus encourages employers' organisations to shift the balance in their staffs towards more technocratic personnel as dealings between the government and employers' organisation increasingly take the form of a constant dialogue in which pressure, lobbying or campaigning seem either irrelevant, or weapons to be used only as a last resort.

Electoral Politics

The tendency in comparative politics in recent years has been to emphasise the importance of actors such as interest groups, corporations and the bureaucracy at the expense of more obviously political actors such as political parties.

It is striking that corporations make no such mistake. In every country covered in this survey, business has a special relationship with one particular political party. Yet in no country is there simply a 'business party'. There are at least two reasons for this. First, the parties most sympathetic to business, like most political parties, are coalitions. Business dominates the LDP in Japan, but the party also pays attention to farmers. Italian business has generally supported the CD, but the party contains more interests than just business. The Republican Party in the United States has tried to attract the support of groups such as the (now defunct) Moral Majority or 'right to life' groups as well as business executives. Although at times business may feel sufficiently slighted by 'its' party to take its support elsewhere – as has happened in Italy with Confindustria and the CD – the intelligent business executive realises that a party dominated solely by business would have little chance of electoral success. The success of the party more sympathetic to business is dependent on its ability to appeal either to a broader range of interests than just business or to pervasive values in society that are not commercial in origin and may indeed run counter to important business interests. The Christian Democratic parties of West Germany and Italy, for example, must appeal to Catholic traditions that can foster ideas critical of corporations. The Republican Party in the United States has usually based its political strategy in modern times on appeals to populist sentiments on 'social issues' that can be hostile to 'Wall Street' or major corporations.

For their part, corporations cannot afford to be too closely tied to parties that might one day lose power. Employers' organisations in Britain, Sweden and Germany adopt postures of technocratic non-partisanship, even while members regularly support a single party. The adaptation of business to political realities in the United States is particularly interesting, particularly as the conservative southern Democrats lose power within their party and are forced by the changing politics of the south to become less conservative, the Republican Party is ideologically attractive to most executives. However, the Democratic Party is almost invariably the party in control of Congress. Corporations therefore follow their hearts and support Republicans when there is an 'open seat' election (ie one in which no incumbent is seeking re-election) but are as likely to back a Democrat as a Republican when an incumbent is running. Corporations would rather buy access to powerful incumbents even if they are Democrats than pursue ideological goals by giving exclusively to Republicans. Perhaps the happiest situation for business is in Japan where the pro-business party is almost certain to constitute the government for the foreseeable future.

The 1980s witnessed an upsurge of support for market economies and societies; slogans such as 'popular capitalism' attracted a following in a surprising range of countries. The more conservative, pro-business party captured power in the United States, Britain and West Germany. Even in Scandinavia and Austria, more conservative parties enjoyed some success. In this context, pro-business parties were obliged to make fewer concessions to other viewpoints or interests than in the past. However, a different problem emerged. Pro-business parties in a number of countries took their pro-market ideologies sufficiently seriously that the consequences for corporations were not always pleasant. In Britain, Mrs Thatcher's tough monetary policies early in her Prime Ministership resulted in numerous bankruptcies and difficulties for major corporations. In the United States the 1986 Tax Reform Act resulted in a massive increase in taxes for corporations as a result of the abolition of tax allowances. In short, although the successes of more conservative parties in the 1980s indicated a more widespread acceptance of the legitimacy of markets and capitalism, in practice pro-business parties could still cause problems for the business community. Business control over the most sympathetic party is never total or, from the viewpoint of business executives, totally satisfactory.

State Intervention in the Economy

It was once traditional in Britain and the USA to depict business and politics as entirely separate spheres of life. Governments might 'interfere' with business through laws or regulations, or business might seek as an interest group to obtain a benefit or subsidy from government, but in principle government and business were separate activities. This way of picturing relations between business and government or the state was never entirely accurate. If one considers market economies, for example, the state still plays a major role. As

Morton Horwitz has described in the American context, judges had to reformulate the common law to rid it of pre-capitalist influences before market forces could operate fully.[5] Markets need the apparatus of the state to protect property, enforce agreements and secure the continuance of the social order.

In practice even states that have been portrayed as embodying free market practices have wandered from that path. The United States, for example, maintained high tariff barriers until the middle of this century and practised extensive regulation of a variety of industries. Although it has also been fashionable to portray Britain as a country instinctively attracted to the view that government should not be involved in detail in industry, most British governments since the 1930s have operated a variety of industrial policies that have cost billions of pounds. Even the Thatcher Government, more committed than any recent Conservative government to allowing market forces to operate, paid billions of pounds in subsidies to declining industries such as coal or loss-making state-owned firms such as Austin Rover. The government also operated a variety of policies to assist market forces through training programmes or grants to assist entrepreneurs start small businesses. The Reagan Administration in the United States, similarly committed to non-intervention in theory, in practice justified plans to spend billions of dollars on an obviously flawed defence programme, the Strategic Defense Initiative, in part by arguing that the programme would benefit high technology industries. In contrast, the Swedish Social Democrats have attempted to avoid close involvement with specific firms while providing generous grants to assist workers adjust to economic change.

Yet if in practice the roles of government in the economies of different nations are complicated, with exceptions existing to most generalisations, there are still important differences in approach. The fundamental differences that exist between the roles of government in the nations we have surveyed relate to contrasting visions of how to make modern capitalism work best. One approach is based on the belief that modern capitalism operates best when government attempts to influence the macroeconomic performance of the economy (through fiscal or monetary policy) while leaving market forces to determine the quantity and nature of production or investment by specific corporations or industries. The other approach assumes that market forces need to be supplemented by detailed government intervention.

As we noted above, no country in practice completely fits the 'ideal type' of reliance on market forces alone to steer specific industries. But it is still possible to make reasonably accurate generalisations. Britain and the United States have pursued policies less determinedly and systematically aimed at changing the behaviour of specific industries than have France and Japan. French planning and, more generally, French industrial policy, was based on specific views of which industries should contract, which should expand, and how these results should be achieved. In its days of glory, the Ministry of International Trade and Industry (MITI) provided similar guidance to Japanese industries. The other countries covered in this book fall somewhere in between these extremes, with West Germany closer to the British and American model, and the neocorporatist countries closer to France and Japan.

Why do countries differ in their attitudes to how much government should be involved in the detailed development of industry? One immediate answer is to say, as Dyson does, that different countries have different 'industrial cultures' i.e. expectations about what role government should play. But as Dyson recognises, we then have to explain why industrial cultures differ.[6] A number of factors are relevant. First, countries differ in their view in general of the role of the state. There is a long tradition in France of asserting (if only in theory) the legitimacy of the power of the state as the embodiment of the popular will or interest; there is a very long tradition in the United States of regarding the state as a threat to the life, liberty and property of the individual. These general differences spill over into industrial and economic policy. Second, nations that have been economic laggards are generally tempted to ascribe a larger role to government than are nations that have industrialised early. Historically, Germany, Japan and France have not been content to wait for market forces alone to allow them to catch up with more advanced nations. Finally, states differ in the degree to which they are capable of playing a leadership role in the economy. Some, such as the United States, are themselves structured in too fragmented a way to allow them to play a coherent role in steering the economy. In Britain the bureaucracy was ill-suited by education, training and tradition to playing the leadership role that the French bureaucracy fulfilled. Some states – again the United States would serve as an example – are too easily swayed from coherent policies by geographically concentrated interests to follow an industrial policy effectively. In other countries, such as Japan, political pressures can be absorbed or deflected by the alliance of the bureaucracy and the permanent ruling party, the LDP.

It might be wise for some nations to recognise that they do not have, and are unlikely to acquire, capacities for pursuing effective industrial policies. In practice, the economic successes of some of the conspicuous practitioners of active industrial policy, notably Japan and France, has naturally encouraged many to try to emulate their policies. Even in the United States, where any attempt to run a detailed industrial policy would surely founder on the power of the Congress and the necessarily parochial interests of legislators, there have been passionate advocates of a federal industrial policy. In practice, arguments that one nation should borrow policy techniques from another run into shoals of unanswerable and hypothetical questions. We do not know how much of the superior performance of France compared to Britain since the Second World War is attributable to French industrial policy. We can only estimate what the consequences might have been of adopting French indicative planning in a very different political economy.

Yet there have been very definite trends in intellectual opinion in what constitutes in general the best type of industrial policy. During the 1960s and 1970s, the predominant approach in academic circles was based on the belief that the more-administered type of capitalism in which government interacted closely with firms or industries produced better results than leaving matters at the microeconomic level to market forces. Shonfield[7] asserted that belief in indicative planning would conquer economic thinking. Schmitter argued that neocorporatist systems coped better with economic difficulties than other nations.[8] Chalmers Johnson celebrated the leadership role of MITI in the Japanese success story.[9]

Whether or not the intellectual tide turned fully in academic circles, i.e. that sphere of intellectual life which has a direct impact on practical thinking about public policy, the tide certainly did turn. While few might have wished to assert as simply as former President Reagan that 'Government isn't the answer, it's the problem', the sentiment was more widely accepted than in the past. Three major factors have weakened faith in the capacities of governments to promote growth through detailed intervention. First, the track records of some governments in identifying prospective future success have been poor. However far-sighted MITI might have been, a long list of commercial decisions by British governments on topics such as supersonic airliners or atomic electricity generating plants have been ill advised. In contrast to the low opinions of its performance in the 1970s, the less-guided economy of the United States seemed to show a capacity for adaptation and growth in the 1980s much admired by Europeans. Experience seemed to show that, contrary to the opinions of many intellectuals, governments could err and market forces succeed.

Second, the fears of government 'overload'[10] in the 1970s highlighted the danger that the more governments do, the more they will be controlled by interest groups. Wide-ranging industrial or regional policies require governments to make decisions on issues on which they will be politically vulnerable to pressure from interest groups or regions with a major vested interest. Governments protect themselves from interest group influence by doing less, emphasising policy techniques such as monetarism where their capacity for control is greatest and their knowledge of the general public lowest.

Third, the internationalisation of all major economies has reduced the degree to which governments can follow policies requiring detailed economic intervention. International agreements such as GATT bar policy techniques that were central to MITI's strategy in the 1950s. More importantly, when foreign consumers have a crucial impact on the state of an economy because exports are a major component in demand, or when foreign investment is much desired, it is impossible for governments to exert as much control over their economies as before. Crucial economic actors lie outside the sovereignty of the government. Significantly, planners in both Japan and France have become steadily more modest about their ability to shape their economies as the involvement of the two countries in the world economy has deepened.

These objections do not invalidate the case for industrial policy. If some countries operate industrial policies, those that do not face major problems. For in an age in which technological change and the diffusion of that change are so rapid that no country can enjoy technological superiority for long in a particular product area, the prize will go to that country which can adapt to new technologies and demands the fastest. There is no guarantee that nations relying on market forces to signal change will adapt the fastest. By the time entrepreneurs have noticed a trend, borrowed money to meet it and moved into production, they may find that a foreign rival, aided by his or her government and government-guided banks, has already become established in the field. Bureaucracies, as is well known, can be very slow to change. But state-guided economic systems, moving resources fast to reinforce market trends, may adapt more speedily to change than systems guided by market forces alone. It is still an open question, therefore, whether state-guided or more purely market-guided systems will operate best in the world economy of the 1990s.

Apart from debates about their relative performance, state-guided systems face another problem. States that wish to follow interventionist economic policies generally prefer to do so in partnership with economic interest groups. Until recently it had seemed reasonable to assume that the general trend in capitalist democracies would be towards the strengthening of economic interest groups. The increasing influence of politics and government on business through regulation, and trade, fiscal and monetary policies would compel business to strengthen its political representation. Stronger business interest groups would be created in recognition of the fact that this is an age of politicised business.

In practice, as we have seen, though there is a trend for business to be more politically active, this trend does not necessarily result in stronger economic interest groups. This is seen most clearly in the United States. Business has become much more politically active, but that activity is carried on at the level of the individual corporation rather than at the level of the Chamber of Commerce or Business Roundtable. In Britain, too, individual corporations have been developing lobbying capacities in London and employing contract lobbyists while the CBI has been declining in power. We also noted the decline in the status of Confindustria in Italy since the 1950s. To some degree, these may be temporary trends. Right-wing governments in the USA and Britain raised issues that divided business (such as tax reform), rather than uniting business (such as stricter environmental regulation). Issues that divide business tend to immobilise trade associations or general employers' organisations as the organisations fear losing members offended by their policy stands. In consequence, there is more scope and need for political activity by the individual corporation. A return to issues prominent in the 1970s such as environmental or safety regulation might tend to reunite business and strengthen its collective interest groups. The election of more left-wing governments would produce similar results. Yet not all industries are equally concerned about pollution controls: even these threats might fail to unite business.

The longer-term problem for business interest groups might be that business is affected by the class decomposition that we noted threatened union federations in neocorporatist systems. Just as members of labour unions might be more likely today than in the past to focus on their interests as workers in a particular industry or corporation than their collective interests, so might their employers. Policies such as monetarism or trade protection affect corporations very differently. Business managers in the age of the leveraged buyout have little incentive to pose as statesmen devoting energy to protecting the general interests of employers that could have been used to increase dividends or stock prices. Business, like labour, might find that it is harder than in the past to mobilise behind collective interests.

If class decomposition does affect employers as well as labour, the more-interventionist states will be faced with a problem. Although states, as we have noted, can reinforce interest groups and increase their status, they may still be unable to counteract long term forces leading to their decline. Current trends in capitalism might well be diminishing the standing of those business organisations that have been the partners of more-interventionist states.

Business and Normative Theory

Until the 1970s, the majority of the very few political scientists interested in business and politics were concerned with the question of how powerful business is, and how its power contrasts with other interest groups. That normative concern attracts little attention today. In a sense, both liberal and conservative writers on business and politics recently have been concerned primarily with a debate over the most appropriate way to reinforce business; the right has argued for reducing tax and regulatory 'burdens' on business while the left has argued for a formalised business–government partnership in pursuit of an industrial policy.

It is easy to see what might have encouraged such a trend. The oil shocks of the 1970s, the world recession of the early 1980s and local factors such as increased awareness in Britain of the comparative economic decline that afflicted the country until the 1980s, all made more vivid the problem of how current living standards were to be maintained or improved. One consequence in the late 1960s and early 1970s of the long economic boom since the Second World War and the optimism instilled by Keynesian economics was a belief that fundamental economic problems had been solved. The management of abundance rather than its creation was the problem facing societies in developed countries. The economic problems of the 1970s and 1980s made such optimism implausible and irrelevant. Even the richest nations looked into an abyss of economic stagnation or decline.

Awareness of the possibility of economic catastrophe had two contradictory effects on policy thought. The first, that proved to be temporary, was to encourage a minority that believed that capitalism was doomed anyway to argue for radical change; the left wings of the British Labour and French Socialist parties are good examples. The more common, and more lasting, impact was to encourage a concentration on practical measures that could be taken now to keep or attract employment. American states and British local governments, irrespective of the dominant party or ideology in their locality, rushed to offer corporations such as Nissan whatever help they could if the corporation would open a plant in their territory.

A second consequence of economic crisis was to remind us of the fact that to some degree business does represent a general interest. Whether or not we believe that profits or dividends are excessive, workers underpaid or consumers cheated, we all have an interest in the success of businesses in our locality or nation. The standard of living of most people in Britain advanced more slowly than in Europe in general between the Second World War and the mid 1980s because of the comparative failure of British industry. In consequence, even valued social services such as the National Health Service became less satisfactory than their equivalents in other European countries. This is not to deny that business raises severe ethical problems. Business is organised in a non-democratic manner, pollutes, encourages artificial demands through advertising and sometimes fails to supply goods or services of adequate quality. It was proved in the United States and many other democratic nations in the 1970s, that it was possible to assert values such as protection of the environment against business and win. In the 1980s, we were reminded of our dependence on the continued success and vitality of business.

Most normative theory has captured only partially the dual character of business as an interest group. On the one hand, theorists such as Lindblom[11] have indeed realised that business is not just another interest group but, because of control over investment decisions, has real power over communities that other interest groups lack. On the other hand, most normative theory has not captured the dependence of the basic interests of communities in the success of business

in order to protect their own interests. If we ask whether
business is too powerful or not, we recognise that the
maintenance of conditions in which business can succeed is
a general as well as a 'special' interest. We may wish
corporations to pollute less or injure fewer workers. Few of
us would pursue those policy goals so vigorously as to
bankrupt industry. In brief, just as our empirical thinking
about the power of business as an interest needs to be guided
by an awareness of its special characteristics and status, so our
normative thinking about whether business is too powerful or
not needs to be guided by an awareness of its dual role as a
social institution geared both to selfish and more general
interests.

Notes and References

1 Introduction

1. DTI, *The Department for Enterprise*, Command 278 (London: HMSO, 1988).
2. John Zysman, *Governments, Markets and Growth* (Ithaca: Cornell University Press, 1983).
3. Zysman, *Governments, Markets and Growth*; Chalmers Johnson, *MITI and the Japanese Economic Miracle, The Growth of Industrial Policy 1925–75* (Stanford: University of Stanford Press, 1982); Andrew Cox (ed) *The State, Finance and Industry* (Brighton: Wheatsheaf Books, 1986); Kenneth Dyson and Stephen Wilks (eds) *Industrial Crisis: A Comparative Study of the State and Industry* (Oxford: Martin Robinson, 1983); Stephen Wilks and Maurice Wright, *Comparative Government Industry Relations, Western Europe, the United States and Japan* (Oxford: Clarendon Press, 1987).
4. Robert B. Reich, *The Next American Frontier* (New York: Times Books, 1983); Robert B. Reich and John D. Donahue, *New Deals; The Chrysler Revival and the American System* (New York: Times Books, 1985).
5. Adam Yarmolinsky, *The Military Establishment* (New York: Harper Colophon, 1971); Paul A. C. Koistiner, *The Military Industrial Complex: An Historical Perspective* (New York: Praeger, 1980); Richard A. Stubbing, with Richard A. Mendel, *The Defense Game: An Insider Explores The Astonishing Realities of America's Defense Establishment* (New York: Harper and Row, 1986); Gordon Adams, *The Defense Game: The Politics of Defence Contracting; The Iron Triangle* (New York: Council on Economic Priorities, 1981).
6. Robert Engler, *The Policies of Oil, Private Power and Democratic Directions* (Chicago: University of Chicago Press, 1961); Peter Odell, *Oil and World Power* (Harmondsworth: Pelican Books, 1981); Robert Engler, *The Brotherhood of Oil* (Chicago: University of Chicago Press, 1977); Anthony Sampson, *The Seven Sisters: The Great Oil Companies and the World They Shaped* (New York: Viking Press, 1973).

7. Ralph Miliband, *The State in Capitalist Society* (London: Quartet Books, 1976); C. Wright Mills, *The Power Elite* (New York: Oxford University Press, 1956); Michael Useem, *The Inner Circle, Large Corporations and the Rise of Political Activity in the USA and the UK* (New York: Oxford University Press, 1984).

8. Elizabeth Drew, *Politics and Money: The New Road to Corruption* (New York: Macmillan, 1983); Amitai Etzioni, *Capital Corruption: The New Attack on American Democracy* (New York: Harcourt Brace Jovanovich, 1984).

9. Miliband, *The State in Capitalist Society*; Mills, *The Power Elite*.

10. Bob Jessop, *The Capitalist State, Theory and Methods* (New York: New York University Press, 1982).

11. James O'Connor, *The Fiscal Crisis of the State* (New York: St Martin's Press, 1971).

12. Theda Skocpol, 'Bringing the State Back In', in Peter Evans, Dietrich Rueschemeyer and Theda Skocpol (eds), *Bringing the State Back In* (Cambridge and New York: Cambridge University Press, 1985).

13. Robert Dahl, *Who Governs?* (New Haven: Yale University Press, 1961).

14. Peter Bachrach and Morton Baratz, 'The Two Faces of Power', *American Political Science Review*, 56 (1962) pp. 947–52.

15. Matthew Crenson, *The Unpolitics of Air Pollution, A Study of Non-Decisionmaking in American Cities* (Baltimore and London: Johns Hopkins University Press, 1971).

16. Steven Lukes, *Power, A Radical View* (London: Macmillan, 1974).

17. Charles E. Lindblom, *Politics and Markets, The World's Political Economic Systems* (New York: Basic Books, 1977).

18. Werner Sombart, *Why Is There No Socialism in the United States?* (re-issue) (London: Macmillan, 1976) (first published 1905).

19. Graham K. Wilson, *Interest Groups in the United States* (Oxford and New York: Clarendon Press, 1981); David Vogel, *Fluctuating Fortunes, The Political Power of Business in America* (New York: Basic Books, 1989).

20. Raymond Bauer, Ithiel de Sola Pool and Lewis Anthony Dexter, *American Business and Public Policy* (New York: Atherton Press, 1963).

21. Theodore Lowi, 'American Business, Public Policy Case Studies and Political Theory', *World Politics*, 16, no. 4 (July 1964) pp. 677–715.

22. Kenneth H. F. Dyson, 'The Cultural, Ideological and Structural Context', in Kenneth Dyson and Stephen Wilks (eds) *Industrial Crisis: A Comparative Study of the State and Industry* (Oxford: Martin Robertson, 1983). See also Stephen Wilks and Maurice Wright (eds), *Comparative Government Industry Relations*.

23. John Keeler, *The Politics of Neocorporatism in France* (Oxford and New York: Oxford University Press, 1987).

24. Wyn Grant and David Marsh, *The CBI* (London: Hodder and Stoughton, 1977).

25. Mancur Olson, *The Rise and Decline of Nations, Stagflation and Social Rigidities* (New Haven: Yale University Press, 1982).
26. Graham K. Wilson, 'Why is there no Corporatism in the United States?', in Gerhard Lehmbruch and Philippe Schmitter (eds) *Patterns of Corporatist Policymaking* (London and Beverly Hills: Sage, 1982); Robert Salisbury, 'Why No Corporatism in the United States?', in Philippe Schmitter and Gerhard Lehmbruch (eds), *Trends Toward Corporatist Intermediation* (London and Beverly Hills: Sage, 1979).
27. Philippe Schmitter, 'Still the Century of Corporatism?' *Review of Politics*, 36, No. 1 (January 1974) pp. 85–131.
28. Alan Cawson, *Organized Interests and the State* (London and Beverly Hills: Sage, 1985). See also Alan Cawson (ed) *Corporatism and Political Theory* (Oxford: Basil Blackwell, 1986).
29. Leo Panitch, *Social Democracy and Industrial Militancy* (Cambridge: Cambridge University Press, 1976).
30. Karel van Wolferen, *The Enigma of the Japanese State* (New York: Alfred Knopf, 1989).
31. For a critical analysis of regional differences, see Dan Clawson and Alan Neustadt, 'Interlocks, PACs and Corporate Conservativism', *American Journal of Sociology*, 94 (January 1989) pp. 749–73).
32. Johnson, *MITI and the Japanese Miracle*.
33. See, for example, James Q. Wilson's introduction to Steven Kelman, *Regulating America, Regulating Sweden, A Comparative Study of Occupational Safety and Health Policy* (Cambridge Mass.: MIT Press, 1981).

2   Business and Politics in the USA

1. *Public Opinion*, June–July, 1980.
2. Andrew Shonfield, *Modern Capitalism: The Changing Balance of Public and Private Power* (Oxford: Oxford University Press, 1969).
3. Anthony King, 'Ideas, Institutions and the Policies of Governments', *British Journal of Political Science*, 3 (July 1973) pp. 291–313.
4. Louis Hartz, *The Liberal Tradition in America* (New York: Harcourt, Brace and World, 1955).
5. Seymour Martin Lipset, 'Why No Socialism in the United States?', in Seweryn Bialer and Sophia Sluzar (eds) *Sources of Contemporary Radicalism*, Vol. 1, pp. 291–313.
6. For a short history see Graham K. Wilson, *Unions in American National Politics* (London: Macmillan, 1979).
7. *Public Opinion*, June–July, 1980; Thomas Ferguson and Joel Rogers (eds) *Right Turn: The Decline of the Democrats and the Future of American Politics* (New York: Hill and Wang, 1986).

8. James Q. Wilson (ed) *The Politics of Regulation* (New York: Basic Books, 1983); Steven Kelman, *Regulating America, Regulating Sweden, A Comparative Study of Occupational Safety and Health Policy* (Cambridge Mass.: MIT Press, 1981); David Vogel, *National Styles of Regulation* (Ithaca: Cornell University Press, 1986); Graham K. Wilson, *The Politics of Occupational Safety and Health* (Oxford and New York: Clarendon Press, 1985).

9. Larry Sabato, *PAC Power: Inside the World of Political Action Committees* (New York: W. W. Norton, 1984).

10. Richard Gable, 'NAM; Influential Lobby or Kiss of Death?', *Journal of Politics*, 15, no. 2 (May 1953) pp. 254–73.

11. Raymond Bauer, Ithiel de Sola Pool and Lewis Anthony Dexter, *American Business and Public Policy* (New York: Atherton Press, 1963).

12. For amplification of this argument see Graham K. Wilson, *Interest Groups in the United States* and David Vogel, *Fluctuating Fortunes, The Political Power of Business in America* (New York: Basic Books, 1989).

13. A book by a British historian Paul Kennedy, *The Rise and Decline of Great Powers: Economic Change and Military Conflict from 1500 to 2000* (New York: Random House, 1987) attracted great attention because of the warnings of American decline.

14. I. M. Destler, *American Trade Politics, System Under Stress* (Institute for International Economics and the Twentieth Century Fund, 1986).

15. For a summary of the evidence, see Vogel, *Fluctuating Fortunes.*

16. Kay Lehman Schlozman and John Tierney, *Organized Interests and American Democracy* (New York: Harper and Row, 1986).

17. Vogel, *Fluctuating Fortunes.*

18. Shonfield, *Modern Capitalism.*

19. Marver Bernstein, *Regulating Business By Independent Commission* (Princeton, NJ: Princeton University Press, 1955).

20. Eugene Bardach and Robert Kagan, *Going By the Book, Unreasonableness in Protective Regulation* (Phildelphia: Temple University, 1981). See also James Q. Wilson (ed) *The Politics of Regulation*; Graham K. Wilson *The Politics of Safety and Health*; Steven Kelman, *Regulating America, Regulating Sweden.*

21. Charles E. Lindblom, *Politics and Markets.*

22. Peter K. Eisinger, *The Rise of the Entrepreneurial State; State and Local Economic Development Policy in the United States* (Madison: University of Wisconsin Press, 1988).

23. Tina Rosenberg, 'Why Tax Incentives Are a Bad Idea for the States', *New Republic*, 3 October 1983, pp. 18–21.

3 Government and Business in Britain

1. Martin Wiener, *English Culture and the Decline of the Industrial Spirit, 1850–1989* (Cambridge: Cambridge University Press, 1981).
2. Philippe Schmitter, 'Regime Stability and Systems of Interest Intermediation in Western Europe and North America', in Suzanne Berger (ed) *Organizing Interests in Western Europe* (Cambridge and New York: Cambridge University Press, 1981).
3. Dyson and Wilks (eds) *Industrial Crisis*, pp. 26–67.
4. Ivor Crewe and Donald Searing, 'Ideological Change in the British Conservative Party', *American Political Science Review*, 82, no. 2 (June 1988) pp. 361–384.
5. Richard Rose, 'Two and One Half Cheers for Capitalism', *Public Opinion*, June–July 1983.
6. Wiener, *English Culture and the Decline of the Industrial Spirit.*
7. Crewe and Searing, 'Ideological Change in the British Conservative Party'.
8. The point is well made by Samuel Beer, *Modern British Politics* (London: Faber and Faber, 1965).
9. For important early works extablishing this see Beer, *Modern British Politics*; S. E. Finer, *Anonymous Empire* (London: Pall Mall Press, 1966).
10. Wyn Grant with Jane Sargent, *Business and Politics in Britain* (London; Macmillan, 1987).
11. Frank Longstreth, 'The City, Industry and the State', in Colin Crouch (ed) *State and Economy in Contemporary Capitalism* (London: Croom Helm, 1979); David Marsh and G. Locksley, 'Capital; The Neglected Face of Power', in David Marsh (ed) *Pressure Politics; Interest Groups in Britain* (London: Junction Books, 1983).
12. Michael Moran, 'Finance Capital and Pressure Group Politics', *British Journal of Political Science*, 11, pt 4 October 1981) pp. 381–404.
13. Commission of Enquiry into Industrial and Commercial Representation (Lord Devlin, Chairman), *Report* (London: Association of British Chambers of Commerce/Confederation of British Industry, 1972).
14. Wyn Grant, 'The Organization of Capitalists in Britain's Company State; A Comparative Perspective', Paper presented to the Annual Convention of the American Political Science Association, Washington DC, 1987.
15. Peter Hall, *Governing the Economy; The Politics of State Intervention in Britain and France* (Cambridge, Mass.: Polity Press, 1988).
16. For an argument that change is possible if not easy see Andrew Cox (ed) *The State, Finance and Industry.*
17. For an example of the problems that are generated, see Graham K. Wilson, 'Planning – Lessons from the Ports', Public Administration, vol. 61, no. 3, 1983, pp. 265–82.

18. Peter Jenkins, *Mrs Thatcher's Revolution: The Ending of the Socialist Era* (London: Jonathan Cape, 1987).
19. Wyn Grant with Jane Sargent, *Business and Politics in Britain.*
20. *DTI – The Department of Enterprise.*
21. Wyn Grant and Jane Sargent, *Business and Politics in Britain.*
22. Karl Polanyi, *The Great Transformation* (New York: Farrow and Rinehart, 1944).
23. For a history of moves towards and away from corporatism, see Keith Middlemas, *Politics in Industrial Society* (London: Andre Deutsch, 1979).
24. Mancur Olson, *The Rise and Decline of Nations.*

4 Germany

1. Barrington Moore (Jr) *The Social Origins of Dictatorship and Democracy, Lord and Peasant in Making the Modern World* (New York: Basic Books, 1967); Ralf Dahrendorf, *Society and Democracy in Germany* (Garden City, New York: Doubleday, 1967). John Zysman, *Government, Markets and Growth.*
2. Eric Owen Smith, *The West German Economy* (London and Canberra: Croom Helm, 1983); Graham Hallett, *The Social Market Economy of West Germany* (London: Macmillan, 1976).
3. On the role of the banks, see Zysman, *Governments, Markets and Growth*; Andrew Cox (ed) *The State, Finance and Industry.*
4. Gerard Braunthal, *The Federation of German Industry in Politics* (Ithaca: Cornell University Press, 1965).
5. For discussion of changes in German policy see Allan G. Gruchy, *Comparative Economic Systems* (Boston: Houghton Mifflin, 1977); Herbert Schatz, 'The Development of Political Planning in the Federal Republic of Western Germany', in Klaus von Beyme (ed) *German Political Systems* (London: Sage, 1976).
6. Kenneth Dyson, 'The Politics of Corporate Crises in West Germany', *Western European Politics*, Vol 7, no. 1, pp. 24–46.

5 Italy

1. Michael Piore and Charles Sable, *The Second Industrial Divide: Possibilities for Prosperity* (New York: Basic Books, 1984).
2. Votaw Dow, *The Six Legged Dog; Mattei and ENI – A Study in Power* (Berkeley: University of California Press, 1964); M. V. Posner and S. J. Woolf, *Italian Public Enterprise* (Cambridge, Mass.: Harvard University Press, 1967); Stuart Holland (ed) *The State as Entrepreneur: New Dimensions for Public Enterprise: The IRI State Holding Formula* (London: Weidenfeld and Nicolson, 1972); Patrizio

Bianchi, 'IRI: Strategic Role and Political Constraints on Italian Public Share Holdings', *Western European Politics*, no. 1, January–March 1987.

3. Joseph Lapalombara, *Interest Groups In Italian Politics* (Princeton: Princeton University Press, 1964).

4. Patrizio Bianchi, 'Privatization of Industry: The Alfa Romeo Case', in Rafaella Y. Nanetti, Robert Leonardi and Piergiorgio Corbetta (eds) *Italian Politics: A Review*, Vol. 2 (London and New York: Francis Pinter, 1988) pp. 109–25.

5. Peter Lange, George Ross and Maurizio Vannicelli, *Unions, Change and Crisis: French and Italian Union Strategy and Political Economy, 1945–80* (London: Allen and Unwin, 1982).

6. Lapalombara, *Interest Groups In Italian Politics*, p. 398.

7. Alberto Martinelli, 'Organised Business and Italian Politics; Confindustria and the Christian Democrats in the Postwar Period', in Peter Lange and Sidney Tarrow (eds) *Italy in Transition; Conflict and Consensus* (London: Frank Cass, 1980).

8. Lapalombara, *Interest Groups In Italian Politics*, p. 286.

9. Ibid, p. 278.

10. Frederic Spotts and Theodore Wieser, *Italy, A Difficult Democracy* (Cambridge: Cambridge University Press, 1986).

6   The Neocorporatist Nations

1. Philippe Schmitter, 'Interest Intermediation and Regime Governability in Western Europe and North America', in Suzanne Berger (ed), *Organizing Interests in Western Europe* (Cambridge: Cambridge University Press, 1984) pp. 287–330.

2. 'Fading Illusions: A Survey of Austria', a special supplement, *The Economist*, 25 February 1989.

3. Schmitter, 'Still the Century of Corporatism?'.

4. Peter Lange, 'Unions, Workers and Wage Regulation: The Rational Basis of Consent', in J. H. Goldthorpe (ed) *Order and Conflict in Contemporary Capitalism* (Oxford: Clarendon Press, 1984) pp. 98–123.

5. For an example of such a scale see Schmitter, 'Interest Intermediation'. For studies of Austria as the exemplar of neocorporatism see Bernd Marin, 'Austria – the Paradigm Case of Liberal Corporatism, in Wyn Grant (ed) *The Political Economy of Corporatism* (London: Macmillan, 1985). See also Gerhard Lehmbruch, 'Liberal Corporatism and Party Government; in Philippe Schmitter and Gerhard Lehmbruch, *Trends Towards Corporatist Intermediation* (London and Beverly Hills: Sage Publications, 1979) pp. 109–32; Peter Gerlich, Edgar Grande and Wolfgang C. Mueller, 'Corporatism in Crisis; Stability and Change in Austria', *Political Studies*, 36 (1988) pp. 209–23 and Kurt Steiner (ed) *Modern Austria* (Palo Alto: Society for the

Promotion of Research and Scholarship, 1981). For an excellent account of Norwegian corporatism see Robert Kvavik, *Interest Groups in Norwegian Politics* (Oslo: Universitetsforlaget, 1976). More generally see Alan Cawson, *Corporatism and Political Theory* (Oxford: Basil Blackwell, 1986); Alan Cawson (ed) *Organized Interests and the State: Studies in Meso Corporatism* (London and Beverly Hills: Sage 1985); Wyn Grant (ed) *The Political Economy of Corporatism.*

6. Peter Katzenstein, *Small States in World Markets* (Ithaca: Cornell University Press, 1985).

7. Graham K. Wilson, *The Politics of Occupational Safety and Health* (Oxford: Clarendon Press, 1985); Wolfgang Streeck and Philippe Schmitter, *Private Interest Government* (London and Beverly Hills: Sage, 1985).

8. Olson, *Rise and Decline of Nations.*

9. Arend Lijpart, *Democracy in Plural Societies: A Comparative Exploration* (New Haven: Yale University Press, 1977).

10. Gerhard Lehmbruch, 'Liberal Corporatism and Party Government', *Comparative Political Studies*, 10 (1), 1977, pp. 91–126..

11. Gerhard Lehmbruch, 'Politische Strategien in der vergleichenden Politikforschung', in Peter Gerlich, Edgar Grande and W. C. Mueller (eds) *Sozialpartnerschaft in der Krise* (Wien: Bohla, 1985) pp. 85–107.

7 Government and Industry in France

1. Lawrence Wylie, *Village in the Vaucluse*, (Cambridge, Mass.: Harvard University Press, 1957).

2. The study is quoted by Suleiman in Steven J. Warneoke and Ezra N, Suleiman (eds) *Industrial Policies in Western Europe* (New York: Praeger, 1975).

3. Suzanne Berger, 'French Business from Transition to Transition', in George Ross, Stanley Hoffman and Sylvia Malzacher (eds) *The Mitterand Experiment* (New York: Oxford University Press, 1987).

4. Alexis de Tocqueville, *The Old Regime and the French Revolution* (Garden City, New York: Doubleday, 1955).

5. Berger, 'French Business'.

6. Jack Hayward, 'Employers' Associations and the State in France and Britain', in Warnecke and Suleiman (eds) *Industrial Policies*, pp. 137–8.

7. John Zysman, *Political Strategies for Industrial Order, State Market and Industry in France* (Berkeley: University of California Press, 1977) p. 63.

8. Henry Ehrman, 'An Exchange Theory of Interest Groups', in R. H. Salisbury (ed) *Interest Groups in America* (New York: Harper and Row, 1977) pp. 43–5.

9. Hayward, 'Employer's Associations', p. 130.

10. Frank L. Wilson, 'Alternative Models of Interest Intermediation: The Case of France', *British Journal of Political Science*, Vol. 12, pt 2 (April 1982) p. 189.
11. Zysman, *Political Strategies*, p. 63.
12. Hayward, 'Employer's Associations', p. 129.
13. J. H. MacArthur and B. R. Scott, *Industrial Planning in France* (Cambridge, Mass.: Harvard University Press, 1969).
14. Ibid. p. 8.
15. Stephen Cohen, *Modern Capitalist Planning: The French Model* (Cambridge Mass.: Harvard University Press, 1969).
16. Shonfield, *Modern Capitalism*.
17. Quoted in Anthony King, 'Ideas, Institutions and the Policies of Governments', *British Journal of Political Science*, 3 (July 1973) pp. 291–313.
18. Stanley Hoffman, 'The State: For What Society?', in Stanley Hoffman (ed) *Decline or Renewal?: France Since the 1930s* (New York: Viking Press, 1970) p. 450.
19. Zysman, *Governments, Markets and Growth*.
20. For a detailed analysis of this issue see Hall, *Governing the Economy*.
21. Andrew Cox (ed) *State, Finance and Industry*.
22. Hall, *Governing the Economy*.
23. Ann Stevens, 'The Higher Civil Service and Economic Policymaking', in Philip G. Cerny and Martin A. Schain (eds), *French Politics and Public Policy Making* (London and New York: Methuen, 1981).
24. Vincent Wright, *The Government and Politics of France* (London: Hutchinson, 1973) p. 90.
25. Suleiman in Warnecke and Suleiman (eds) *Industrial Policies* p. 37.
26. Hall, *Governing The Economy*.

8 Japan

1. For strong statements of this perspective see the regular columns by James Fallows in *The Atlantic* in 1988 and 1989; see also Karel van Wolferen, *The Enigma of the Japanese State* (New York: Alfred Knopf, 1989).
2. For an argument that Japan has lessons to teach that other countries can learn see Ezra Vogel, *Japan As Number One: Lessons for America* (New York: Harper Colophon, 1982).
3. The classic statement of this view is Chalmers Johnson, *MITI and the Japanese Miracle, The Growth of Industrial Policy 1925–75* (Stanford: Stanford University Press, 1982). See also T. J. Pempel, *Policy and Politics in Japan: Creative Conservativism* (Philadelphia: Temple University Press, 1982); US Department of Commerce, *Japan – The Business Government Relationship* (Washington DC: Government Printing Office, 1974).
4. Johnson, *MITI and the Japanese Miracle*.

5. For a more qualified view of Japanese policy as market reinforcing see Richard J. Samuels, *The Business of the Japanese State: Energy Markets in Comparative and Historical Perspective* (Ithaca: Cornell University Press, 1987. See also 'Once Mighty MITI Loses Power', *New York Times*, 9 July 1989.
6. Zysman, *Governments, Markets and Growth.*
7. Samuels, *The Business of the Japanese State.*
8. Zysman, *Governments, Markets and Growth.*

9 The Multinationals – Companies without Governments?

1. Much of the evidence is summarised conveniently in Anthony Sampson, *The Sovereign State of AT and T* (New York: Stein and Day, 1973).
2. US Senate, Subcommittee on Multinational Corporations of the Committee on Foreign Relations, 93rd Congress, *The International Telephone and Telegraph Company and Chile, 1970–71*; US Senate, Committee to Study Government Operations with Respect to Intelligence Activities, Staff Report, *Covert Operations in Chile* (Washington DC: Government Printing Office, 1975).
3. Quoted in Charles E. Kindleberger (ed), *The International Corporation* (Cambridge, Mass.: MIT Press, 1970).
4. 'US Business Loosen Ties to Mother Country', *New York Times*, 21 May 1989.
5. Barbara Stallings, *Banker to the Third World: Latin America and US Capital Markets 1900–86* (Berkeley: University of California Press, 1987); Barbara Stallings and Robert Kaufman (eds) *Debt and Democracy in Latin America* (Boulder: Westview Press, 1988).
6. Raymond Vernon, *Storm Over Multinationals, The Real Issues* (London: Macmillan, 1977)
7. For some excellent work on multinationals, see Raymond Vernon, *Storm Over Multinationals, The Real Issues* (London: Macmillan, 1977); G. Modelski (ed) *Transnational Corporations and World Order* (San Francisco: W. W. Freeman, 1979); D. K. Fieldhouse, *Unilever Overseas: The Anatomy of a Multinational 1895–1965* (London: Croom Helm, 1978).

10 Conclusions

1. David Truman, *The Government Process* (New York: Alfred Knopf, 1951).
2. Alfred Stepan, *State and Society: Peru in Comparative Perspective* (Princeton, NJ: Princeton University Press, 1978).

3. Samuel Beer, *Modern British Politics* (London: Faber and Faber, 1965).
4. For an examination of the importance of this factor in the United States see Graham K. Wilson, 'Corporate Political Strategies', *British Journal of Political Science* (forthcoming).
5. Morton Horwitz, *The Transformation of American Law 1780–1960* (Cambridge, Mass.: Harvard University Press, 1977).
6. Kenneth Dyson, 'The Cultural, Ideological and Structual Context' in Dyson and Wilks (eds) *Industrial Crisis.*
7. Shonfield, *Modern Capitalism.*
8. Schmitter, 'Interest Intermediation'.
9. Johnson, *MITI and the Japanese Miracle.*
10. See for example, Anthony King (ed) *Why is Britain Becoming Harder to Govern?* (London: BBC Publications, 1976).
11. Lindblom, *Politics and Markets.*

Bibliography

Adams, Gordon, *The Defense Game: The Politics of Defense Contracting; The Iron Triangle* (New York: Council on Economic Priorities, 1981).

Almond, Gabriel, 'Corporatism, Pluralism and Professional Memory', *World Politics*, 35 (1983) pp. 245–60.

Almond, Gabriel, 'A Return to the State', with replies by Eric Nordlinger, Theodore Lowi and Sergio Fabbrini, *American Political Science Review*, 82 (1988) pp. 853–904.

Bachrach, Peter and Morton Baratz, 'The Two Faces of Power', *American Political Science Review*, 56 (1962) pp. 947–52.

——, *Power and Poverty, Theory and Practice* (Oxford and New York: Oxford University Press, 1970).

Badie, Bertrand and Pierre Birnbaum, *The Sociology of the State* (Chicago: University of Chicago Press, 1983).

Bauer, Raymond, Ithiel de Sola Pool and Lewis Anthony Dexter, *American Business and Public Policy* (New York: Atherton Press, 1963).

Beer, Samuel, *Modern British Politics* (London: Faber and Faber, 1965).

Beer, Samuel, *Britain Against Itself* (London: Faber and Faber, 1982).

Berger, Suzanne (ed) *Organizing Interests in Western Europe* (Cambridge and New York: Cambridge University Press, 1981).

Bernstein, Marver, *Regulating Business by Independent Commission* (Princeton, NJ: Princeton University Press, 1955).

Berry, Jeffrey, *The Interest Group Society* (Boston: Little, Brown, 1984).

Bianchi, Patrizio, 'IRI: Strategic Role and Political Constraints on Italian Public Share Holding', *Western European Politics*, no. 1 (January–March, 1987).

——, 'Privatization of Industry: The Alfa Romeo Case', in Rafaella Y. Nanetti, Robert Leonardi and Piergiorgio Corbetta (eds) *Italian Politics: A Review*, Vol. 2 (London and New York: Francis Pinter, 1988) pp. 109–25.

Birch, Anthony, 'Overload, Ungovernability and Delegitimation', *British Journal of Political Science*, 14 (1984) pp. 135–60.

Block, Fred, 'The Ruling Class Does Not Rule: Notes on the Marxist Theory of the State', *Socialist Review*, 33 (1977).

Braunthal, Gerard, *The Federation of German Industry in Politics* (Ithaca: Cornell University Press, 1965).

Campbell, John, 'Compensation for Expatriates: A Case Study of Interest Group Politics and Party Government Negotiation', in T. J. Pempel (ed) *Policymaking in Contemporary Japan* (Ithaca: Cornell University Press, 1977).

Carnoy, Martin, *The State and Political Theory* (Princeton N. J.: Princeton University Press, 1984).

Cawson, Alan, *Corporatism and Political Theory* (Oxford: Basil Blackwell, 1986).

—— (ed), *Organized Interests and the State* (London and Beverly Hills: Sage, 1985).

—— (ed), *Corporatism and Political Theory* (Oxford: Basil Blackwell, 1986).

Cerny, Philip G. and Martin A. Schain (eds), *French Politics and Public Policy Making* (London and New York: Methuen, 1981).

Chubb, John, *Interest Groups and the Bureaucracy* (Stanford: Stanford University Press, 1983).

Clawson, Dan, and Alan Neustadt, 'Interlocks, PACs and Corporate Conservatism', *American Journal of Sociology*, 94 (January 1989) pp. 749–73.

Cohen, Stephen, *Modern Capitalist Planning: The French Model* (Cambridge, Mass: Harvard University Press, 1969).

Cox, Andrew (ed) *The State, Finance and Industry* (Brighton: Wheatsheaf Books, 1986).

Crenson, Matthew, *The Unpolitics of Air Pollution, A Study of Non–Decisionmaking in Cities* (Baltimore and London: Johns Hopkins University Press, 1971).

Crewe, Ivor and Donald Searing, 'Ideological Change in the British Conservative Party', *American Political Science Review*, 82, no. 2 (June 1988) pp. 361–384.

Dahl, Robert, *A Preface to Democratic Theory* (Chicago: University of Chicago Press, 1956).

Dahl, Robert, *Who Governs?* (New Haven: Yale University Press, 1961).

Dahl, Robert, *Dilemmas of Pluralist Democracy* (New Haven: Yale University Press, 1982).

Dahrendorf, Ralf, *Society and Democracy in Germany* (Garden City, New York: Doubleday, 1967).

Dennis, Jack, 'Groups and Political Behaviour: Legitimation, Deprivation and Competing Values', *Political Behaviour*, 9 (1987) pp. 323–371

Destler, I. M., *American Trade Politics, System Under Stress* (Institute for International Economics, Washington DC, and the Twentieth Century Fund, New York, 1986).

Donnelly, Michael, 'Setting the Price of Rice; A Study in Political Decisionmaking' in T. J. Pempel (ed) *Policymaking in Contemporary Japan* (Ithaca: Cornell University Press, 1977).

Dow, Votaw, *The Six Legged Dog; Mattei and ENI – A Study in Power* (Berkeley: University of California Press, 1964).

Drew, Elizabeth, *Politics and Money: The New Road to Corruption* (New York: Macmillan, 1983).

Dyson, Kenneth, 'The Politics of Corporate Crises in West Germany', *Western European Politics*, Vol 7, no. 1, pp. 24–46.

Dyson, Kenneth and Stephen Wilks (eds) *Industrial Crisis: A Comparative Study of the State and Industry* (Oxford: Martin Robertson, 1983).

Eckstein, Harry, *Pressure Politics, The Case of the BMA* (Berkeley: University of California Press, 1963).

Ehrman, Henry, 'An Exchange Theory of Interest Groups', in R. H. Salisbury (ed) *Interest Groups in America* (New York: Harper and Row, 1977) pp. 43–5.

Einhom, Eric and John Logue, *Welfare States in Hard Times, Problems, Policy and Politics in Denmark and Norway* (Kent, Ohio: Kent Popular Press, 1982).

Eisinger, Peter K., *The Rise of the Entrepreneurial State: State and Local Economic Development Policy in the United States* (Madison: University of Wisconsin Press, 1988).

Engler, Robert, *The Politics of Oil: Private Power and Democratic Directions* (Chicago: University of Chicago Press, 1961).

—— *The Brotherhood of Oil* (Chicago: University of Chicago Press, 1977).

Etzioni, Amitai, *Capital Corruption: The New Attack on American Democracy* (New York: Harcourt Brace Jovanovich, 1984).

Evans, Peter, Dietrich Rueschemeyer and Theda Skocpol, *Bringing the State Back In* (Cambridge and New York: Cambridge University Press, 1985).

Ferguson, Thomas and Joel Rogers (eds), *Right Turn: The Decline of the Democrats and the Future of American Politics* (New York: Hill and Wang, 1986).

Fieldhouse, D. K., *Unilever Overseas: The Anatomy of a Multinational 1895–1965* (London: Croom Helm, 1978).

Finer, S. E., *Anonymous Empire* (London: Pall Mall Press, 1966).

Gable, Richard, 'NAM; Influential Lobby or Kiss of Death?', *Journal of Politics*, 15, no. 2 (May 1953) pp. 254–73.

Gais, Thomas, M. Peterson and J. Walker, 'Interest Groups, Iron Triangles and Representative Government in American National Government', *British Journal of Political Science*, 14 (1984) pp. 161–86.

Garson, G. David, *Group Theories of politics* (Beverly Hills: Sage Publications, 1978).

Gerlich, Peter, 'Government Structure' in Kurt Steiner (ed) *Modern Austria* (Palo Alto, California: Society for the Promotion of Science and Scholarship, 1981).

——, Edgar Grande and Wolfgang C. Mueller, 'Corporatism in Crisis; Stability and Change in Austria', *Political Studies*, 36 (1988) pp. 209–23.

Goldthorpe, John (ed), *Order and Conflict in Contemporary Capitalism* (Cambridge and New York: Cambridge University Press, Clarendon Press, 1984).

Grant, Wyn (ed), *The Political Economy of Corporatism* (London: Macmillan, 1985).

——, 'The Organization of Capitalists in Britain's Company State; A Comparative Perspective', Paper presented to the Annual Convention of the American Political Science Association, Washington DC, 1987.

Grant, Wyn (with Jane Sargent) *Business and Politics in Britain* (London: Macmillan, 1987).

Grant, Wyn and David Marsh, *The CBI* (London: Hodder and Stoughton, 1977).

Greenstone, J. David, *Labor in American Politics* (Chicago: University of Chicago Press, 1977).

Gruchy, Allan G., *Comparative Economic Systems* (Boston: Houghton Mifflin, 1977).

Habermas, Jorgen, *Legitimation Crisis* (trans. Thomas McCarthy) (Boston: Beacon Press, 1975).

Hall, Peter, *Governing the Economy; The Politics of State Intervention in Britain and France* (Cambridge, Mass.: Polity Press, 1988).

Hallett, Graham, *The Social Market Economy of West Germany* (London: Macmillan, 1976).

Hartz, Louis, *The Liberal Tradition in America* (New York: Harcourt, Brace and World, 1955).

Hayes, Michael, *Lobbyists and Legislators, A Theory of Political Markets* (New Brunswick: Rutgers University Press, 1981).

Heclo, Hugh, and Henrik Madsen, *Policy and Politics in Sweden* (Philadelphia: Temple University Press, 1987).

Hoffman, Stanley, 'The State: For What Society?', in Stanley Hoffman (ed) *Decline or Renewal? France Since the 1930s* (New York: Viking Press, 1970) p. 450.

Holland, Stuart (ed), *The State as Entrepreneur; New Dimensions for Public Enterprise; The IRI State Holding Formula* (London: Weidenfeld and Nicolson, 1972).

Horwitz, Morton, *The Transformation of American Law 1780–1960* (Cambridge, Mass.: Harvard University Press, 1977).

Jenkins, Peter, *Mrs Thatcher's Revolution: The Ending of the Socialist Era* (London: Jonathan Cape, 1987).

Jessop, Bob, 'Recent Theories of the Capitalist State', *Cambridge Journal of Economics*, 1 (1977) pp. 353–73.

Jessop, Bob, *The Capitalist State, Theory and Methods* (New York: New York University Press, 1982).

Johnson, Chalmers, *MITI and the Japanese Miracle, The Growth of Industrial Policy, 1925–75* (Stanford: Stanford University Press, 1982).

Jordan, Grant, and J. J. Richardson, *Government and Pressure Groups in Britain* (Oxford: Oxford University Press, 1987).

Katzenstein, Peter, *Small States in World Markets, Industrial Policies in Europe* (Ithaca: Cornell University Press, 1985).

—— *Corporatism and Change, Austria, Switzerland and the Politics of Industry* (Ithaca: Cornell University Press, 1982).

Kaufman, Herbert, *The Administrative Behavior of Federal Bureau Chiefs* (Washington DC: Brookings Institution, 1981).

Keeler, John, *The Politics of Neocorporatism in France* (Oxford and New York: Oxford University Press, 1987).

Kelman, Steven, *Regulating America, Regulating Sweden, A Comparative Study of Occupational Safety and Health Policy* (Cambridge, Mass.: MIT Press, 1981).

Kennedy, Paul, *The Rise and Decline of Great Powers: Economic Change and Military Conflict from 1500 to 2000* (New York: Random House, 1987).

Kindleberger, Charles E. (ed), *The International Corporation* (Cambridge, Mass.: MIT Press, 1970).

King, Anthony, 'Ideas, Institutions and the Policies of Governments', *British Journal of Political Science*, 3 (July 1973) pp. 291–313.

—— (ed), *Why is Britain Becoming Harder to Govern?* (London: BBC Publications, 1976).

Kingdon, John, *Congressmen's Voting Decisions* (New York: Harper and Row, 1973).

Koistiner, Paul A. C., *The Military Industrial Complex: An Historical Perspective* (New York: Praeger, 1980).

Kumar, Martha Joynt and Michael Baruch Grossman, 'The Presidency and Interest Groups', in Michael Nelson (ed) *The Presidency and the Political System* (Washington DC: CQ Press, 1984).

Kvavik, Robert, *Interest Groups in Norwegian Politics* (Oslo: Universitetsforlaget, 1976).

Lange, Peter, 'Unions, Workers and Wage Regulation: The Rational Basis of Consent', in J. H. Goldthorpe (ed) *Order and Conflict in Contemporary Capitalism* (Oxford: Clarendon Press, 1984) pp. 98–123.

——, George Ross and Maurizio Vannicelli, *Unions, Change and Crisis: French and Italian Union Strategy and Political Economy, 1945–80*, (London: Allen and Unwin, 1982).

Lapalombara, Joseph, *Interest Groups in Italian Politics* (Princeton: Princeton University Press, 1964).

Lehmbruch, Gerhard, 'Politische Strategien in der vergleichenden Politikforschung', in Peter Gerlich, Edgar Grande and W. C. Muller (eds) *Sozialpartnerschaft in der Krise* (Wien: Bohla, 1985) pp. 85–107.

—— and Philippe Schmitter (eds), *Patterns of Corporatist Policymaking* (London and Beverly Hills: Sage, 1982).

Lijpart, Arend, *Democracy in Plural Societies: A Comparative Exploration* (New Haven: Yale University Press, 1977).

Lindblom, Charles E., *Politics and Markets, The World's Political Economic Systems* (New York: Basic Books, 1977).

Lipset, Seymour Martin, 'Why No Socialism in the United States?', in Seweryn Bialer and Sophia Sluzar (eds) *Sources of Contemporary Radicalism*, vol. 1, pp. 291–313.

Longstreth, Frank, 'The City, Industry and the State', in Colin Crouch (ed) *State and Economy in Contemporary Capitalism* (London: Croom Helm, 1979.

Lowi, Theodore, 'American Business, Public Policy Case Studies and Political Theory', *World Politics*, 16, no. 4 (July 1964) pp. 677–715.

——, *The End of Liberalism*, 2nd edn (New York: W. W. Norton, 1979).

Lukes, Steven, *Power, A Radical View* (London: Macmillan, 1974).

Marin, Bernd, 'Austria – The Paradigm Case of Liberal Corporatism?', in Wyn Grant (ed) *The Political Economy of Corporatism* (London: Macmillan, 1985).

MacArthur, J. H. and B. R. Scott, *Industrial Planning in France* (Cambridge, Mass.: Harvard University Press, 1969).

Marsh, David and Gareth Locksley, 'Capital in Britain; Its Structural Power and Influence Over Policy', *Western European Politics*, 6, no. 2 (April 1983) pp. 36–60.

——, 'Capital; The Neglected Face of Power', in David Marsh (ed) *Pressure Politics: Interest Groups in Britain* (London: Junction Books, 1983).

Martinelli, Alberto, 'Organized Business and Italian Politics; Confindustria and the Christian Democrats in the Postwar Period', in Peter Lange and Sidney Tarrow (eds) *Italy in Transition; Conflict and Consensus* (London: Frank Cass, 1980).

Middlemas, Keith, *Politics in Industrial Society* (London: Andre Deutsch, 1979).

Milbrath, Lester, *The Washington Lobbyists* (Chicago: Rand McNally, 1963).

Miliband, Ralph, *The State in Capitalist Society* (London: Quartet Books, 1976).

Mills, C. Wright, *The Power Elite* (New York: Oxford University Press, 1956).

Modelski, G. (ed) *Transnational Corporations and World Order* (San Francisco: W. W. Freeman, 1979).

Moore, Barrington (Jr), *The Social Origins of Dictatorship and Democracy, Lord and Peasant in Making the Modern World* (New York: Basic Books, 1967).

Moran, Michael, 'Finance Capital and Pressure Group Politics', *British Journal of Political Science*, 11, pt 4 (October 1981) pp. 381–404.

Nanetti, Rafaella Y., Robert Leonardi and Piergiorgio Corbetta (eds), *Italian Politics: A Review* (London and New York: Francis Pinter, 1988).

Nordlinger, Eric, *On the Autonomy of the Democratic State* (Cambridge, Mass.: Harvard University Press, 1981).

O'Connor, James, *The Fiscal Crisis of the State* (New York: St Martin's Press, 1971).

Odell, Peter, *Oil and World Power* (Harmondsworth: Pelican Books, 1981).

Offe, Claus, 'The Attribution of Public Status to Interest Groups' in Suzanne Berger (ed), *Organizing Interests in Western Europe* (Cambridge: Cambridge University Press, 1981) pp. 123–58.

Offe, Claus, and H. Wisenthal, 'Two Logics of Collective Action; Theoretical Notes on Social Class and Organisational Form, *Political Power and Social Theory*, 1, pp. 67–115

Offe, Claus, *Disorganized Capitalism* (Cambridge, Mass.: MIT Press, 1985).

Olsen, Johann, *Organized Democracy; Political Institutions in A Welfare State* (Oslo: Universitetsforlaget, 1983).

Olson, Mancur, *The Logic of Collective Action, Public Goods and the Theory of Groups* (New York: Schocken Books, 1968).

Olson, Mancur, *The Rise and Decline of Nations, Stagflation and Social Rigidities* (New Haven: Yale University Press, 1982).

Orren, Karren, 'Standing to Sue; Interest Group Conflict in the Federal Courts' *American Political Science Review*, no. 3 (September 1976).

Panitch, Leo, *Social Democracy and Industrial Militancy* (Cambridge: Cambridge University Press, 1976).

Pempel, T. J., *Policy and Politics in Japan; Creative Conservatism* (Philadelphia: Temple University Press, 1982).

Piore, Michael and Charles Sable, *The Second Industrial Divide: Possibilities for Prosperity* (New York: Basic Books, 1984).

Polanyi, Karl, *The Great Transformation* (New York: Farrar and Rinehart, 1944).

Posner, M. V., and S. J. Woolf, *Italian Public Enterprise* (Cambridge, Mass.: Harvard University Press, 1967).

Reich, Robert B., *The Next American Frontier* (New York: Times Books, 1983).

—— and John D. Donahue, *New Deals: The Chrysler Revival and the American System* (New York: Times Books, 1985).

Rokkan, Stein, 'Norway, Numerical Democracy and Corporate Pluralism', in Robert Dahl (ed), *Political Oppositions in Western Democracies*, (New Haven: Yale University Press, 1966).

Rose, Richard, 'Two and One Half Cheers for Capitalism', *Public Opinion*, June–July 1983.

Rosenberg, Tina, 'Why Tax Incentives Are A Bad Idea for the States', *New Republic* 3 October 1983, pp. 18–21.

Ross, George, Stanley Hoffman and Sylvia Malzacher (eds) *The Mitterrand Experiment*, (New York: Oxford University Press, 1987).

Sabato, Larry, *PAC Power: Inside the World of Political Action Committees* (New York: W. W. Norton, 1984).

Salisbury, Robert, 'Interest Representation – The Dominance of Institutions', *American Political Science Review*, 78, no. 1 (1984) pp. 64–76.

——, John P. Laumann and Robert L. Nelson, 'Who Works With Whom? Interest group Alliances and Opposition', *American Political Science Review*, 81, (1987) pp. 1217–1234).

Sampson, Anthony, *The Seven Sisters: The Great Oil Companies and the World They Shaped* (New York: Viking Press, 1973).

——, *The Sovereign State of AT and T* (New York: Stein and Day, 1973).

Samuels, Richard J., *The Business of the Japanese State: Energy Markets in Comparative and Historical Perspective* (Ithaca: Cornell University Press, 1987).

Schattschneider, E. E., *Politics, Pressures and the Tariff* (reprint) (New York: Arno Press, 1974) (original 1935).

——, *The Semi-Sovereign People* (New York: Holt, Rinehart and Winston, 1960).

Schatz, Herbert, 'The Development of Political Planning in the Federal Republic of Western Germany', in Klaus von Beyme (ed) *German Political Systems* (London: Sage, 1976).

Schlozman, Kay Lehman and John Tierney, *Organized Interests and American Democracy* (New York: Harper and Row, 1986).

Schmitter, Philippe, 'Regime Stability and Systems of Interest Intermediation in Western Europe and North America', in Suzanne Berger (ed) *Organizing Interests in Western Europe* (Cambridge: Cambridge University Press, 1981).

——, 'Interest Intermediation and Regime Governability in Western Europe and North America', in Suzanne Berger (ed), *Organizing Interests in Western Europe* (Cambridge: Cambridge University Press, 1984).

——, 'Still the Century of Corporatism?', *Review of Politics*, 36, No. 1 (January 1974) pp. 85–131.

——, 'Modes of Interest Intermediation and Models of Societal Change in Western Europe' *Comparative Political Studies*, 10 (1977) pp. 7–38.

—— and Gerhard Lehmbruch (eds), *Trends Toward Corporatist Intermediation* (London and Beverly Hills: Sage, 1979).

Self, Peter and Herbert Storing, *The State and the Farmer* (London: Allen and Unwin, 1962, 1971).

Shapiro, Martin, 'The Supreme Court's "Return" to Economic Regulation', *Studies in American Political Development*, vol. 1 (New Haven and London: Yale University Press, 1986).

Shonfield, Andrew, *Modern Capitalism: The Changing Balance of Public and Private Power* (Oxford: Oxford University Press, 1969).

Smith, Eric Owen, *The West German Economy* (London: Croom Helm, 1983).

Sombart, Werner, *Why Is There No Socialism in the United States?* (re-issue) (London: Macmillan, 1976) (first published 1905).

Spotts, Frederic and Theodore Wieser, *Italy, A Difficult Democracy* (Cambridge: Cambridge University Press, 1986).

Stallings, Barbara, *Banker to the Third World: Latin America and US Capital Markets 1900–86* (Berkeley: University of California Press, 1987).

—— and Robert Kaufman (eds), *Debt and Democracy in Latin America* (Boulder: Westview Press, 1988).

Steiner, Kurt (ed) *Modern Austria* (Palo Alto: Society for the Promotion of Research and Scholarship, 1981).

Stepan, Alfred, *State and Society: Peru in Comparative Perspective* (Princeton, NJ: Princeton University Press, 1978).

Stewart, Richard, 'The Reformation of American Administrative Law', *Harvard Law Review*, 88, no. 81 (1975) pp. 1667–1813.

Streeck, Wolfgang, *Industrial Relations in West Germany* (London: Heinemann Educational, 1984).

—— and Philippe Schmitter, *Private Interest Government* (London and Beverly Hills: Sage, 1985).

Stubbing, Richard A., with Richard A. Mendel, *The Defense Game: An Insider Explores the Astonishing Realities of America's Defense Establishment* (New York: Harper and Row, 1986).

Tocqueville, Alexis de, *The Old Regime and the French Revolution* (Garden City, New York: Doubleday, 1955).

Truman, David, *The Governmental Process* (New York: Alfred Knopf, 1951).

Useem, Michael, *The Inner Circle, Large Corporations and the Rise of Political Activity in the USA and the UK* (New York: Oxford University Press, 1984).

Van Wolferen, Karel, *The Enigma of the Japanese State* (New York: Alfred Knopf, 1989).

Vernon, Raymond, *Storm Over Multinationals, The Real Issues* (London: Macmillan, 1977).

Vogel, David, *Fluctuating Fortunes, The Political Power of Business in America* (New York: Basic Books, 1989).

——, *National Styles of Regulation*, (Ithaca: Cornell University Press, 1986).

——, 'The Power of Business in the United States, A Re-Appraisal', *British Journal of Political Science*, 17 (1987) pp. 385–408.

Vogel, Ezra, *Japan as Number One: Lessons for America* (New York: Harper Colophon, 1982).

Walker, Jack, 'The Origins and Maintenance of Interest Groups in America', *American Political Science Review*, 77, no. 2 (1983) pp. 390–406.

Warnecke, Stephen J., and Ezra N. Suleiman, (eds) *Industrial Policies in Western Europe* (New York: Praeger, 1975).

Wiener, Martin, *English Culture and the Decline of the Industrial Spirit 1850–1980* (Cambridge: Cambridge University Press, 1981).

Wilks, Stephen and Maurice Wright, *Comparative Government Industry Relations, Western Europe, the United States and Japan* (Oxford: Clarendon Press, 1987).

Wilson, Frank L., 'Alternative Models of Interest Intermediation: The Case of France', *British Journal of Political Science*, Vol. 12, pt 2 (April 1982) p. 189.

Wilson, Graham K., *Special Interests and Policymaking, Agricultural Politics and Policies in Britain and the United States* (Chichester and London: John Wiley and Son, 1977).

——, *Unions in American National Politics* (London: Macmillan, 1979).

——, *Interest Groups in the United States* (Oxford and New York: Clarendon Press, 1981).

——, 'Planning – Lessons from the Ports', *Public Administration*, vol. 61, no. 3, 1983, pp. 265–82.

——, *The Politics of Occupational Safety and Health* (Oxford and New York: Clarendon Press, 1985).

——, 'Corporate Political Strategies', *British Journal of Political Science* (forthcoming).

Wilson, James, Q., *Political Organizations* (New York: Basic Books, 1974).

——, (ed) *The Politics of Regulation* (New York: Basic Books, 1983).

Winkler, J., 'The Coming Corporatism' in R. Skidelsky (ed), *The End of the Keynesian Era* (London: Macmillan, 1977).

Wright, Vincent, *The Government and Politics of France* (London: Hutchinson, 1973) p. 90.

Wylie, Lawrence, *Village in the Vaucluse* (Cambridge, Mass.: Harvard University Press, 1957).

Yarmolinsky, Adam, *The Military Establishment* (New York: Harper Colophon, 1971).

Zeigler, L. Harman, 'Interest Groups in the American States', in Virginia Gray, Herbert Jacobs and Kenneth Vines (eds), *Politics in the American States* (Boston: Little, Brown, 1983) pp. 97–131.

Zysman, John, *Governments, Markets and Growth* (Ithaca: Cornell University Press, 1983).

——, *Political Strategies for Industrial Order, State Market and Industry in France* (Berkeley: University of California Press, 1977).

Index